Toward a Generous Orthodoxy

June 2013

To Todd

With great appreciation
for a friend and colleague.

Jason

AMERICAN ACADEMY OF RELIGION

REFLECTION AND THEORY IN THE STUDY
OF RELIGION SERIES

SERIES EDITOR
James Wetzel, Villanova University

A Publication Series of
The American Academy of Religion
and
Oxford University Press

OPTING FOR THE MARGINS
Postmodernity and Liberation in Christian Theology
Edited by Joerg Rieger

MAKING MAGIC
Religion, Magic, and Science in the Modern World
Randall Styers

THE METAPHYSICS OF DANTE'S *COMEDY*
Christian Moevs

PILGRIMAGE OF LOVE
Moltmann on the Trinity and Christian Life
Joy Ann McDougall

MORAL CREATIVITY
Paul Ricoeur and the Poetics of Moral Life
John Wall

MELANCHOLIC FREEDOM
Agency and the Spirit of Politics
David Kyuman Kim

FEMINIST THEOLOGY AND THE CHALLENGE OF DIFFERENCE
Margaret D. Kamitsuka

TOWARD A GENEROUS ORTHODOXY
Prospects for Hans Frei's Postliberal Theology
Jason A. Springs

Toward a Generous Orthodoxy

Prospects for Hans Frei's
Postliberal Theology

JASON A. SPRINGS

OXFORD
UNIVERSITY PRESS

2010

OXFORD
UNIVERSITY PRESS

Oxford University Press, Inc., publishes works that further
Oxford University's objective of excellence
in research, scholarship, and education.

Oxford   New York
Auckland   Cape Town   Dar es Salaam   Hong Kong   Karachi
Kuala Lumpur   Madrid   Melbourne   Mexico City   Nairobi
New Delhi   Shanghai   Taipei   Toronto

With offices in
Argentina   Austria   Brazil   Chile   Czech Republic   France   Greece
Guatemala   Hungary   Italy   Japan   Poland   Portugal   Singapore
South Korea   Switzerland   Thailand   Turkey   Ukraine   Vietnam

Copyright © 2010 by American Academy of Religion

Published by Oxford University Press, Inc.
198 Madison Avenue, New York, New York 10016

www.oup.com

Oxford is a registered trademark of Oxford University Press

Library of Congress Cataloging-in-Publication Data
Springs, Jason A.
Toward a generous orthodoxy : prospects for Hans Frei's postliberal
theology / Jason A. Springs.
p. cm.
Includes bibliographical references and index.
ISBN 978-0-19-539504-4
1. Frei, Hans W. 2. Postliberal theology. I. Title.
BX4827.F74S57   2010
230'.046—dc22   2009050151

9 8 7 6 5 4 3 2 1

Printed in the United States of America
on acid-free paper

In Memoriam
William C. Placher

Acknowledgments

I owe thanks to many people for assisting me in completing this book. During its time as a dissertation for Harvard University's Committee on the Study of Religion, Francis Fiorenza and David Lamberth commented upon several drafts with a helpful suspicion, pressing me to maintain a critical, self-reflective edge at every turn. Thanks also go to the cadre of young theologians and philosophers from (at the time) Princeton, Princeton Seminary, and Duke Divinity School for their critical feedback on the early drafts of this project—especially Steve Bush, Todd Cioffi, Kevin Hector, and Bryan Langlands. Portions of the manuscript benefited tremendously from questions, criticisms, and passing conversations with Grant Brooke, Jacob Goodson, Katherine Grieb, Sam Houston, Keith L. Johnson, Paul Dafydd Jones, Kate Sonderegger, and Nicholas Wolterstorff. I am grateful to Ted Vial, editor of the AAR/Oxford Reflection and Theory in the Study of Religion series, for seeing beyond the revised dissertation I first submitted to him for consideration, and on toward the makings of a book. Mike Higton and Paul DeHart shared generously of their own manuscripts on Frei's thought and postliberal theology, in both cases prior to publication. Higton's meticulous work in retrieving the contents of Frei's archival papers in *Christ, Providence and History*, along with DeHart's acute exposition of Frei's late engagement with Schleiermacher and reframing of the "postliberal-revisionist" debate in *The Trial of the Witnesses*, have helped to clear the field on which I here attempt to further elucidate, expand, and make Frei's theological approach available for novel conversations.

Thanks to the generous sponsorship of Princeton University's Center for the Study of Religion I spent the year following my doctoral studies revising this book as the Center's Post-doctoral Fellow in Christian Thought and Practice (2005–06). Robert Wuthnow and the participants of the Center's Religion and Public Life colloquium provided critical feedback to key portions of this project from sociological, anthropological, philosophical, as well as theological angles—precisely the kind of multidisciplinary feedback that Hans Frei would have relished. Martin Kavka, the Carpenter Fellow in Public Theology that year, applied his keen editor's eye to each of my revised chapters. He responded with the insight and perceptiveness of a Jewish philosopher well-versed in the debates surrounding Frei's approach to scriptural reasoning and Robert Brandom's inferential pragmatism.

I have been fortunate to work with several teachers and mentors who knew Frei personally as a colleague and friend. They provided a wealth of resources in personal conversation and correspondence. Cornel West generously regaled me with stories of his many conversations with "Hans Wilhelm" during their days together at Yale. It was, more significantly, Cornel's witness as an unapologetically Christian philosopher and public intellectual of deep pragmatist sensibilities that first motivated me to explore the congruities of pragmatist thinking and "postliberal" theology. In many ways the path that came to fruition in this project began with West. Cornel's personal attention and support (in concert with that of Jeffrey Stout) made it possible for me to complete the dissertation phase of this project as an Exchange Scholar in the Princeton University Religion Department (2004–05). Ronald Thiemann, my dissertation director at Harvard, invested the time and effort to walk with me step by step through Frei's work when I was a first-year doctoral student. Even more fortuitously, that semester Thiemann conscripted me into his seminar on Karl Barth—reportedly the first seminar on Barth's theology taught at Harvard in decades. This combination of Frei and Barth planted the seeds for the project that eventually grew into this book.

The deepest debts of gratitude I owe to Jeffrey Stout and George Hunsinger. Stout took me into his classroom and under his guidance when I was a first-semester seminary student at the school across the street from his own. The engagement with theological voices I encountered in conversation with him—always presented at their best—modeled for me the kind of complex equilibrium that a modestly pragmatist philosophical posture can find with theological voices in the study of religion. Stout first led me through the works of Ludwig Wittgenstein, Wilfrid Sellars, and Robert Brandom over the course of a semester-long, weekly conversation that often lasted four or five hours per session. His meticulous analysis of my writing and criticisms of several early chapter drafts helped me to produce whatever here is readable and might pass philosophical muster. Whatever does not is surely the result of the stubborn streak in my philosophical sensibilities.

George Hunsinger's sustained interest in this project assisted my progress tremendously. Through a series of reading group sessions and seminars on Barth and Frei dating back to the summer of 2001, George tirelessly demonstrated how to go about unlocking the majesty of Barth's theology, and the intricacy of Frei's. He modeled a charity and passion that never strayed far from the lessons taught him by his own instructor in Barth's theology, Mr. Frei. His criticisms of a penultimate draft of the project pushed me to continue refining it. At the same time, his theologically motivated, relentless opposition to the concurrently unfolding U.S. war in Iraq, and the torture controversies surrounding it in particular, kept me acutely aware of the practical, ethical, and potentially radical political implications and obligations of scriptural reasoning generally, and Frei's and Barth's theological approaches more specifically.

Finally, I owe words of gratitude for the life and work of Bill Placher. Reports of Placher's dreadfully early passing arrived moments after I signed the final publication agreement for this book. Though I never knew him as teacher or mentor, I feel as though I did. Bill shared generously with me from his own continuing conversation with the memory of Hans Frei on several occasions in recent years. Much of what follows would not have been possible without his influence. In particular, Placher's *Unapologetic Theology* and *Narratives of a Vulnerable God* conspired with my first encounters with West and Stout to set the course for my seminary and doctoral studies. More importantly, Placher's witness as a dedicated teacher, academic theologian, and devoted participant in the life of the church modeled precisely the kind of theological sensibility written of by his teacher. Just as important was his diligence and clarity in making Frei's work available for the scholarly community and unfolding its implications for future generations of seminarians, students of religion, and (as Placher would say) church folk. We already miss him so.

To all of these I owe debts of gratitude that I cannot repay in kind. I hope that they will accept as a down payment my attempt to reread and expand with charity and imagination the legacy of their teacher, mentor, colleague, and friend. Whatever here does not withstand critical scrutiny, or might have been presented better, is certainly my own doing.

Of course, the very condition for the possibility of this project was the unwavering care and support of my parents, Lance and Kathy Springs, my grandparents, Alois and James B. Lewis, E. W. and Frances Springs (both of blessed memory), and my sister and brother-in-law, Amanda and Bryan Lang-lands. These are the people who first nurtured me in faith and intellect. They supported and sustained me throughout a decade of graduate studies and beyond. Any sanity that remains, I owe to them. My wife and colleague, Atalia Omer, read and interrogated every word that follows. She knows the full depths of the process through which this book came into being, and suffered and celebrated its occasional *in*sanity with me time and again. In some moments she carried me through. Atalia and the new additions to our journey together—Yehonathan Daniele and Pnei'el Alois Omer-Springs—continually challenge and inspire me. They will have to be thanked on a more intimate occasion.

Portions of chapters 2 and 7 appeared in the article "Between Barth and Wittgenstein: On the Availability of Hans Frei's Later Theology," *Modern Theology* 23 (July 2007): 393–413.

Contents

Toward a Generous Orthodoxy

Introduction

Hans Frei found his voice as a theologian at the close of an era of theological giants. The span of twelve years leading up to the publication of Frei's first book, *The Eclipse of Biblical Narrative*, witnessed the passing of his teacher and mentor H. Richard Niebuhr (1962), Paul Tillich (1965), Karl Barth (1968) and Reinhold Niebuhr (1971).[1]

Rudolf Bultmann passed away two years later (1976). Protestant theology in North America found itself in a precarious transition. Accounts of secularization proliferated nearly as rapidly as did liberation theologies. Theological voices in North American public life were mere echoes of what they had been at the height of the civil rights movement several years earlier. The idea of theology as an academic enterprise increasingly required justification. Theologians faced a set of dichotomous options. To remain within the academy meant surrendering much of theology's distinctively theological content in order to justify the legitimacy of its place there. How could a theologian speak in the full particularity of her theological convictions without becoming unintelligible to her nontheological interlocutors? Or if she adopted more broadly acceptable language and presuppositions, what could she say that was not already available to fellow scholars without the assistance of her theological commitments? In a shifting institutional and cultural context, theology appeared to be dispatched to the professional confines of seminaries and divinity schools.[2]

One alternative tempted theologians to draw back into the life of the church. If this avoided compromising theological distinctiveness, however, it risked implicating them in a sectarian posture and retreat into a theological ghetto. This alternative was complicated by the fact that lay people in many church contexts found the terms of academic theology as obscure as those of any nontheological scholarly discipline. Attempting to straddle the church/academy divide led some theologians to occupy themselves so intently with "theological method" that academic theology became nearly synonymous with "seemingly endless methodological foreplay."[3] Amidst the challenges presented by this transitional moment for theology in North America, Hans Frei emerged as one of the most influential theologians of his generation.[4]

In *The Eclipse of Biblical Narrative* Frei provided a meticulous historiographic analysis of the development of biblical hermeneutics in eighteen- and nineteenth-century Europe. There he demonstrated how scriptural reasoning and interpretation had come to be regulated by fairly recent and heavily theory-laden conceptions of "meaning," "reference," "interpretation" and "understanding." The story he told captivated theologians, historians, literary critics, and biblical scholars for more than a decade. At one level, it provided an historical and genealogical account of academic theology's late twentieth-century predicament. "Frei has helped to raise ghosts from the eighteenth and nineteenth centuries who are going to put insistent questions to us in the coming years," one discerning critic put it. "One of the hopes aroused by this book is that he himself will make a distinctive and outstanding contribution to answering them."[5] This is precisely what Frei set out to do.

In the wake of Eclipse, Frei sought to critically retrieve approaches to reading Scripture that early Christian communities had drawn from ancient Jewish scriptural practices. According to Frei, those approaches had been employed in various forms roughly through the time of the Protestant Reformation.[6] He took up this project fully aware of the ease with which one might valorize a bygone era of "precritical" biblical interpretation. Frei sought, by contrast, to recover and critically enrich those textual practices with the help of whatever twentieth-century philosophical and literary tools might lend themselves to his purpose and subject matter. Frei thought that critically enriching textual concepts like "realistic narrative" and the "literal sense of Scripture" might provide a way beyond a deepening theological and interpretive stalemate occurring between modern evangelicalism and theological liberalism.[7]

On one hand, textual literalists and theological apologists defended the biblical truth against the tools of "higher criticism." So-called "higher critics," in turn, charged scriptural apologists with deploying protective strategies and wishful thinking, even as they asserted their own enterprise as thoroughly scientific and historical, and thus legitimate in the halls of the modern academy. Still others claimed that the true religious significance of the Christian Scriptures was, in fact, wrapped in the garb of myth or symbol and required translation into terms of meaning that would be relevant to the modern worldview. Frei presented the case that, whether they recognized it or not, the various parties to this dispute held certain basic presuppositions in common. He thought the impasse between theological "liberals" and "conservatives" was largely characteristic of Christian thought in modern European and American contexts. As the deadlock between these camps of scriptural interpretation deepened, the predicament confronting late twentieth-century theologians intensified.

Frei's primary concerns were far more concrete than reconciling the apparent church/academy and church/world dichotomies that confronted him at midcareer. He sought, rather, to excavate and reframe many of the challenges to scriptural authority and theological exegesis posed by eighteen- and nineteenth-century thinkers. He sought, further, to avoid justifying his theological presuppositions from the standpoint of allegedly universally-available rationality free of prejudice. He refused to appeal to an "anthropological flash point for faith" apart from, or prior to, God's activity of special revelation. For these reasons among others, Frei is credited by some—indicted by others—with having formulated a *postliberal* theology.

Postliberal theologians are often characterized as privileging theological terms by refusing to translate them into nonscriptural and nonconfessional language. By some accounts, they insist that the terms used by their interlocutors be translated into Christian scriptural or ecclesial terms, or else face elimination. Critics from all sides worry that postliberal theology precludes serious and edifying conversation with nontheological voices and abandons concern for public discourse, owing to its focus upon the church.[8] "Postliberal" treatments of biblical narrative often are identified with nostalgia for the unified conception of Scripture allegedly enjoyed by "precritical" biblical studies.[9] They have been criticized for subsuming the rich diversity of nonnarrative biblical forms under a one-dimensional and too easily harmonious narrative of "salvation history."[10] Still others identify postliberal theology as forgoing all concern for historical accuracy of the Bible and fixating instead upon an autonomous "world inside the text."[11] Hermeneuticians have charged that postliberal instruction to "absorb" the contemporary world into the world of the biblical text ties postliberals to a reading of Ludwig Wittgenstein's "forms of life" as autonomous and discrete. Such a reading curtails the possibility of understanding across different forms of life (if the very idea of the biblical world "absorbing" the modern world is not preposterous to begin with).[12]

Evangelical critics charge that postliberal refusals to historically verify the events reported in Scripture yields the upper hand to modern forms of skepticism.[13] Thus, postliberals lack faith in the historical accuracy of the scriptural witness and are derelict in their apologetical duties. Postliberal theology seals itself into a "closed epistemological circle," some critics claim, "a fideism from within which everything can be seen clearly but which remains necessarily opaque to those outside."[14] At the same time, the single-minded preoccupation with the theological interpretation of Scripture of postliberal theology isolates it—perhaps even alienates it—from other academic disciplines. "When theology limits itself to the task of interpreting Scripture, it gains the advantage of peaceful coexistence with the other faculties of the university," writes Nancey Murphy. "Yet the price of conceiving of theology as the science of revelation is estrangement from and irrelevance to the secular sciences."[15] In the book that follows I argue that these criticisms related to "postliberal" theology fail to fit Frei's theological approach.

The overarching purpose of this book has two distinct but interrelated parts. It aims, first, to provide a critical and methodical exposition of Frei's theology. This objective is neither small nor uncontroversial. The sheer quantity of the critical responses that Frei's work continues to inspire nearly twenty-five years after his death is startlingly disproportionate to the two monographs and handful of articles that he produced over the span of his career. Moreover, as broadly influential as his work has been, it has stirred a comparable breadth of misunderstandings from all across the theological and philosophical spectrum. There are several reasons for this. Frei's thinking generally is unsystematic in ways that make it hard to follow. His writing style is, on occasion, positively obscure. His theology is highly eclectic, even improvisational and ad hoc. Frequently it does not cohere (or coheres only haphazardly) with any single or established theological option. In addition, the association of his work with the label 'postliberal'—and, occasionally, the outright assimilation of his later work to George Lindbeck's—has made Frei's work a target of criticism, polemic, and occasionally caricature. More significantly in my judgment (and a primary motivation for this book) is that insufficient attention to the thoroughly multidimensional character of Frei's work has led to many of the persistent misunderstandings that still vex it today.

Frei's work was a rich and textured mixture of intuitively articulated insight, occasionally excruciating rigor in the details, tortured prose, and a delicate balance between philosophical and theological sensibilities. In many ways he worked as a *bricoleur*—one who cobbles together the bits and pieces of whatever fragments are adequate for the subject matter and task at hand. As remarkable as was Frei's ability to discern family resemblances and develop inconspicuous connections, it was the unsystematic character of his work that left so many questions begged and lingering points of confusion. This book aims to help alleviate these confusions by elucidating Frei's project in terms of the full range of resources upon which he drew, the ends at which he aimed, and the basic coherence that his body of work exhibits.

The second purpose of this book, perhaps a necessary consequence of the first, is to critically challenge, expand, and enrich the history, character, and viability of so-called "postliberal" theology. My aim here is not to defend postliberal theology per se. In my judgment, the fact that Frei often gets pigeonholed as simply a "postliberal" theologian is itself a problem. Hence, my explication, clarification, and (where appropriate) defense of Frei's work does not result in an outright embrace of the "postliberal" nomenclature. Neither, however, does it result in pronouncing the demise of "postliberal theology," intentionally avoiding the category or declaring it useless. Reading Frei as I propose will charitably complicate it as a theological option. I aim to contribute to a more flexible and complex appreciation of the range of family resemblances that might be said to constitute loosely a "postliberal" approach to theology.[16] This term has found sufficient currency in theological reference tools, curricula, and scholarly literature to suggest that reports of its demise are greatly exaggerated. If so, the question becomes how to cultivate uses of the term that are sufficiently precise to be helpful, yet underdetermined enough to avoid Ralph Waldo Emerson's caution against such monikers—"if I know your sect, I anticipate your argument."[17] On one hand, I aim to demonstrate the ways that Frei's thinking resists certain customary and monochromatic uses of the category. On the other hand, a complex account of Frei's theology requires attending carefully to his ad hoc uses of (and contributions to) the various features of recent theology that might fairly, and illuminatingly, be described as "postliberal."

A central premise of this book is that unlocking the full resourcefulness of Frei's theological approach requires sustained attention to its interdisciplinary and conversational character from start to finish. I make the case that Frei's uses of Ludwig Wittgenstein, Gilbert Ryle, Erich Auerbach, Clifford Geertz, ordinary language philosophy, and nonfoundational philosophical insights—while christologically motivated and oriented—do not relegate his theological approach to critical quietism, methodological separatism, or a so-called "theological ghetto." Moreover, understanding these dimensions of Frei's work is not simply a matter of identifying similarities or appreciating elective affinities. An accurate grasp of Frei's thinking propels us into extensive engagement with nontheological forms of thought and opens opportunities for mutual enrichment. Sustained attention to the multidimensionality of Frei's work will demonstrate that Frei cannot be pigeonholed simply a "church theologian" whose work bears certain quizzical flashes of relevance or interest to nontheological discourses. In fact, his work challenges many of the received conceptions of what it means to be a theologian of "academic" or "church" or "public" varieties. Arguably, it exposes these received options as a set of false dichotomies. Read in this way, Frei's pragmatic application of nontheological resources for theological purposes provides a model for church-oriented academic theology in a religious studies context.

Unapologetic Theology

Frei thought that theology ought not seek to justify itself in nontheological terms nor by criteria outside the witness of the gospel narratives. Neither can it take its raison d'etre to be its relevance to society or use-value to the world at large. That said, theology cannot do without resources from nontheological disciplines and interlocutors, and neither can it simply forgo attention to its broader relevance. Theology engages nontheological resources not because it is incomplete in itself nor incapable of self-expression. It must seek these resources *because* it is capable of expressing itself. Theology, Frei thought, is licensed—if not compelled—to explicate and expand its implications by every means available. It cannot be sequestered by the boundaries of professional and academic propriety, nor by the methodological equipment by which specialized academic domains differentiate and legitimate themselves. All such resources avail themselves to the theological task because that task first belongs to Christ. "Belonging to Christ" means that this task is initiated and oriented by the gospel witness in which the person and work of Christ confronts its readers as a range of stories whose unity rests upon a Name. Whatever tools might help clarify and illuminate these stories are fair game for the theologian.

To say that theology belongs to Christ is to say, as well, that theology belongs to the church. Dogmatic theology was, as Frei conceived it, divine *Wissenschaft*—spinning out, testing, ordering, redescribing, and correcting the inferences and implications of the rationality intrinsic to faith. It was Karl Barth's influence that led Frei to claim that theology must be unapologetic, and Frei found Barth's pithy definition of dogmatic theology particularly helpful in expressing this idea. Barth had characterized dogmatics as "the scientific test to which the Christian Church puts herself regarding the language about God which is peculiar to her."[18] The language peculiar to the church was not the medium that the church had invented in order to talk about the revelation of God. It was, rather, the medium that had created the church.

The point of origin of the church's peculiar language—and the church itself—was the life, death, and resurrection of Christ to which the Scriptures witness. On this account, the "church" has no unrevisable form or fixed meaning apart, that is, from the fact that it belongs to Christ. The "church's" modifier, "Christian," has its significance in pointing to the One who calls, commands, and gathers the followers into communities of various shapes and forms. Scripture's witness to the person and work of Christ presents the *fons et origo* ("fount and origin") of that peculiar language in which the church is gathered and through which its life unfolds. Frei was keenly attuned to how *under-determined* Barth's account of the church remains. He treated the topic with a similar delicacy.[19]

Frei found Barth's account of revelation especially compelling. Scripture, on this account, is not a distinct and separable medium of God's revelation. It is, authentically yet indirectly, that revelation. God acts to manifest the person of Christ in and through the apostolic witness of Scripture through the activity of the Holy Spirit. The result is that the *content* of revelation becomes inseparable from its *form*, while remaining qualitatively distinct from it. The Word of God occurs conceptually, and thus linguistically, in God's continuing activity of revelation. Yet there is no simple or univocal correspondence between the words of Scripture and the Word of God as it comes in and through Scripture. Rather, God takes up human conceptual practices—words, concepts, and the claims and assertions they constitute—and breaks and transforms them for the purposes of revelation.[20] "[W]e don't have more than our concepts of God," Frei articulated the point. "We don't have a separate intuition, a preconceptual or prelinguistic apprehension or grasp of God in his reality, not unless we are mystics (and we honor them). But we don't need it either; for the reality of God is given in, with, and under the concept and not separably, and that is adequate for us."[21] As Barth put it, God's revelation comes as the gift to humankind in human form. "[T]he transparency of these human words [of the prophets and apostles] is God's free gift," Barth had written. "But this gift is placed in their hands, and it is theirs to make their own insofar as they will make use of it. Thus the exposition of the prophetic-apostolic witness becomes a human task and activity."[22] "Divine gift in human form" could not result in a synthesis of the two on this view. It could not compromise the qualitative distinctiveness of the divine and the human. God's revealing activity leaves intact the social and practical identities of human concepts, words, and speech.

Friedrich Schleiermacher had claimed, by contrast, that language was an anthropomorphic addition to revelation. As long as God's revelation remained within immediate (and thus prelinguistic) consciousness, it was wholly separate from its anthropomorphic mode of representation.[23] Barth countered

Schleiermacher with the claim that, because we have it only conceptually, revelation is, in a sense, *essentially* anthropomorphic. "Since all our language inevitably arises from and is formed by the human and creaturely sphere," George
Hunsinger helpfully captures the point, "the question in speaking about
God was not whether but how to be 'anthropomorphic'." [24] And yet, because
God's act of revelation is the condition of the possibility of such anthropomorphism, it differs entirely from the creeping anthropo*centrism* that Barth
diagnosed as a central disorder of modern theology and then worked tirelessly
to invert. It would be fair, if overly simple, to say that Frei spent his career figuring out how to speak and think about, conceptually redescribe, and expand
upon the peculiar kind of anthropomorphism that was central to Barth's
account of revelation.

From the time of his work in the early 1960s to his latest writings, Frei's
eclectic and ad hoc borrowing was central to the task of theology as he understood it. "The logic of religious discourse is odd," he wrote in the preface to *The
Identity of Jesus Christ*, "connecting things and categories that may be disparate
in other contexts, for example, the mode of factual affirmation with that of a
religious life." [25] At the same time, this same logic of religious discourse required
Frei to abandon any borrowed theoretical tool if it risked tying him down to a
general theory or larger philosophical system.

For instance, to expand upon Barth's definition of dogmatics as the testing
and self-examination of the language about God that is peculiar to the church,
Frei first drew a philosophical connection. [26] "Incidentally," he wrote, "Barth
wrote this passage in 1931 when most theologians still thought that the tools
for knowing God were faith with or without concepts, in either case an 'inward,'
mental instrument and not an 'outward' or linguistic skill. *Now* it's commonplace, philosophically as well as theologically. But it was quite remarkable for
Barth intuitively to reach that far ahead." [27] Here Frei pinpoints the idea—
increasingly commonplace at the time he wrote—that concepts are not ghostly
entities occurring somewhere inside an interior region of "the mind." They
are, rather, products of the practical skills of language use (paradigmatically,
words), an insight he found most profoundly articulated by Ludwig Wittgenstein and several of his students. [28] Frei thought that Barth was onto this insight
at least as early as Wittgenstein, and long before other theologians. While it
will prove to be far from the case that Frei can adopt some theoretical tool only
if he first finds it theologically articulated by Barth, there is something to the
suggestion that Frei was schooled philosophically and anthropologically by
Barth's theology.

As Frei read him, Barth's account of God's revelation, the church, and the
task of theology could be elucidated and expanded in practical and social terms.

The rationality intrinsic to faith does not present a set of conceptual relations abstracted from practice and action. It is self-involving. This does not mean, we will see, that this peculiar rationality is intelligible only for those involved in it. It means, rather, that "unlike other cases of factual assertion, that of the resurrection of Christ shapes a new life."[29] This rationality with the person of Christ at its center is embodied, practical, and therefore exhibited in all the practices that constitute the communities that participate in the life of the Christian church and engage the world.

Frei recognized concept and language use as two of the practical and social skills most basic to the constitution of the church, but without deriving this insight from a general anthropological theory. In other words he recognized language and concept use as basic practices for the church *not* because human beings are most fundamentally language and concept users. He thought of social practices as basic to God's revelation, the church, and the life of faith because God's Word "became flesh and dwelt among us . . . full of grace and truth" (John 1:14). This was the reason that Frei thought developments in ordinary language philosophy, the philosophy of mind, and cultural anthropology might serve as particularly helpful tools for theological redescription.

The practical and social character of faith and the church comes clearly to the fore when theology executes its task of reflecting upon and redescribing the practices that constitute the communities of those who follow Christ. "[T]he subject matter of theology (the very word itself involves it) is 'God'; that is the 'object' or 'referent' of the language," Frei wrote. "For Barth we have the reality only under the description, only linguistically, not independently of the concept as we use it in preaching and liturgy, in action in church and world, in prayer and praise."[30] In other words, the content of God's revelation is inseparable from—yet not identical to—its form. We do not have the Word of God in abstraction from the person and work of Christ as narratively depicted in Scripture. And we have that depiction as it is used in particular contexts. God's use of Scripture's witness to mediate the person of Christ implicates all the embodied practices to which that witness gives rise, and thus all the practices that constitute the church.

At the same time, the Word cannot simply be reduced to Scripture's narrative accounts nor to the uses of those accounts in particular contexts. Frei spent much of his career working to move past this apparent opposition. And while he clearly spent little time articulating what could be called a formal "ecclesiology," the priority he ascribed to the social and the practical embodiment of Christ's witness meant that ecclesial interests could never be tangential to his thinking. In fact, they informed much of his work from *The Identity of Jesus Christ* to his latest writings. Even when Frei did not speak explicitly of them, ecclesial implications of his work were never far away.

Much is made of the fact that Frei's thinking about the contextual character of the church and scriptural practices developed considerably over the course of his career. So much, in fact, that he is often treated as two different theologians—the "early" and the "later" Freis. The following chapters make the case that the development in Frei's thinking is just that, a continuous development. I argue that Frei's increasingly explicit attention to social and practical contexts occurred as an expansion and elucidation that made explicit the inferences and implications implicit in much of his earlier work. It is from the vantage point of the end of his career that Frei most overtly articulated his philosophical and anthropological borrowings. There these insights visibly interacted with his markedly Barthian orientation. I will show, however, that this increased explicitness does not become disjoined from the basic trajectory of Frei's earlier thinking. In fact, a central claim of this book is that the development of Frei's thinking over the course of his career displays greater continuity than discontinuity. Moreover, it is in attending meticulously to the philosophical and anthropological facets of Frei's work that we might draw its overarching continuity into full precision and clarity.

Frei departed from Barth in important ways. The reading of Barth in the paragraphs above, for instance, is uniquely Frei's. "Here I admit to doing a bit of finagling or making Barth say what I want him to say," he quipped in a characteristically plainspoken aside. "The word for that is 'interpretation'."[31] Even so, Barth's work enchanted Frei. It was his quiet but passionate interest that made Frei one of Barth's most provocative readers. And Frei transmitted that passion to several generations of his students.[32] Even at his most innovative and eclectic, Frei's work exemplified the basic spirit of Barth's claim that "the truth of the Word must be sought precisely, in order to be understood in its deep simplicity. Every possible means must be used: philological and historical criticism and analysis, careful consideration of the nearer and more remote textual relationships, and not least, the enlistment of every device of the conjectural imagination that is available."[33]

One of the earliest tools Frei used to make explicit the hermeneutical bases of dogmatic theology was Gilbert Ryle's debunking of a conception of consciousness and inner intentionality that had plagued modern thinking since Descartes—a conception Ryle called "the ghost in the machine."[34] Frei began reading Wittgenstein by the early 1960s and found the most salient themes in Wittgenstein's later writing worked out philosophically by Ryle and anthropologically by Clifford Geertz. He deployed these thinkers' theoretically low-flying treatments of terms like "meaning," "understanding," "identity," and "culture" eclectically and unsystematically in order to make sense of the theological claim that God's revelation comes to us conceptually.[35]

Of course, such an appeal to conceptual articulation—such a "linguistic turn"—did not imply the "autonomy of language." To put the point in the philosopher's terms, Frei's *semantics* presupposes a *pragmatics*. Concepts have meaning as *concepts in use*, and use presumes embodiment and context. Frei gradually came to understand biblically oriented concept and language use as a social and practical skill orienting and incorporating the practices and contexts that make up Christian communities.

Philosophy as the Handmaiden of Theology

Frei's uses of philosophical and anthropological tools for theological purposes invites a persistent misreading that I grapple with in various forms throughout the chapters that follow. While this misreading acknowledges value in Frei's use of nontheological resources for theological purposes, it does so with insufficient flexibility. I must briefly address it here lest some otherwise friendly reader proceeds with the misapprehension that my account of Frei is flatly "correlationist"—that I construe Frei as conferring a flat-footed independence to, and parity between, theology and nontheological disciplines. Such allegations misunderstand the nature and basis of the theological commitments that motivate Frei's work. They too rigidly demarcate the boundaries between theology and nontheological disciplines without paying attention to specific engagements between them.

Frei's theological interests and purposes are normative throughout his work without question. However, he remained insistent that this is not to be captured in a method or a formal rule. It is, rather, a matter of approach—of theological sensibility—a practical skill exercised on a case-by-case basis. Thus, Frei wrote to one inquiring philosophical interlocutor:

> I am a Christian theologian and do not regard philosophy as ever having achieved that clearly demonstrated set of even formal certainties (and agreements) in 2500 years which would allow it the kind of authoritative status you seem to want to accord it; and yet I believe theology cannot do without philosophy. Furthermore theology cannot even invest so much in the foundational/anti-foundational debate as to come out (*qua* theology) *in principle* on the anti-foundational side. Christian theologians will have to make use of philosophy, whichever way philosophers decide that particular issue is to be resolved. In other words, I'm saying two things simultaneously: First, Christian theology is quite distinct from philosophy . . . Second,

despite their mutual distinctness, theology as a second-order
discipline cannot dispense with philosophy, and their relation
remains complex and has constantly to be worked out, rather than
being of invariable shape.[36]

This passage exemplifies that, in Frei's view, the relationship between theology
and philosophy cannot be captured in a formal rule. Even a principle as platitu-
dinous as "philosophy will be Christian self-description's handmaid" gives the
encounter between philosophy and theology precisely the kind of invariable
shape that Frei thought we ought not presume to ascribe to it. Such a principle
risks fashioning an a priori conception that will constrain assessments of this
complex relationship across cases. This relationship, Frei thought, should be
assessed situationally. Any *pre*conception about the shape of their relationship
risks manipulating the theologian's task. The deficiency of such a rule is not
that there is no validity in it, but that it mistakes the claim that in *some* instances
philosophy will serve as theology's "handmaid" for the demand that such a
relationship must obtain in every case. The latter conception is not sufficient to
capture the multidimensionality and situation-specific character of the ways
that theologians will engage—and be engaged by—nontheological resources
and interlocutors. Some occasions may take this form. Others will not.

The point to keep in mind is that an a priori rule is insufficient because it
fails to take into account God's concrete activity. The case-by-case approach
Frei describes is not a claim that in every instance theology will subvert philosophy, disassemble it for useful pieces, or even appear to subsume it. Nor do
nontheological discourses find their true identity only in service to theology.
Such claims would abstract the faith-inscribed theological sensibility that
Frei's work exhibits by reducing it to a rule that presupposes a method for
application. While Frei described the theologian's use of philosophy as a "ruled
use," his is a fairly idiosyncratic application of that term.[37] He used it to indicate a practical skill or sensibility "most likely to have been learned in or by
application." Such uses are likely to be articulated and applied quite dispa-
rately, depending upon contextual specifics. Such uses are "ruled" in the sense
that any application of nontheological tools will not be arbitrary or accidental.
They will be ordered in accord with the centrality of the person of Christ.
But this ordering will appear differently—sometimes radically different—as
circumstances of application differ. As we will see, this is what Frei meant
when he said that the relationship of philosophy and theology stands as
"complex and has constantly to be worked out."[38]

Frei keeps the whole of the gospel in mind precisely because he leaves space
for, and fully expects, God's activity in particular circumstances of application.

The particular form that God's activity will take at a given point is impossible to predict antecedently. It could mean, in some instances, that philosophy serves as theology's tutor, standing on its own as friendly critic or adversary. Philosophy may be a fellow laborer in the field. From time to time, moreover, philosophical or anthropological claims may challenge, subvert, or scramble theological categories.[39] But this can be so only in virtue of a larger sense of the whole—a whole with the person of Christ at its center. So understood, the theologian's primary objective is neither to be distinctive nor normatively prior to other disciplines. The concepts characteristic of theology stand just as much under God's judgment as any others. Rather, the theologian's primary objective is to be faithful to the witness of Christ. And when faithfulness norms the theologian's task, her investigations cannot but come to bear an unpredictable flexibility and expectancy.

It is simply not the case, then, that theology must always come first in the order of presentation, or even that a theologian's explicitly theological interests and purposes will always plainly be in view. The distinctive feature of the whole is that Christ is the centerpoint that orients it. In this way, Frei modeled anthropological and philosophical workings after Barth's in that his ultimate end is to point back to that centerpiece. "[P]hilosophy is *not* the handmaid of theology," Barth declared. "Theology, along with philosophy, can only seek to be the handmaid of the church and the handmaid of Christ."[40] Frei, we will see, was inclined to agree.

On the Very Idea of "Church Theology"

Frei practiced theology as an interdisciplinary exercise. And yet, he understood that theology could forgo the final particularity of its vantage point only at its own peril. In the book that follows I clarify and expand upon precisely this delicate balance in Frei's work. I aim to demonstrate the kinds of engagements that are possible when a theological approach and sensibility of the kind that Frei exhibited converses with its nontheological conversation partners, as it must. Conceived in this way, theology is anything but sequestered from the broader concerns of intellectual discourses, academic or otherwise. Nor does it engage them to only plunder and steal from them. Neither, moreover, does it describe and redescribe its inner workings as a matter of "show and tell" in interdisciplinary conversation.[41]

Theology can—in fact it must—open itself, press beyond itself, engaging its interlocutors in ways that recognize their integrity. And yet, it does this on the basis of its conviction that "the final word of the final word" is the same for both. As Frei put it, what we say now we say with an "eschatological edge."[42] The theologian opens himself to his interlocutors under the conviction that God's promises are true, and that the command of the One who has called him or her is "the light which will burn the longest."[43] So conceived, the theological endeavor is not oriented by privileging the discursive practice formally known as *theology* per se. The theologian's allegiance is to the command and promise of God. And yet, the theological task is not *ultimately* guided by the theologian's faithfulness, but by God's. It is the particular commitments, normative attitudes, dispositions, and actions that arise from her being confronted by, conformed to, and working in light of God's commands and promises that make the theologian a theologian. These chart the course for what she does, and how she does it. However, what they imply and where they might lead far outrun exclusively theological precincts of her chores and tools. How can they not? God's promises and commands will transgress any disciplinary boundaries purporting to mark out theology *proper*.

The ways that the Word of God may come outrun even the practices that *formally* constitute the church. This does not imply that God's grace, as it comes to us, is extricated from language and social practices. It means, rather, that God's grace can announce itself in *any* language, as Barth put the point, "even by quite other tongues than those which have been given to us."[44] If God is the central actor in any theological endeavor, then it is God's freedom and sovereignty that must order the indispensability and standing complexity of theology's interrelation with philosophy on the one hand and their irremediable distinctiveness on the other. In this important sense, then, theology is *essentially* interdisciplinary. That is, it will be interdisciplinary insofar as it is faithful to the freedom of God's free grace. "Because it [God's grace] is free, it is not bound to human ways and means," Barth wrote, "the area of 'the Church's concern' is not a prison, but a platform open on all sides for the word of God's grace." He continued:

> The language of the Church, theological language, the edifying
> language of Canaan, may not be the fetters of this word, nor may the
> history and tradition of the church. . . . We must reckon with the fact
> that [God's free grace] can always be at work outside the walls of the
> Church and can be announced even by quite other tongues than
> those which have been given to us. Its being so free brings fresh air
> again and again into the Church. We need this fresh air, and we
> should not try to shut it out with the holy games of our churchly
> speaking and behavior. . . . The Lord God could be more liberal than
> we think or like. But we are speaking of God's liberalism and
> therefore about the freedom of God's grace.[45]

I take this description to convey the theological sensibility that Frei had in mind when he spoke of a "generous orthodoxy."

Of course, the radical unpredictability of God's Word cannot be abstracted from God's love. God's freedom is not like human caprice. Sovereignty does not render God unknown or unknowable. Rather, God comes to humankind—graciously, miraculously—as the One who loves in freedom, in the person and work of Jesus Christ through the continuing activity of the Holy Spirit.[46] The unpredictability of God's grace requires that it be discerned with specific attention to the witness of Scripture and its portraiture of Christ's life, death and resurrection. "[A] word from outside is not self-validating," Eugene Rogers cautions. "It is not entitled a prophetic authority within the church, until tested by exegesis. To make the test *is* the task of dogmatics, 'the *wissenschaftlich* self- examination of the Christian church with respect to the content of its distinctive talk about God.'"[47] Rogers' caution here pinpoints the centrality of the practices of reading and consulting Scripture in the life of the church, and the task of theology. But these, and all of the practices surrounding the exegesis of Scripture, are notoriously messy and continually contested. Affirming the necessity and centrality of scriptural exegesis can be only the first step in a perhaps interminable investigation.

The complex tension generated between a scripturally centered orientation and ceaseless interpretive contestation is no deficiency, of course. It is the substance of a living tradition. Frei sought to articulate, explicate, apply, and expand the historical and conceptual dimensions of all the practices that constitute the tradition of Christian scriptural reading and exegesis. He sought to conceive of this tradition broadly as, at once, orthodox *and* generous.[48] He thought that the inevitable conflict and contestation internal to scriptural practices presented an opportunity for Christ-oriented thought and practice to be, and to become, generous. Such generosity would identify and integrate the best insights of theological liberalism and evangelicalism at the same time that it sought to diagnose and move beyond the deficiencies that kept them locked in apparently irremediable conflict.

As Frei conceived it, a *generous orthodoxy* will attune itself to the best insights of various Christian theological traditions. It will reach beyond itself in order to engage the full wealth of resources made available by nontheological interlocutors, remaining keenly attentive to the ways that the Spirit might work through nontheological voices. For Frei, the dynamic, unpredictable, and at times painful interplay of traditional constraints with innovation and improvisation did not indicate strife, intractable opposition, or unfaithfulness in a tradition. It is blessing, and likely a sign that the tradition in question is flourishing. Such a tradition has much to teach, as well as much to learn. It has much to preserve, but also much to expect in the way of transformation.

The Structure and Claims of this Project

The early chapters of this book are primarily exegetical. In chapter 1 I sort through the details of Frei's early project on biblical interpretation published as *The Identity of Jesus Christ*. I argue that an adequate understanding of that project requires a cautious grasp of its complex integration of hermeneutical, confessional, and ecclesial dimensions. Perhaps more significantly, a detailed grasp of the complex interaction of these dimensions in *Identity* is required for an accurate conception of the deep continuity running from that work through Frei's thinking of the 1970s and 80s.

Chapter 2 explicates this trajectory of Frei's thinking over the course of his career. It challenges the prevailing belief that Frei's theology divides neatly into two distinct periods, the "early" and "later" Freis.[49] The earlier period is frequently characterized by Frei's attention to an essential meaning in the scriptural text; the later, by his turn to a cultural-linguistic framework, largely under the influence of the "cultural-linguistic" theory of his colleague at Yale, George Lindbeck. I argue that what is frequently understood as a "break" in which Frei turns his attention from Scripture "in itself" to the impact that cultural and linguistic considerations have upon scriptural practices is not, in fact, a *break* or *turn* at all. My rereading of the development of Frei's work demonstrates that so-called "cultural-linguistic" insights are, in fact, evident in some of his earliest writing. At the same time, his later writing does not forgo textual constraints exerted by Scripture in order to comply with the (markedly un-Wittgensteinian) slogan injudiciously extracted from Wittgenstein's later work and taken to encapsulate a Wittgensteinian theory of meaning—that of "meaning as use." I aim to demonstrate that even at his most explicitly "cultural-linguistic," Frei did not collapse meaning into use.

It is true that Frei's emphases upon the social and practical character of theology place him in close proximity to the work of George Lindbeck. And Frei was deeply appreciative of Lindbeck's work.[50] At moments he drew upon several insights directly from Lindbeck's formulations and endorsed certain of his claims. The intricacies of their similarities and differences lead many to view their projects as components of a larger single project or school of thought. In chapter 3 I argue that positioning their work in this way is a mistake. I argue that the differences between Frei and Lindbeck, while often quite subtle, are, on balance, more definitive than their similarities. Here I most explicitly take up questions of theology's relationship to philosophy and other nontheological disciplines. I make the case that Frei ascribed a *regional* (as opposed to all-fields encompassing) grasp to the theological task without compromising the final ultimacy of the claims that are its ground and goal. This distinguishes his position from several other theologians broadly classified as postliberal. At the same time, it further illuminates the basically conversational and interdisciplinary character of Frei's approach to theology.

Chapter 4 addresses two of the most pressing challenges to Frei's understanding of his own work. The early part of the chapter sifts through Frei's debate with the evangelical theologian Carl F. H. Henry. My purpose is to draw the most opaque feature of Frei's theology into the greatest possible transparency (arguably the point most criticized from evangelical quarters)—the question of historical reference. Here I take up two criticisms frequently leveled at Frei. The first is that he forgoes all concern for whether or not the biblical accounts of Jesus do, in fact, truly correspond to actual historical events. The second is that Frei reduces the biblical witness to a self-contained literary world. These are two of the criticisms that Henry raised against Frei. They have been reiterated by numerous critics in the twenty-five years since the Frei-Henry exchange. Indeed, Frei's writings on the question of historical reference are elusive. Nonetheless, I demonstrate that they are coherent and that his position can be made clear.

The second part of chapter 4 takes up another pressing criticism, this time from Barth scholars. Throughout his career Frei understood himself to be in an extended engagement with Karl Barth. Several critics allege, however, that Frei's reading of Barth suffers a central deficiency. Specifically, in treating Barth's 1931 book on St. Anselm of Canterbury as a "revolutionary turn" in Barth's thinking (from dialectical method to analogical thought form), Frei's account of Barth became infected with two persistent inaccuracies. Perhaps more significantly, these inaccuracies have been transmitted to many of the so-called "American neo-Barthians" influenced by Frei and have thus become two hallmarks of "postliberal theology."

First, positioning Barth's *Anselm* text as a turn from dialectic to analogy results in an "undialectical" treatment of Barth's theology. This restricts God's revelatory activity to an analogical mode of reference, thereby collapsing it into the biblical text and resulting in a "positivist Biblicism." Theology, then, becomes "just one more complacent, bourgeois discipline" rather than a task dependent upon God's actually doing something time and again as a condition for its very possibility.[51] A second deficiency in Frei's reading of Barth is that it conjoins its undialectical reading of Barth with "non-foundational philosophical epistemologies." On this basis Frei reconceived theology as "communal self-description" understood as the task of explicating the rules implicit in Christian practices. This account forgoes the realism of Barth's theology. It overlooks Barth's claim that God's miraculous activity makes human concepts refer to the otherwise unintuitable reality of God as God outside of the creaturely sphere. The result, if not a terminal deficiency in its own right, is a positive misconstrual of Barth's theology. Frei and the postliberal thinkers influenced by him deploy Barth for their own specific purposes. Such uses of Barth are not inherently illicit, of course. However, postliberal thinkers engage in a bit of false advertising insofar as they claim to present an accurate account of Barth's theology.

These are powerful charges, but they are ultimately erroneous when applied to Frei. Frei's understanding of Barth's *Anselm* text is far more complex than they permit. To access this complexity, I engage in a critical retrieval of material in Frei's dissertation, his earliest publications, and recently circulated material from his archived papers. Frei, we will see, identified a complex inter-relation of dialectic and analogy in Barth's theology dating back as far as the second edition of Barth's *Romans* commentary, and reaching forward into the *Church Dogmatics*. I argue that it is equally inadequate to view Frei's ad hoc use of "non-foundational epistemology" as implicating him in a *reductive* account of theology as "reflexive ethnography of Christian practices" that precludes propositional truth claims. I devote the remainder of the book to addressing the difficulties raised by the complex position that Frei articulates.

Chapters 5 and 6 together take up the feasibility of Frei's likening his theological approach to the cultural ethnographer's task of "thick description." Some claim that Frei's borrowing from cultural anthropology results in an overly integrated and unified conception of "the church" and its practices. Others charge his philosophical borrowings with contributing to a kind of "faith foundationalism" and conceptual or practical "fideism." Still others charge that his approach reduces theology to redescription of the logic internal to Christian practices, thereby eliminating the capacity to make truth claims or to correct Christian malpractice. Several questions follow in train. For instance, if Frei articulated a historically and socially situated conception of God's revelation, how did he avoid compromising the *objectivity* of that revelation? Once we focus our attention upon the contingencies of cultural context and the formation of revelation within social practices, have we not rendered God's revelation a function of human understanding? Moreover, as far as Frei utilized insights from Wittgenstein's so-called "linguistic turn"—a turn to the irreducibility and inescapability of linguistic social practices—how does he not "lose the world?" How, in other words, did he avoid sliding down the slippery slope into linguistic idealism? Reservations or criticisms couched in terms of a "linguistic turn" are often driven by assumptions of a necessary dualism between realism and antirealism. These latter questions I take up in the remainder of the book, in the context of a broader exposition of Frei's work on the plain and literal senses of Scripture.

Chapters 7 and 8 are the most philosophically technical chapters of the book. Here I hope to clarify and sharpen the cogency of Frei's claims about plain sense and literal reading. This issue has been of particular interest in biblical hermeneutics and the theological interpretation of Scripture. It is also a topic on which Frei's thinking was most in progress at the time of his death as it posed a central concern of the material posthumously collected and published as *Types of Christian Theology*. My aim in these chapters is to administer sustained attention to the difficulties produced by Frei's increased emphasis upon context, practice, and tradition in his account of Scripture's meaning. On one hand, I hope to illuminate Frei's uses of Geertz and Wittgenstein for these purposes. At the same time, I aim to identify and explore the limitations of these tools. For it is at their most anthropological and philosophical turns that Frei's claims about literal reading receive their most persistent criticisms.

It should come as no surprise that several of the central philosophical insights that Frei employed parallel—and, at points, overlap with—developments in recent philosophical work on social practices. Frei sought to sidestep many of the same perennial philosophical conundrums that praxis-oriented philosophers have worked to dissolve.[52] Chapters 7 and 8 explicate how the insights and advances in recent philosophical work might be used to further clarify and sharpen—and to overcome certain descriptive limitations of—the tools that Frei employed to circumvent the above difficulties. Attempting to imitate Frei's knack for bricolage, I briefly turn to the work of Wilfrid Sellars and his colleague Robert Brandom to further clarify, enrich, and expand Frei's account of literal reading and the plain sense of Scripture. My aim here will be to identify and sort out the several delicately interwoven strands of normative constraint that easily become tangled in Frei's latest writings. These tangles obscure the nuances of his claims and open the door to charges that Frei, for instance, merely offers cultural-linguistic correction of his earlier claims about realistic narrative, and that what inevitably ensues is a textual "warranted assertability" that collapses meaning into the community of readers' uses of the text. Brandom's conceptual pragmatism affords redescriptive insights with which I propose to clarify Frei's seemingly contradictory claim that the recognition of the *sensus literalis* as plain or obvious in Christian scriptural practices was not a "logically necessary" development, but was nonetheless obliged by the "rule of faith" or "rule of truth" in the life of the community. These resources should, at the same time, illuminate how Frei additionally factored in the biblical text's grammatical/syntactical features on one hand, and its "literary-literal" (what Frei calls its "storied") sense on the other.[53]

Conclusion

It might appear to some that an analysis of Frei's thinking focused so persistently upon the methodological facets of his work cannot but confirm its contrary; that is, in fact, Frei's theology never gets past a fixation upon theological method indicative of so many theologians of his generation as a last-ditch effort to retain some glimmer of relevance and respectability for theology in the academy. And yet, the viability of Frei's central claims about the church and its scriptural practices does not stand or fall with my success in clarifying or defending the tools Frei used. More importantly, Frei would politely demur in response to any characterization of his work that rested the success of his theological claims upon his precision about, for instance, some Wittgensteinian methodology (a markedly un-Wittgensteinian idea to begin with). As we will see in chapter 1, Frei learned from Barth that scriptural readers and theologians can never simply dispense with philosophy. The legitimacy of such insights and tools will depend upon how they were used.[54] It was in light of these observations that Frei found the philosophical approach portrayed in Wittgenstein's later work redescriptively helpful precisely because it was eclectic, ad hoc, nonreductive—even "vacillating." "There is not *a* philosophical method," Wittgenstein had written, "though there are indeed methods, like different therapies." Just as important as his eclecticism for Frei's purposes was Wittgenstein's aim to cultivate the kind of philosophical sensibility "that makes me capable of stopping doing philosophy when I want to. . . . that gives philosophy peace, so that it is no longer tormented by questions which bring *itself* in question."[55]

Frei took the unavoidability of second- and third-order reflection in theology as a constant reminder that the insights and tools of "theological method" serve their proper purposes only if, first, they arise in engagement with the biblical witness, and second, they are oriented by and used in ways that ultimately point back to that witness. In his own way, then, Frei sought to articulate a sensibility for which theological method was properly ordered and that was capable of "stopping doing theological method" when it needed to. And yet, Frei's was not simply a Wittgenstein-inspired attempt to relieve late twentieth-century theology of its methodological obsessiveness. Frei viewed the subject matter that motivated and oriented his theological investigations as unique in kind and finally defying any exhaustive framework or methodological container (even of a Wittgensteinian variety). Accordingly, at times in his writing Frei falls conspicuously silent, makes an appeal to "common sense," or interposes a proviso that speculation and system-building need to be avoided. From time to time he reminds his readers that "extra-scriptural" implements, while indispensable, must finally remain fragmentary and ad hoc.[56] Occasionally he will register such provisos at points where his interlocutors (theological apologists, "higher" critics, and analytic philosophers in particular) most want to pin him down in detail. This has led some to try to determine for themselves what Frei's theory of truth, meaning, or reference must be by force of logical inference. Such an approach to Frei's work is surely to frustrate and confuse. Frei frequently points his readers back to Barth's theology and, ultimately, to the biblical accounts themselves.[57]

Frei remained keenly attuned to the priority of the church for theology's vocation throughout his career. At the same time, it was precisely this sense of vocation that impelled him to continuously transgress the boundaries between church, academy, and world. His theological approach caught him up in a constant shifting and catching of balance that is not easy to emulate, and perhaps impossible to master. Explicating and expanding upon the dynamics of this theological gait cannot be done without at least attempting to resolve the confusions that arise from insufficient attention to its multidimensionality. At the same time, while Frei may have avoided a number of the errors ascribed to him by sympathetic readers and critics alike, by no means is his work free from error or inconsistency. My hope is to alleviate the inconsistencies and errors in his work that are merely apparent and to explore the prospects for further developing a theological sensibility of this type. These critical occasions afford the opportunity to affect a little theological therapy— to untie a few conceptual knots that do not have to be there. And *theological therapy* this is. For whatever philosophical explication I employ in redescriptively expanding upon Frei's theological approach ultimately points us back to Frei's unwavering focal point—the passion, death, and resurrection of Jesus Christ.

More than two decades after Frei's passing, contemporary theology finds itself characterized by a new set of dichotomous oppositions. Some of the most strident theological voices today retrieve notions of "tradition" and "orthodoxy" in the name of becoming as distinctive and uncompromising as possible. Frequently, such voices seek to counter theological postures that are so reserved or open-handed as to invite questions about what makes them theological at all. Both of these currents of theological reasoning stand in contrast to hegemonies of so-called secular reason that would eliminate theology from the conversation altogether on the grounds that the academic study of religion at large remains, purportedly, far too "residually Christian." Frei's work offers a wealth of resources with which to chart a path through these apparent dichotomies—a path that will be marked primarily by its concern to be charitable and faithful, and generous.

I

The Hermeneutical Bases
of Dogmatic Theology

Hans Frei's aversion to theoretical systems is nowhere more evident that in his approach to the practice of reading Scripture. His work reflects Karl Barth's influence in Frei's basic conviction that Scripture is the cornerstone of Christian faith because it manifests a person to its readers—the person of Jesus Christ. Moreover, any doctrine saying as much had to be based upon, and point back to, Scripture's witness. Understanding the scriptural accounts of Jesus, as Frei saw it, could not finally depend upon any particular preunderstanding on the part of the reader, whether that be his or her perspective, life experience, or even "reading through the eyes of faith." Imposing such categories upon the text would obscure, or dangerously anthropocentrize, its witness.

At the same time, Frei recognized—as Barth had—that readers do not approach Scripture in a conceptual vacuum. Some concepts and categories are necessary for the very possibilities of reading and comprehending Scripture in the first place. "[I]t is really quite impossible for us to free ourselves of our own shadow," Barth had written, "that is, to make the so-called *sacrificium intellectus*" by attempting to alleviate ourselves of the "external" influences of every set of concepts, interests, purposes, and perspective—as though assuming a 'view from nowhere'—prior to taking up and reading Scripture. Barth continued:

> Even in what [a reader] says as an observer and exponent [of what
> Scripture declares to us], he will everywhere betray the fact that,
> consciously or unconsciously, in cultured or primitive fashion,
> consistently or inconsistently, he has approached the text from the
> standpoint of a particular epistemology, logic or ethics, of definite
> ideas and ideals concerning the relations of God, the world and man,
> and that in reading and expounding the text he cannot simply deny
> these. Everyone has some sort of philosophy, i.e., a personal view of
> the fundamental nature and relationship of things—however
> popular, aphoristic, irregular and eclectically vacillating.[1]

Frei recognized that Barth had not taken a principled stand against all forms of "extratextuality." Barth's position was far more subtle and complex than that. "[W]e cannot basically contest the use of philosophy in scriptural exegesis," Barth had written. "Where the question of legitimacy arises is in regard to the *How* of this use."[2] To a great extent, it was this *how* of scriptural exegesis that Frei explored in his 1967 cycle of essays that later became *The Identity of Jesus Christ*.[3]

Identity remains a drastically underappreciated book compared to the critical attention received by *The Eclipse of Biblical Narrative*. And yet, *Identity* may be more instructive than *Eclipse* for understanding the multidimensionality and complex unfolding of Frei's theology. *Eclipse* is history written under a thesis. A fairly explicit agenda motivates the story Frei tells there and his painstakingly fine-grained excavation of the seemingly negligible figures over which he at times labors.[4] His aim is a cumulative account of the sea change in Christian scriptural practices that resulted in a detachment of the meaning of scriptural texts from their form as realistic narrative and the scope of their reach through figural reading. These latter had been central features of Christian scriptural practice through the time of the Protestant Reformation. *Eclipse* is not simply a story of decline and loss, however. The historical account carries within it implicit criticism of the impoverished condition of late twentieth-century Christian theology and scriptural practices. He gestures toward Barth's work as a promising means for course correction.

Identity presented Frei's own sketch of the prospects for the kind of realistic reading of the Gospels that would be possible if one took seriously the critical-historiography account that he had set forth in *Eclipse*. It is a complicated endeavor, to say the least. Theoretically austere, concerned to make Scripture both the starting point and culmination of its analysis, there Frei grapples with the two problems around which modern theology revolved: (1) "the endeavor to see a unique revelation in history [in and through the person of Christ] as an option that made sense"; and (2) the real presence of Christ, that is, "the presence of God in Christ to our present age, or any given present age."[5] Frei sought, as well, to investigate a set of exegetical practices that might successfully navigate the challenges raised by traditional thinking about Christ's identity and presence within the modern context without purporting to revert to a "precritical" state of affairs. In so doing, he could not but contrast critically this approach with the scriptural practices that had prevailed amongst readers of Scripture (believers and nonbelievers alike) since the early eighteenth century. This adds a subtly polemical aspect to the book. Interestingly, Frei took up all of these concerns with Christian lay readers as his intended audience.

Identity's multiple dimensions make it easy to conflate the several distinct but interrelated tasks that Frei undertakes there. It is easy either to underestimate the delicacy with which Frei interwove these various strands or to misorder their importance. Frei's interests and purposes in Identity are deeply hermeneutical and, at the same time, situated within and directed toward the textual practices in which Christian communities engage, and which are largely constitutive of those communities. A precise grasp of Frei's project in this text is prerequisite for understanding the full significance and development of his work in the 1970s and 80s.

My task in this chapter is to explicate the several dimensions of Frei's project in Identity. The first section situates Frei's motivating concerns against the backdrop of the general account he provides in Eclipse. Section two attends to Frei's more specifically theological aims, namely, the proper ordering of the identity and presence of Jesus Christ. Section three addresses the theoretical ambitions of the project and the extent to which it may implicate Frei (however inadvertently) in the kind of hermeneutical endeavor he sought to avoid.

I. Frei's Objectives in The Identity of Jesus Christ

Frei's investigation of what Barth had called the how of biblical exegesis highlighted an apparent dilemma. On one hand stood the complex indispensability, yet ultimate inadequacy, of nonscriptural concepts and categories. On the other hand, as Barth had pointed out, the name of Jesus Christ is the object mirrored in the biblical text, and must be orientational for engaging it. "These texts can be understood only when understood as determined by this object," Barth had written.[6] Hence, while necessary, both philosophical and theological modes of thought would have to remain "hypothetical, relative and incidental" in the exposition of the biblical witness. They must be oriented by the subject matter, by "the object mirrored in the text" of Scripture—the name of Jesus Christ in his person and work as concretely set forth in evangelical witness and apostolic proclamation.[7]

Frei proposed to navigate this dilemma by remaining as formal as possible with the concepts and categories used to read and enrich the Gospels' renderings of Jesus. He thought that modern approaches to scriptural exegesis tended to apply such schemes in ways that overwhelmed the subject matter.[8] As a result, reading and interpretation become abstracted from the concrete renderings of Christ that the scriptural narratives portray. If kept "suitably formal," Frei thought, extrascriptural interpretive insights and tools might "enable us to see who Jesus is without determining better than the text itself the meaning and importance of what the Gospels have to say about him."[9] With such a reserved approach in mind, Frei set out to demonstrate the kinds of reading he thought most appropriate specifically for scriptural exegesis. This task entailed finding tools with which to open up, enrich, and aid in critically reflecting upon Who the gospel narratives concretely portray. Proper use of such tools would need to ultimately point back to those accounts, leaving them as theoretically unencumbered as possible. In order to avoid overwhelming the subject matter, the exegete's interpretive interests, purposes, and theoretical tools would all need to be administered in consistently piecemeal, occasional, and ad hoc ways. Moreover, readers would need to take up the exegetical task expecting to have their categories, interpretive schemes, and expectations scrambled from time to time by the One who confronts them in these stories.

If such an approach to scriptural reading were itself to be oriented by the centrality of Christ in the gospel narratives, Frei thought it necessary to first accurately grasp the unique affirmation at the center of Christian faith—"not only that [Christ] is the presence of God but also that knowing his identity is identical with having him present or being in his presence."[10] Accurately grasping this affirmation would mean properly ordering its elements. Frei worked to show that Christ's real presence to believers presupposes the manifestation of Christ's identity by the scriptural narratives. Moreover, the former cannot be disconnected from the latter without harmful repercussions. If Christ is present to believers as the Word of God in Scripture, then one cannot properly have Christ's presence in abstraction from Scripture's witness to his identity. Christ's presence is dependent upon Christ's identity.

Frei's motivations for this task were several. First, he thought that this order of identity and presence was simply true to Christian faith, and he sought to clarify how these logical interworkings were based upon the biblical witness. This meant neither eliminating nor diminishing Christ's *presence* in relation to his *identity*. It meant, rather, properly ordering the two. The person and work of Christ appear in and through the evangelical narration as the gospel narratives that tell Christ's story. Hence, placing Christ's identity and presence in proper order presupposes the gospel narratives of Christ as the hermeneutical bases for the task. Frei intended, furthermore, to demonstrate the kind of approach to reading Scripture that fit this scriptural witness. Frei turned his attention to the *surface* of the scriptural narratives in order to avoid two persistent modern quandaries: (1) *reference* as the basis for meaning and credibility, and (2) *intention* as the basis for identity and agency. With this facet of Frei's project, the polemical element of *Identity* comes into view, illuminating the story that Frei told in *Eclipse*.

Modern approaches to Scripture generally viewed the narrative form of the gospel accounts of Jesus as a function of their attempt to report historical events. As reports, these texts could be considered "historical" and "reliable" insofar as they accurately corresponded to the facts of the events in question. Historical-critical tools of investigation presented the most promising means for determining the probability that the events recounted in the Gospels actually had occurred. As evidence-oriented models of rationality ascended in eighteen- and nineteenth-century Europe, however, less and less of the gospel accounts could achieve credible status.[11] Amidst these developments, two general strategies prevailed for salvaging the Gospels' credibility.[12] These strategies attempted either to reconcile the biblical reports with "the facts of history" or to sidestep questions of history and factuality all together by focusing upon the symbolic or mythical significance of the stories.[13]

Readers employing the first approach tried to square miracle accounts with the lawlike workings of nature and the probabilistic character of historical reasoning. This approach accommodated a range of "naturalist" and "supernaturalist" perspectives. Naturalists believed that there must be some perfectly ordinary explanation for events reported in miraculous terms. Wherever some gospel writer reported a miracle, a "naturalist" interpreter claimed that the event had been either misunderstood or misinterpreted. Supernaturalist readers, by contrast, appealed to divine inspiration in response to challenges posed by historical reference and factual credibility. While Supernaturalist accounts varied by degrees, by the middle of the eighteenth century even the most conservative defenders of the faith relied upon the claim that God revealed himself through the book of nature.[14] These claimed that the most dubious points in the biblical narratives could be rendered compatible (at least) with the basic tenets of natural religion. "The biblical revelation," Frei restated the position, "though disclosing mysteries above nature and reason, contains nothing contrary to them."[15] The reports conveyed in the Bible "could be brought to the highest degree of probability or the greatest possible moral certainty in accordance with all the logical rules of historical proof," wrote the eighteenth-century

University of Halle professor S. J. Baumgarten.[16] Frei pointed out that, with precisely these claims, Supernaturalists had gradually come to presuppose a thoroughly modern conception of historical reasoning "at least in their acknowledgment of responsibility to a court of general credibility for anything, sacred or secular, that claims to be a fact."[17]

Others responded to the treatment of biblical narratives as the reporting of historical facts by claiming that the stories do not exactly mean what they appear to say. Rather, they speak elliptically. A report of Jesus' resurrection, for instance, does not actually mean that he defied the laws of nature in an event of literal resurrection. Rather, reports of this event function symbolically, for instance, as narrative symbols of the rise of the disciples' faith in Jesus. Accounts portraying the life of Jesus cannot be restricted by a lack of corroborating evidence from outside the text. The Jesus stories function symbolically to convey certain general truths and religious meaning. They are thus freed from the constraints of evidential reasoning and historical verification.

In *The Life of Jesus Critically Examined*, David Friedrich Strauss drew upon the symbolic significance of biblical narrative in order to articulate his own response to the challenge of historical verification. Strauss argued that miracle stories function as myths that reflect the consciousness of their sincere yet primitive authors. As Frei restated Strauss's central claim, "[E]ach miracle story is simply typical of the folklore inhabiting the spiritual climate of the area and era, given the Old Testament tradition and the common anticipation then and there of the advent of the Messiah."[18] Strauss found a way to sidestep the need to reconcile these reports with "factuality" and "history" altogether. Readers of the book of Scripture need neither reconcile its contents with the book of nature nor resort to an appeal to supernatural claims. Strauss was genuinely surprised by the vitriolic response that *The Life of Jesus* inspired from the most devout of its readers. He understood himself to have opened up new possibilities for the religious meaning of Scripture by refining away their "primitive mythical dross."[19] Of course, in so doing, his account reduced the meaning of these myths to "the working of the religious mind or spirit" of their writers, thus bringing the anthropocentric meaning of the gospel accounts full circle.

Frei pointed out that the various symbolic approaches to scriptural meaning presupposed that the content of the biblical narratives was separable from their form. On this view, Christ could be "present" wholly apart from the concrete accounts portrayed in the Gospels. He could be present in a symbolic sense to those affected by the story quite apart from the concrete accounts of his words and work that the gospel narratives portray. For instance, he might be present as the moral ideal of the fully realized human personality, or as the personification of the power of human belief to resist oppressive circumstances. Such readings were possible because the gospel narratives really mean something other than what they appear to say.

Each of these approaches shared an overriding concern with what lay behind the text—"the facts" to which these stories referred. Either they took factuality as a legitimate burden of proof that the biblical reports must meet or as a criterion from which the mythical significance of Scripture could happily exempt itself. Frei was convinced that such concerns gave normative sway to relatively recent and quite theory-laden notions of "history," "reference" and even "the facts." He thought that these concepts and their theoretical presuppositions had come to govern the interpretation and exegesis of Scripture in the eighteenth and nineteenth centuries. The result was an eclipse of the tradition of scriptural reading that had sustained Christian communities since their earliest time. *Identity* responded to these developments by outlining an approach to reading Scripture that treated the form and content of the biblical narratives as indissoluble.

II. From "Presence" to "Identity"

The question of "the presence of God in Christ" had haunted Protestant theology since the early nineteenth century.[20] This tradition tended to explain "presence" in terms of "the phenomenon of consciousness," a conception that had underpinned both the symbolic and supernaturalist ways of comprehending Christ's identity in the modern era. The referential conception of Scripture's meaning relied upon a notion of subjectivity inaugurated much earlier by Rene Descartes in the seventeenth century. On the Cartesian view, individual self-consciousness, or a "thinking thing" (*res cogitans*), stands over against the objects that furnish the world, "extended things" (*res extensae*). Objects are known "objectively" insofar as ideas representing them in the inner theatre of the subject's mind accurately correspond to those objects out in the world. When "clear" and "distinct," such representations present themselves immediately to "the mind's eye." As such, they are incorrigible. One cannot be mistaken that some object seems to appear to one's mind's eye, even if that seeming (the representation that presents itself) ultimately turns out to be inaccurate. Immediacy and incorrigibility thus became two of the salient features of the Cartesian conception of consciousness. And *self*-consciousness—the thinking mind's presence to itself in the very act of cognition—became the most immediate and incorrigible feature of all. *Cogito ergo sum.*

As Frei told the story, the advent of consciousness as a "private subject world" that consisted in a "perspective on all objective existence including its own psychophysical organism" came of age in the work of Immanuel Kant.[21] On this account, Christ's real presence to the believer was construed as an interior, unmediated (and thus incorrigible) occasion. The embodied actions of the man Jesus might be said to function as the particular container of his discrete and separable "God consciousness." Christ, occurring fully in that "God consciousness," could be present wholly apart from his embodied words and work that the gospel accounts portrayed. As an event internal to the believer's consciousness, Christ's presence might occur as a "limit experience," either cognitively or affectively immediate. It might occur in the form of a clear and distinct idea present to the mind's eye. It might manifest itself as a warming of the heart. From this perspective, theological rationalists and religious pietists were, in effect, siblings beneath their skins. Whatever the specifics of the account, the basic point they all shared is that Christ's *presence* occurs as some kind of immediate event construed broadly in terms of "consciousness." In each case Christ's presence is abstractable from the concrete witness of Scripture to the accounts of his life, death, and resurrection.[22] As such, the rise of this "private subject world" was yet another development that marked the demise of realistic or history-like reading of biblical narrative.[23]

Frei sought to counter the prevailing models with an account of Christ's identity and God's presence in Christ that was at once faithful to the scriptural portraits and consistent with the logic intrinsic to faith—specifically, with the axiom that Christ's presence presupposes his identity. Such a conception could neither employ nor presuppose the pervasive understandings of personal identity and presence taken for granted in most modern thinking on the subject, namely, "identity as consciousness" and presence as "immediate presence to consciousness."[24] By contrast, Frei focused on the inseparability of the form and content of the Gospels' witness. "[W]e cannot have what [the Gospels] are about without the stories themselves," he wrote.[25] These stories are "history-like—in [their] language as well as [their] depiction of a common public world (no matter whether it is the one we all think we inhabit), in the close interaction of character and incident, and in the non-symbolic quality of the relation between the story and what the story is about."[26] He would later expand the point:

> If we say, for example, that Jesus is the Christ, or if we say simply
> Jesus Christ, what we mean by that is exactly the story of the
> enactment of his life and death and resurrection. He is not Jesus
> Christ apart from that story of his. It is precisely in that story that he

is the Christ. And this already begins to suggest something of where the difference is located between consciousness or liberal theology and what I am trying to shape. The self in the consciousness theology is precisely that: a consciousness perspective on the world. In a realistic story the self is a specific agent. There is no *general* anthropology here; the self is a *specific* agent who is what he does, not the consciousness lying behind. He is what he does and what is done to him, so that (if I may put it in theological terms) Jesus Christ the person is nothing other than the enactment of his person in his work. Who is Jesus Christ in the story? Not a messianic consciousness: no, he is the obedient Christ who died and rose again. He is what he does and what is done to him.[27]

With such claims Frei began to present his case that the gospel stories depictively render or open up a world to their readers because the meaning of the scriptural portraits of Jesus is inseparable from their narrative shape.

Frei identified this shape in terms of the formal "structures" of those narratives, namely, the interaction of character, circumstance, and theme. "[N]arrative meaning is identical with the dynamics of its descriptive shape—for which the characters, their social context, the circumstances or incidents, and the theme or themes are all interdependent," he wrote.[28] He explained, further, that "[r]ealistic narrative is that kind in which subject and social setting belong together, and characters and external circumstances fitly render each other. Neither character nor circumstance separately, nor yet their interaction, is a shadow of something else more real or more significant. Nor is the one more important than the other in the story."[29] In other words, the elements of realistic narrative interweave. Characters are portrayed in their social contexts in virtue of interacting with the circumstances and incidents they encounter. The story's "sense" is just its depictive rendering of its subject matter in the interaction of character, circumstance, and theme. Moreover, to abstract any one of these elements at the expense of the others is to distort the narrative form, and thus the sense of the story. Likewise, to reduce the story to some more basic element (even, for instance, a set of propositional assertions) is to render it something other than the depictive rendering that it is, and thus, to diminish the orientational significance of its narrative sense.

Given these "formal structures" of realistic narrative, how best to open up and redescribe the events that the gospel narratives portray? What kind of conceptual tools might aid in such redescription without distorting those narrative descriptions?[30] In response to such questions, Frei proposed that the exegesis most appropriate for stories such as the gospel accounts simply looks for the *sense* of the story. And yet, such exegesis must be more than repeating or reiter-ating those stories. It must seek, rather, to make reading "more alert, appro-priate, and intelligent." As such, it needs interpretive tools that will illuminate and open up those stories in order to "enable us to see who Jesus is without determining better than the text itself the meaning and importance of what the Gospels have to say about him."[31] In other words, the tools must remain as delicate as possible. To that end, Frei devised certain "formal questions" to pose to the narratives—questions that, when properly deployed, would not "force an answer that would risk overwhelming either the person or the story."[32] To the accounts of Jesus in the Gospels Frei posed the questions "Who is he?" and "What is he like?" Frei thought that such questions were sufficiently formal to cast into relief the identity of Jesus in the gospel narratives without over-whelming the texts' portrayal of his identity with a general theory.

To answer the question "What is he like?" Frei focused on the public and socially embodied interaction of character and circumstance with the help of a device called "intention-action description," which he borrowed from the Oxford philosopher of mind, Gilbert Ryle.[33] "Intention-action description" takes as primary the public and practical makeup of a character's story, "the changes that he undergoes, and his acts at a given point or over a limited stretch of time." So understood, the character's actions do not *represent* his more essen-tial identity. They embody his identity. To know someone, according to this view, to "access his true identity," is simply to observe what she does and what is done to her in a given context and her interaction with a set of circumstances. To answer the question "Who is he?" Frei employed what he called the "sub-ject's self-manifestation." According to this descriptive approach, a character exhibits his identity by virtue of his words ("verbal medium") and embodiment ("its peculiar and unexchangeable location that is called *mine*").[34] "In each instance there is a strong relation between the inward and the outward," wrote Frei. At the same time, "neither case has a 'ghost in the machine' character, and each illustrates a healthy regard for the intrinsic significance of the outward life."[35] Readers need not conduct psychoanalysis upon the character of Jesus in the Gospels to *really* understand what he is up to and what his claims mean. Nor do readers need to seek the significance of his actions by symbolically transposing them. Basically, what you see is what you get.

Of course, the normative priority of the biblical narrative over any interpre-tive tools meant that even Frei's use of these formal textual implements must ultimately be subordinated to the stories themselves. And not surprisingly, the categories of identity description that Frei borrowed from Ryle, as useful as they are, eventually break down when applied to the scriptural account of Jesus.[36] Frei's central point here is that once Ryle's categories of description have served their purpose, one must simply retell the story in order to convey the identity of this story's central character. Frei meant to sidestep any attempt to explain the "ontological unity" of intention and action, as well as precisely how who and what one encounters further contributes to the formation and extension of one's identity.[37] Reflecting upon the story in terms other than those that the story itself presents, as one must, finally brings the reader full circle back to the sense of the story as a whole. However, this return to the story comes *after* the tools have been redescriptively applied and have enriched the story's sense. Frei described the results of his own analysis with Ryle's tools as follows:

> I would say that the person of Jesus, and not only his message, is both indispensable to, and known in, the story. Who is Jesus in the Gospel story, and under what identification or description do we know him? He is who he is by what he does and undergoes, and chiefly we must say that he is Jesus crucified and raised. That is the simple fruit of identity analysis of the New Testament narrative, both in the mode of intention-action description (with its categories finally transcended) and in the mode of subject–self-manifestation description. Hence my claim that we have in these narratives a high Christology—not before, but after any 'demythologization' or transfer of the 'meaning' of the story to 'our day' that may be necessary.[38]

With this claim Frei pressed home the point that the meaning of the story is finally just that—the story. Frei's emphasis on the person and work of Christ depictively rendered in Scripture casts a curious light on the tools he borrowed from Ryle. Borrowing this apparatus for opening up the text implicates him in a sort of hermeneutics, and thus, some conceptions of "understanding," "meaning," and "interpretation." Did Frei, however inadvertently, fall into precisely the kind of theorizing he set out to avoid?

III. Anti-Antihermeneutics

It is possible to read Frei's emphasis upon the normative priority of the gospel narratives—"to keep the theological horse before the methodological cart," as Frei put it—as indicative of a general aversion to hermeneutics. Clearly, he sought to illuminate and follow the history likeness of the gospel narratives so as to leave them as theoretically unencumbered as possible. Moreover, whatever tools Frei used in service of that purpose he kept secondary to the particular story of Jesus. In other words, Frei consistently sought to avoid hitching his theological horse to some general theory about "the process that goes into understanding or interpreting linguistic phenomena."[39] However, Frei's reserve toward *general* hermeneutical theory does not result in an aversion to hermeneutics altogether. Imprecision about his interpretive aims at this point will have major repercussions for our grasp of the rest of Frei's work.

Frei was by no means "prohermeneutics" in what he called "the ambitious, indeed all-encompassing view of hermeneutics as inquiry into the process that goes into understanding or interpreting linguistic phenomena."[40] Neither, however, was he, in principle, "antihermeneutics." To take a principled "anti" position would implicate him in the same kind of mistake committed by full-fledged hermeneutics—an "antitheory theory." In the preface to *Identity* he offered his own definition of hermeneutics as "the old-fashioned, rather narrow, and low-keyed manner as the rules and principles for determining the sense of written texts, or the rules and principles governing exegesis."[41] This notion of hermeneutics, Frei explained further on, "appeal[s] to just enough theory to describe the rules and principles used in actual exegesis, and no more, even if it means that we have only fragments of one or several theories rather than a single all-inclusive theory of interpretation."[42]

Frei identified two central parts to his exegetical task in *Identity*. He sought to offer a realistic (or "history-like") reading of the gospel narratives on one hand. He sought, likewise, to demonstrate the use of "hermeneutical instruments" that avail themselves to such a reading.[43] To overlook this hermeneutical dimension of Frei's project risks unhitching altogether the "methodological cart" from the "theological horse." As Frei used the word, "hermeneutics" meant neither developing a method nor a general conception of "understanding." He understood hermeneutics as *praxis*—as second-order reflection upon the concrete practices of reading these particular stories.

Granting priority to the narrative shape of the scriptural story does not preclude Frei's use of hermeneutical approaches. Theory remains valuable, but on an ad hoc and pragmatic basis. In other words, Frei's claim for the normative priority of the gospel narratives was a claim about *proper ordering* rather than *exclusion*. He draws a distinction, and then places the components into their proper order in relation to the centrality of the person of Christ. By treating the gospel stories as stories *first* (because it is in storied form that the words and work of Jesus come to their readers), Frei thought that the story could orient the reader's understanding of it.[44] But the normative priority of the story eliminated neither the need for interpretive tools nor questions about "understanding" and "meaning." Rather, the story's priority influenced which tools should be selected, how those tools were ordered and used, and how readers might best think about "understanding" and "meaning" ("remember: for this particular exegetical task!").[45] Frei explained:

> I am only saying that to the extent that the Gospel stories are, indeed, in the form of narrative, let us treat them that way when we ask about their meaning. This does not deny the validity of source, form, and redaction criticism—in other words, of a variety of historical approaches both to the fact estimation and meaning of these stories. Nor does it deny—on the contrary, it affirms—the active, though unsystematic, interplay of historical, aesthetic, and religious understanding in comprehending a text. Who knows what may result when we scramble methods? The only plea I make is for distinction and priority choice. . . . [D]epending on what we do, one kind of reading will have priority. And if we try to understand the text internally (to itself), we must try for a reading in which the text itself is the meaning.[46]

In other words, the christological content that these stories "depictively render" should order whatever additional interpretive tools and theoretical presuppositions a reader might have. If the story remains the centerpiece of the exegetical practice, then its narrative form and christological content—namely, its witness to, and manifestation of, the person of Jesus—would order the results. In this way, ideas about reference, meaning, and understanding were not eliminated altogether but became oriented by the storied sense of the text.

To say that Frei's approach is not a method means that he was not concerned to fashion a system or general theory of how to read or a set of rules that hold across contexts. He did not execute his exegetical task "as if it were composed of a series of distinctly demonstrable steps which together form a whole, subject to independent description, and then, as a separate and subsequent procedure, applicable to the textual materials to be exegeted!"[47] He sought, rather, to demonstrate a situated, practical sensibility for reading these stories that is first oriented by the stories. Learning to read these stories in this way entails developing the sensibility and practical wisdom for selecting and applying the tools that may fit them. Frei borrowed tools from nonscriptural sources and then let them go either when they ceased to be of use or began to encumber the sense of the story with weightier philosophical questions and claims. The tools are ordered by their usefulness to the stories and thus stand in an asymmetrical relationship to those stories.

As we saw in Frei's borrowing and application of Ryle's tools, this asymmetry is neither mysterious nor complicated. Frei employed Ryle's descriptive terms insofar as they rendered the history likeness of those stories all the more clear and basic and illuminated the identity of their central character. At the point that these tools ceased to be useful for this purpose, Frei let them go. Notice that these tools are not derived from the textual accounts themselves. Nor is there any indication that Frei reconfigured them in order to fit a scriptural worldview or system. His application was more ad hoc and unsystematic than that. He selected the tools in light of the kind of depiction rendered by the New Testament. He used them to open and expand these realistic narratives in ways that would not divert attention from the person that these stories present. When these tools ceased to be of use, Frei turned his attention back to the stories themselves.

But why should Frei have bothered mentioning hermeneutics at all? Why not sidestep this concern in favor of simply reading the story? Another glance in Barth's direction helps to further clarify Frei's claim that "without some perspective of our own the story has no discernibly significant shape for us."[48] To do anything more than simply reiterate the words of the story required tools for commenting on, redescribing, and elucidating these stories. That is, some such tools were necessary even to engage in exegetical practices as theoretically uncomplicated as asking our fellow readers if they agree with what we find in the story and why and, as Frei put it, in order to "discover its patterns to one another." Otherwise, exegesis would be reading and rereading the stories. Such reading would be, at best, a "mechanical exercise, no more than the reiteration of words."[49] Addressing what he called "the problem of interpretation," Frei wrote, "we must approach the Gospels with some conceptual tool in hand, otherwise we understand nothing at all."[50]

> Without some perspective of our own the story has no discernibly significant shape for us; but on the other hand we must not imprint either our own life problems or our own ideological analyses on it. The proper approach is to keep the tools of interpretive analysis as minimal and formal as possible, so that the character(s) of the narrative of events may emerge in their own right.[51]

As we saw above, here Frei has borrowed a move from Barth that he would deploy throughout his career.[52] "We must be clear that every scheme of thought which we bring with us is different from that of the scriptural word which we have to interpret, for the object of the latter is God's revelation inspired by the Holy Ghost, and it can become luminous for us only through the same Holy Ghost."[53] Applying any such tools or categories to Scripture must remain an ad hoc affair. What such an engagement with Scripture looks like, and the claims Scripture makes in such an engagement, will vary to some degree on a case-by-case

basis. The tools for exegesis may vary by context, according to immediate concern, and on the basis of particular engagements with the biblical narratives.[54]
But the gospel witness to the person and work of Christ will remain orientational. Engaging the biblical narratives is a context-specific practice requiring
practical wisdom, so as to avoid eclipsing the narratives themselves.[55]

Conclusion

Frei made the case that the gospel narratives portray a history-like world that
demands "to be read in ways which allow that world to unfold in its own time
and space." And yet in *Identity*, ultimately, he articulated these insights with an
insufficiently asymmetrical emphasis upon "realistic narrative" as a general
literary category. Despite Frei's own caution, "realistic narrative" became a conceptual tool that risked overpowering the gospel story. The temptation was,
first, to establish the basic structure and function of this type of narrative and,
then, turn to reading the gospel accounts in light of those dimensions of the
narrative.[56] This overemphasis risked conferring normative priority upon the
form of the story, when both form and content ought to be subordinated to
the person of Christ. As a result, Frei would have to soften his claims on behalf
of "realistic narrative" as a literary genre of which the Gospels present particular
instances.

The following chapter examines how Frei corrected the extent of his depen-
dence upon realistic narrative in order to maintain his basic point in *Identity*
that the history likeness of these stories should be basic to how readers
approach them. Frei discovered that he could make much the same point about
these stories primarily in the terms of a tradition of reading in Christianity that
orbits around the concept of the *sensus literalis* or literal sense of the text. This
approach alleviated neither his need to reflect critically about "understanding"
and "meaning" nor his need to work deliberately with "extratextual" instruments and insights. Opting to focus upon the *sensus literalis* required Frei's
increasingly explicit attention to contexts of use and an expanded account of
scriptural practices. While these represent marked developments in his work, I
argue that Frei's refocusing his project along these lines occurs in the form of
a refining and expansion of his earlier claims about Scripture. They do not
present a simple rejection of his previous claims in favor of new ones. I aim to
demonstrate, moreover, that even his early emphasis upon the realistic narratives is never presented in abstraction from a concern for the practical, public,
and ecclesial contexts in which Christians engage Scripture. In other words,
Frei did not forgo concern for the history likeness of gospel narratives so

central to his earlier work for the historical and social character of believers' uses of those stories in his later work, as is often argued. Rather, he gradually came to reposition his concern for the history likeness of these stories—no less central to his description than before—within this broadened and explicit concern to account for the essentially historical, social, and practical character of these history-like stories.

2

Between Barth and Wittgenstein

Frei's account of the meaning of the biblical texts lends itself to ambivalent readings. Recent treatments have highlighted, in particular, the way that it appears to diverge problematically over the course of his career. This apparent divergence creates the impression of two distinct phases of his work. Frei's early work is commonly understood to locate the meaning of biblical narrative in the structures of those texts. "The meaning, pattern, or theme, whether upon literal or figural reading or, most likely, upon a combination of both, emerges solely as a function of the narrative itself," quotes Dan Stiver from a passage at roughly the midpoint of Frei's career. "It is not imprinted on the text by the interpreter or by a multifarious interpretive and religious 'tradition.'"[1] Stiver reads Frei here as rejecting outright several hermeneutical options: reader-response theory, Gadamer's "fusion of horizons," as well as Paul Ricoeur's claim that the world is "textually construed" due to the "intertextuality" of human experience. This rejection leads to several liabilities. It overlooks the ways that readers' preunderstandings inevitably participate creatively in following the text. At the same time, it overlooks that hermeneutics provides critical tools which aid vigilance against ideological distortions and inadvertent "replacement of the text by the prejudices of the reader."[2]

Stiver goes on to point out that certain emphases in Frei's later work lead in the opposite direction—"to a sociological approach which suggests that a community shaped by a particular tradition can become the virtual arbiter of what a text can mean."[3] He pinpoints trends in Frei's thinking that associate Scripture's meaning with the *use* of that text within a community of faith. "We can therefore go in two different directions with Frei," Stiver concludes. "One emphasizes the sufficiency of the immanent meanings of the text, the other emphasizes the community of faith as determining the meaning of the text."[4]

This apparent divergence in Frei's thinking generally inspires two responses from friendly readers and critics alike. The first identifies this divergence as a discrepancy and attributes it either to simple self-contradiction or perhaps inevitable tensions owing to the unsystematic character of Frei's thinking. A second response attributes it to a "conceptual turn" that Frei's thought underwent at roughly the midpoint of his career. According to the second version, Frei turned from an essentialist understanding of scriptural meaning to a social and practical account that attended to the uses of that text within ecclesial contexts.

The later, distinctively sociological developments in Frei's thinking are often attributed to the influence of his colleague at Yale, George Lindbeck.[5] Lindbeck first formulated a "cultural-linguistic" account of religion in *The Nature of Doctrine*, deploying insights that he cobbled together from Ludwig Wittgenstein, Clifford Geertz and Thomas Kuhn.[6] Religion, he claimed, is like a culture or language. It functions as a framework "that makes possible the description of realities, the formulation of beliefs, and the experiencing of inner attitudes, feelings, and sentiments."[7] In his work of the late seventies and eighties, Frei similarly drew upon insights provided by Geertz and Wittgenstein in order to describe the Christian church as a set of cultural practices. Moreover, his use of these insights appeared to coincide with his having reframed Scripture's "meaning" as a function of the way that text is used by readers in particular times and places. It is common among Frei's readers to identify these developments as the marks of his "turn" to a cultural-linguistic framework. They are thought to reflect perhaps the most salient difference between Frei's earlier and later work.

Recent readings of Frei's work attempt to improve upon these dichotomous options. In the first book-length treatment of Frei's theology, for instance, Mike Higton softens the stark distinction between "earlier" and "later" Frei.[8] He resists the common account that would identify the "cultural linguistic" developments in Frei's thinking as either equivalent to, or derived from, Lindbeck's articulation of those categories. In particular, he points to a crucial distinction between Lindbeck's use of general philosophical insights to frame a theory of religion, within which Christianity presents a distinctive instance, and the christological ground and goal that orient Frei's sociological redescriptions of

Christian scriptural practices.[9] Rather than positioning his later work as an independent project that stands on the far side of a break with his earlier thinking, Higton reads Frei as having shifted his attention to ecclesial contexts at the midpoint of his career. Frei accomplished this repositioning, in part, by simplifying the "methodological scaffolding" that had surrounded his earlier account of biblical narrative.[10] "Frei's aim in all this later work," Higton explains, "was to bring theology more closely into contact with the ordinary practices of Christian communities in our world, and to clear away that great methodological thicket which too often separates theological experts from the believing communities they intend to serve."[11] Higton characterizes this change in Frei's writing as largely stylistic in character—from a "purely intellectual" form to a style more "sociologically aware of itself."[12] This shift was, in turn, "accompanied and supported by a clarification of the ordinary, practical, ecclesial grounds of theology, a clarification which involved Frei distancing himself from some aspects of his original, more theoretical grounding of dogmatic theology," Higton writes, "and his re-establishment of a slightly altered version of his theology on new ground, 'cultural-linguistic' and theological."[13]

The virtues of this account are several. First, it makes clear that Frei's emphasis of the historical character of concepts and concept use served his christological aims. Secondly, it reflects how Frei articulated his attention to historical contingency and social location with increasing explicitness throughout his writing of the 1970s and 80s. Moreover, this account strives to discern a basic coherence in the development of Frei's thought by refusing to treat the later work as an independent project. And yet, even in light of the refined account that Higton provides, the reasons that Frei relocated his theology on new, "cultural-linguistic" ground at midcareer remain puzzling.[14] In fact, fully accounting for these sociological developments in Frei's thinking continues to be difficult, which comes as no surprise.[15] Several of the writings in which Frei most explicitly and articulately reflected upon those developments were still in progress at the time of his death.[16] With great sensitivity to this fact, Higton opts to treat Frei's work during the last years of his life as *commentary* upon his earlier work. "In the absence of the more substantial work that Frei would have gone on to produce had he not died so suddenly, I think his later work is most appropriately presented as commentary upon his earlier work, rather than as an independent project," Higton cautions his readers.[17] Construed as commentary, the later work is to be treated as clarifying and qualifying Frei's thinking of the 1960s and early 70s. Higton then cautiously sets out to explicate how Frei's later "modifications" of his earlier work offer insight into his "original intentions" and, accordingly, restrains his treatment of this dimension of Frei's work to a single (albeit rigorous) chapter.[18]

In the following chapter I explore the possibility that emphasizing the role of Frei's later work as commentary upon the earlier unnecessarily constrains the possibilities for grasping its full reach and significance. Perhaps more importantly, so situating that work might inhibit the prospects for expanding upon and carrying forward the important innovations that Frei developed in the final decade of his career. Are the only available options to either frame Frei's work of the 1980s as *commentary* or as an *independent project*? Is his later work merely a "cultural-linguistic correction" of his earlier claim that "the Bible means what it says?"[19] In order to refine our grasp of the development of Frei's theology, as well as survey the prospects for further expanding a theological approach of this type, in the following pages I explore the extent to which "cultural-linguistic" insights do—or do not—present "new ground" upon which Frei relocated his theology during the late 1970s. I make the case that, rather than confronting us with points on which Frei distanced his later thinking from his earlier, the pragmatic and sociological developments in his work of the late 70s and early 80s actually present important continuous threads in his thinking from early to late. I demonstrate that many of the "cultural-linguistic" insights ascribed to his later work are, in fact, central to his thinking as far back as the early 1960s. I aim to show, furthermore, that the developmental character of Frei's work over the course of his career exhibits a coherent trajectory from earlier to later—a trajectory that is consistently Wittgensteinian in sensibility and indebted to his career-long conversation with Barth's theology. Reading Frei with attention to the full reach of these insights, I argue, permits us to treat the methodological developments in the last decade of his career as more than clarification and qualification of his earlier claims.

If successful, the reading I propose here may help resolve the persistently vexing motivations and sources of Frei's apparent turn to "cultural-linguistic" insights. Viewed in genealogical perspective, insights usually considered novel to Frei's later work can be recognized, instead, as resulting from a trajectory of thought that Frei had been grappling with and refining since early in his career. Clearly, such developments include moments of adjustment and critical revision. Nonetheless, the fact that we have much of Frei's later material only as it was "in progress" at the time of his death turns out to be no special reason to treat it with hesitancy. In fact, its "in progress" character becomes largely consistent in tenor with the rest of his work. Frei was constantly in motion as a thinker, self-critical of his best insights, revising, gleaning new insights from his colleagues and students. Refining the precision of our grasp of this dimension of his work should illuminate how the recurring "in progress" character of Frei's work is, in fact, one of its several virtues. So positioning Frei should provide a clearer picture of the kind of thinker that he was—one whose thinking about a set of material insights and conceptual tools unfolded in a "lengthy, even leisurely" manner over the course of several decades. We will see that Frei's early work is more innovative, and his later work less derivative, than is often recognized.

I. Methodological Continuities in the Development of Frei's Thought

As in *The Identity of Jesus Christ*, Frei's concern for the centrality of the biblical narratives motivated his writing throughout the 70s and 80s. And as before, the narrative accounts were central in virtue of the Person manifest in and through them. Moreover, throughout the development of Frei's thought, his methodological prescriptions consistently intended to demonstrate the kinds of tools appropriate for scriptural exegesis conceived as opening up, redescribing, and critically reflecting upon those texts. In short, while the relationship between the methodological concerns and the subject matter of these texts is necessarily delicate, it is delicately necessary. Frei's methodological concerns are a central feature to the priority that he gives to the biblical narratives. These two concerns must be properly ordered, and neither can be abstracted from the other. Frei's tools and his approach presuppose his subject matter, namely, the unity of narrative form and christological content of the gospel accounts of Christ's death and resurrection. This required conceptual tools that were at once theoretically austere and sensitive to history and context.

Frei's ideas about the historical character of concepts, linguistic practices, and the social and practical constitution of the church begin to surface in various forms in his theological work of the 1960s. These appear perhaps nowhere more explicitly than in the conceptual tools by which he expanded upon those claims in terms of culture and language. In his "Remarks on a Theological Proposal" of 1967, for instance, Frei cited the increasing influence of the philosopher he would consult as the primary resource for redescribing what he took to be Barth's chief historicist insights.[20] By Frei's own account, as early as 1962 he had been earnestly reading this thinker, arguably the philosopher of historicized concepts and situated practices *par excellence*—Ludwig Wittgenstein.[21]

Looking back from the vantage point of an interview in 1975, Frei recounted drawing two general insights from his earliest readings of Wittgenstein's work. "First, it described how we actually use language in ordinary conversation and so weaned me from a specialized vocabulary and thought form both for philosophy and theology," he reported. "Second, it weaned me away from high-flown ontological reflection in order to understand theology."[22] If we take Frei at his word here, then as early as the mid-1960s he concerned himself with ordinary social practices like concept and language use and sought to sidestep theoretically weighty claims in his theology. If this is correct, then it remains to be seen just how Frei's work at that time demonstrates these basic interests and purposes. The "methodological scaffolding" surrounding his work at the time may not have set the theological expert so far apart from the community of believers after all.

In several essays of the 1960s, Frei's Wittgensteinian proclivities appeared most pointedly in his description of both the narrative portrayal of Christ's identity and the church as publicly and socially constituted. And the redescriptive tools he used to articulate these insights (those borrowed from Ryle, in particular), in fact, materially implicate the insights he would invoke more explicitly later on (namely, Wittgenstein and Clifford Geertz). These connections make it possible to trace a continuity of approach running through the developments that many readers casually refer to as the "earlier" and "later" Freis. In fact, the philosophical and anthropological appropriations that Frei made from early to late in his career bear marks of Wittgenstein's influence.

In his article "Theological Reflections on the Accounts of Jesus' Death and Resurrection" and again in the articles that became *Identity*, Frei articulated a social and practical conception of Christ's identity. As detailed in the previous chapter, the gospel accounts of Christ's identity, on this view, do not rely upon the modern philosophical notions of "inner intention," "consciousness," or "self-presence." Rather, they portray Christ's identity in the publicly available, socially situated, complex interaction of character, circumstance, and theme. Frei used Ryle's work to displace the notion of "inner lives" with what characters in the biblical narratives do as they interact with the circumstances confronting them. As we saw in the previous chapter, Ryle's criticism of "the ghost in the machine" enabled Frei to sidestep construing "consciousness" as "a perspective on the world" that anchored an agent's "intention," or the real meaning of his actions and, allegedly, the true seat of his identity.

In the Preface to *The Eclipse of the Biblical Narrative*, Frei identified Ryle and Erich Auerbach, along with Barth, as the primary influences on his thinking up to that point.[23] This 1974 citation brings to culmination roughly a decade of their influence upon his thinking. Frei read Auerbach's *Mimesis* for the first time in 1964. He sharpened his understanding of Ryle's work in 1965 while advising a dissertation entitled *The Concept of Personal Agency as a Theological Model*.[24] By the mid-1960s Frei began to characterize intention and action, as well as thought and speech, as "unified"—as "causal knowledge internally connected with bodily movement in an external context." The resources from which he derived these insights illustrate the case-by-case basis on which he worked out the complex interaction of philosophy and theology. On the philosophical side, Frei cites Ryle as well as Elizabeth Anscombe's text *Intention*, Stuart Hampshire, and Peter Strawson. He was equally influenced on these points by the theological work of Austen Farrer, and of course, Karl Barth.[25] On the basis of these insights, Frei brought thought, intention, and identity out of the internal space of "consciousness."[26] "[F]or descriptive purposes," he wrote, "a person's uniqueness is not attributable to a super-added factor, an invisible agent residing inside and from there directing the body."[27] Highlighting the basically *linguistic* character of this descriptive account he added, "[i]ntention and action logically involve each other in verbal usage."[28]

Frei deployed Ryle's view that "intending" was simply an "implicit action" in order to help illuminate the christological character of the "realistic narratives" in Scripture.[29] The events and persons at the "surface" of the realistic narrative text present themselves to readers in virtue of the public interactions of socially constituted characters and practically generated circumstances. In other words, Ryle's public conception of identity located the meaning of the text in the world wrought *in* the narrative *through* the shape of the story. From this Frei extrapolated:

> [N]either from the side of paying attention to oneself nor from that of
> paying heed to what others are about is it necessary to enter a
> mysterious realm of being and meaning, or an equally mysterious
> private-subject world in order to discover what makes any intelligent
> action publicly or commonly intelligible. Especially in narrative,
> novelistic, or history-like form, where meaning is most nearly
> inseparable from the words—from the descriptive shape of the story
> as a pattern of enactment, there is neither need for nor use in looking
> for meaning in a more profound stratum underneath the structure
> (a separable "subject matter") or in a separable author's "intention,"
> or in a combination of such behind-the-scenes projections.[30]

Did Frei's use of these tools implicate him in a general theory? Did it conflict with his effort to remain theoretically unencumbered in order to grant priority to the gospel accounts? The reason that it did not is apparent in how he responded to the criticisms leveled at Ryle's project when it was treated as a general, explanatory theory.

Frei was acutely aware that in his attack on "the ghost in the machine" Ryle appeared to go so far as to deny the very possibility of "inner episodes," and perhaps any conception of "interiority" whatsoever. Ryle viewed all talk of "mind" and "mental states" as metaphysically tainted with the Cartesian picture of an "animating ghost." Critics labeled his position a form of "behaviorism" because it allegedly reduced all talk of "mental processes" and cognition to forms of behavior. Moreover, Ryle never made convincingly clear how his criticisms of "the ghost in the machine" did not render meaningful action "non-cognitive," nor that talk about minds was, at bottom, nothing more than another way of talking about bodies caught up in habituated, material processes.[31]

Frei found the full extent of Ryle's claims oddly counterintuitive. "There is a real or hypothetical 'inside' description of that transition [from intention to action], of which all of us are aware but of which it is not easy to give an account," he wrote.[32] However, Frei was convinced that to theorize an explanation of this occurrence would overpower the subject matter that the Gospels portrayed. He thought that behaviorist charges would surface only against the background of an attempt to *systematically* explain intention and action. And this he was not concerned to do. He simply sought tools adequate for *redescribing* the content of the gospel narratives in light of their particular form. "It is my conviction that the interaction of character and circumstance, subject and object, inner and outer human being cannot be *explained*," Frei wrote. "But it can be described, and that is the point." He continued, "One can, up to a point—and only up to a point—render a description, but not a metaphysics, of such inter-active unity. It is done by the rendering of certain formal categories; but finally, the categories themselves are outstripped, and then all one can and must do is narrate the unity."[33]

In his conclusion to *The Identity of Jesus Christ*, Frei expanded his conception of the world depictively rendered in Scripture to encompass not merely authors and readers but the church and all of history.[34] Having first applied Ryle's account to the characters and circumstances in the gospel narratives, he then expanded that account of 'intention-action description' to include the intentional actions of the gospel writers in writing these texts. "'[T]o perform intelligently is to do one thing and not two things,'" Frei quoted Ryle, "And this is as much to be remembered in the reading of texts as in understanding any other intelligent activity."[35] Thus we have grounds to take the gospel writers as simply meaning what they say rather than as employing words that approximately reflect a separable—and ultimately interior— "intended meaning." We need not presume that the author's *true* intention somehow stands hidden within or behind the account that he provides, any more than we must of necessity deduce psychologically the *genuine* intentions of the characters whose actions the gospel accounts narratively render.

Frei should not be read here as suggesting that there is no such thing as "authorial intention," nor that "what the author intended to communicate" may not need to be clarified, contextualized, or be subject to different readings. His point is more modest than that—only that we need not be locked into, and need not presume, a conception of authorial intention as something hidden and waiting to be decoded. Especially in genres of realistic, novelistic and history-like writing ("where meaning is most nearly inseparable from the words—from the descriptive shape of the story as a pattern of enactment"[36]) the author's intention likely will be as plain to view and humdrum as the words and phrases that the author uses. Such determinations will need to be negotiated on a case-by-case basis.

By applying this redescriptive tool to the life of the church, Frei construed it as gathered around and oriented by its historically situated and extended engagement with—and gathering under—the biblical witness.[37] In his final essay of *The Identity of Jesus Christ* cycle of 1967, he wrote:

> [T]he Church has a history, indeed it is nothing other than its as yet
> unfinished history transpiring from event to event. The identity
> description that we applied to Jesus in the Gospels must, to a lesser
> extent and in merely analogous fashion, be applied also to the
> Church as his people. . . . Jesus' identity was the intention-action
> sequence in which he came to be who he was. His being had to be
> narrated, as historians and novelists must always narrate the matters
> they describe. He was constituted by the interaction of his character
> and circumstances. So also is the Church. Like Jesus, like the people
> of Israel, the Church is its history, its passage from event to event in a
> mysterious pattern that is dictated neither by a mechanical fate nor
> by an inner and necessary rhythm of the human psyche.[38]

These redescriptive insights Frei drew from Ryle's text *The Concept of Mind* present a point at which Wittgenstein significantly influenced Frei's thinking during the 1960s.[39] In fact, many of the central insights in Ryle's text of 1949 owe much to Wittgenstein's later thought, even well before the *Philosophical Investigations* appeared in print in 1953.[40]

Ryle and Wittgenstein first met at a joint session of the Mind Association and the Aristotelian Society in 1929 and later at meetings of the Moral Sciences Club at Cambridge. By the early 1930s Ryle recounts long walks and conversations with Wittgenstein about the issues and concerns that would come to be known as Wittgenstein's "later thought."[41] Along with just a few others, Ryle was in a unique position to work through these ideas as a student and young professor. The ideas Wittgenstein shared with him in their many conversations of the 1930s and 40s were otherwise not available beyond the immediate Oxbridge context until the publication of the *Philosophical Investigations*.[42]

Though the influences are considerable, to characterize Ryle as a follower of Wittgenstein would overstate the case. Characterizing Frei as a card-carrying Wittgensteinian would be equally incorrect. My account has a stake in neither of these claims. However, the insights that drew Frei to borrow from Ryle's work bear deep family resemblances to Wittgenstein's later thought and reflect his influence. Frei recognized these resemblances and drew freely and innovatively upon these tools insofar as they aided his theological interests and purposes—at least until those tools were finally outstripped.[43]

The usefulness of Wittgensteinian tools led Frei to further resources and insights. For instance, Frei gradually came to speak of the church in terms of a social organism, and found it helpful to describe the theological task as analogous to nonreductive, reflexive ethnography.[44] In much the same way he treated the identity of Jesus, he sought not to explain or justify the practices and understandings uniquely constitutive of the church. He sought, rather, to describe them for purposes that could range from self-clarification and intellectual devotion to self-criticism and self-correction, as well as interdisciplinary conversation. This redescriptive conception of theology Frei likened to what Clifford Geertz had famously called "thick description."[45]

Frei's borrowing from Geertz to redescribe the church and the theological task is an important marker in the development of this thinking. Geertz's influence appears most explicitly in his "'Literal Reading' of Biblical Narrative" essay and the material published as *Types of Christian Theology*.[46] These insights helped Frei become increasingly precise in his explication of the inseparability of the theological task and the contextually situated practices of the church, again in markedly Wittgensteinian terms. Geertz relied upon multiple facets of Wittgenstein's later work. He wrote:

> Wittgenstein's attack upon the idea of a private language, which
> brought thought out of its grotto in the head into the public square
> where one could look at it, his notion of a language game, which
> provided a new way of looking at [thought] once it arrived [in the
> public square]—*as a set of practices*—and his proposal of 'forms of
> life' as (to quote one commentator) the 'complex of natural and
> cultural circumstances which are presupposed in . . . any particular
> understanding of the world. [These] seem almost custom designed to
> enable the sort of anthropological study I, and others of my ilk, do.[47]

Frei did not dispatch the insights he drew from Ryle and Auerbach in his later writings, though he ceased to mention either of these thinkers as frequently as before. In fact, he was quite clear that Geertz's conceptions of meaning, culture, and descriptive approach most appealed to him at precisely those points at which Geertz clearly draws upon Ryle's and Wittgenstein's accounts of the public meaning of actions on the basis of *know-how*.[48] Geertz provided Frei a social and practical framework for thinking of culture that complements the intention-action construal of character and identity that Frei had earlier derived from Ryle and Auerbach.[49] Both cases presuppose a social and practical conception of the context and action in which people "act intelligently" in virtue of interacting in and coping with the practical circumstances within which they find themselves. These tools helped Frei to position reading and consulting Scripture as practices within, and unique to, that particular, Christian social organism—the church.

Of course, Frei's thinking evolved in important ways as it proceeded along the trajectory that I have described above. For instance, he came to temper his earlier reliance upon the notion of realistic narrative out of concern that it gave priority to a general literary category. He feared that insufficiently nuanced claims about the nature of this literary genre risked overpowering the biblical story's rendering of the person of Christ. In particular, Frei grappled with the temptation to, *first*, establish the basic structure and function of realistic narratives and, *second*, read the gospel accounts as a particular instance of those dimensions of the narrative. This risked conferring normative priority to the literary category.[50] And yet, Frei nonetheless preserved a christological sense to the surface of the biblical accounts even as he softened his use of literary categories to redescribe them. In other words, his work of the 1980s reconciled his earlier claims for the normative priority of the plainly christological character of these history-like (formerly "realistic") narratives with his increasingly explicit articulation of the social-practical character of engaging Scripture. How he did this, and whether or not he was successful, are concerns I take up in extended detail in chapters 7 and 8.

As in his work of the 1960s, Frei refused to sidestep all concern for hermeneutics in his later work. As before, he construed textual interpretation in a manner sufficiently delicate to avoid overwhelming the subject matter of the gospel accounts. "'Understanding' involves a capacity combining a variety of skills rather than a single unitary phenomenon," Frei wrote in 1982. "Understanding texts may differ in accordance with different texts and their differing contexts."[51] Moreover, he persisted, we will have to continue to explore what it is to "understand" as a set of technical questions that reflect upon situated scriptural practices as a second-order level. His claims at this point bear a great deal of consistency with the account of "understanding" that Frei described in his reflections on *The Identity of Jesus Christ*.[52] At roughly the time he wrote those articles, he had commented:

> In regard to understanding, (remember: for this particular exegetical task!) I find myself influenced increasingly by Wittgenstein and J. L. Austin. . . . There is, it seems to me, a variety of descriptions for any given linguistic phenomenon and hence, above all, no ontological superdescription or explanation. Furthermore, the "grammar" (use according to rules of such a construct) is more readily exhibited or set forth than stated in the abstract.[53]

Notice that, even at this early point, Frei's account of understanding is situation specific. He avoids technically freighted explanatory claims. The difference is that Frei's later formulation reflects a far more refined and explicit attention to the complex interaction of text and context. Frei is increasingly explicit that any such task of interpretation, and second order reflection upon the terms of the interpretive task itself such as "meaning" and "understanding," is a set of embodied skills employed on a context-by-context basis. Moreover, he expands his earlier conception of "the world wrought in scriptural narratives" and the sense in which it embraces the historical situation of the church. Thus, Frei came to characterize the communal life of the church as an "acted document"— a historically extended, socially and practically embodied organism that is oriented by the narrative world depictively rendered by its engagements with Scripture.[54] Believers are "embodied agents," Frei writes, "who understand what we do, suffer, and are in the contexts in which we are placed as the world is shaped upon and by us. In that way the gospel story and we ourselves inhabit the same kind of world."[55]

These refined insights about the cultural and historical situatedness of ecclesial contexts are neither wholly novel to Frei's "later" work nor do they mark a "turn" or "break" from his "earlier" work. They redescriptively expand and render increasingly explicit his characterization of the church as socially embodied and historically extended. Glimpses of this characterization are evident in the closing chapters of *The Identity of Jesus Christ*. As we saw above, there Frei had claimed that the identity of that historically extended social organism (the church) has to be narrated—that we have it only under some set of descriptive terms—much like the identities of Jesus and the people of Israel.[56] Running throughout his work—early to late—this theme most clearly evinces the influence of both Barth and Wittgenstein upon Frei's thinking. Frei drew the connection most explicitly in a lecture of 1974, writing:

> [Barth] suggested that our very knowledge of ourselves as creatures, but even more our very knowledge of ourselves as sinners is a knowledge, an apprehension, a tactile direct contact that has to be mediated to us. We have to learn it, in an almost Wittgensteinian way.

(And there is, incidentally I think for me, a lot of relationship, a lot of similarity between the later Wittgenstein and Karl Barth). We have to learn in an almost Wittgensteinian way how to use the concepts that apply to the way we know ourselves, because the world, the true, real world in which we live—the real world in which the Second World War took place in which Barth was so much engaged, in which the conflict with Nazism took place, in which the conflict or the adjustment with Communism took place later—that real world is only a figure of an aspect in that one overall real world in which the covenanted God of grace lives with man.[57]

As these lines indicate, Frei found helpfully redescriptive tools in Wittgenstein's thinking. And yet, even here Frei is cautious to properly order Wittgenstein and Barth. The relation is *almost* Wittgensteinian, he says. Frei finds similar claims robustly articulated by Barth. Wittgenstein provides terms for redescription in virtue of similarities that Frei recognizes between Barth and Wittgenstein. But we must be precise on this point. Frei is drawn to Wittgenstein's thinking and finds it helpful because, first, he is persuaded by Barth's theology. To misorder this relation—to view Frei as first or primarily a Wittgensteinian—is certain to veer off the rails.

The problem with reading Frei as a card-carrying Wittgensteinian is that it ties the success of his theological project to the success of Wittgenstein's philosophical project. This was a problem that Frei was vigilant against—a lesson he learned from Barth. Hence, while Wittgenstein's praxis-oriented, unsystematic approach and antipathy to grand theorizing all conspire to form a sensibility that keenly appealed to Frei (for Barthian reasons), it always entailed the risk of becoming an "antitheory theory" and thus implicating Frei in the very situation that he continually warned against—"getting the cart before the horse."

As this sketch of Frei's thinking should indicate, there are important continuities internal to the development of Frei's thought about both scriptural and ecclesial practices from the 1960s onward. There is enough continuity, at least, to mediate any simple opposition between his "earlier" and "later" work on these issues. While sketchy, Frei's ecclesial interests and purposes nevertheless convey practical and public implications even in *The Identity of Jesus Christ*. When we take the continuity internal to Frei's development as our focus, the earlier work may be seen to implicate the later. The later may be seen as the fruit of a long period of development. If successful, such a framework can account for the development of Frei's thought without attributing to him either superficial treatment of his subject matter, flagrant self-contradiction, or a sudden realization that historical and ecclesial contexts matter. Adding this dimension to our account of Frei's work helps him appear as a thinker who deeply and carefully engaged a set of ideas and conceptual tools over the course of several decades.

In the remaining pages of this chapter I take up a second thread of continuity in Frei's thinking—a thread far less attended to and more controversial than the "methodological" continuities in Frei's thinking illuminated above. In the remainder of this chapter I highlight the continuities in his ecclesial concerns.

II. Ecclesial Interests and Purposes in *The Identity of Jesus Christ*

To claim that Frei's ecclesial interests are an important part of *The Identity of Jesus Christ* lands us directly in the middle of controversy. In fact, many readers think Frei qualified the claims he made about realistic narrative in *Identity* in order to correct his earlier lack of attention to ecclesial contexts.[58] And yet, I think the case can be made that attention to ecclesial and liturgical context is inscribed in the very terms in which Frei executes his argument in *Identity*.

Stanley Hauerwas takes issue with Frei's inattentiveness to ecclesial context. "Even though his primary thesis concerning the narrative character of the Scripture has been fruitful for recent biblical scholarship, Frei argues that to be convincing, the emphasis on realistic narrative must reflect the authority structure of a community's tradition."[59] This observation sets up a criticism that Hauerwas levels in a footnote, writing:

> What is frustrating about Frei's position is the failure to specify the liturgical context through which such consensus is formed. This is not just a genetic point, for without the liturgy the text of Scripture remains just that—text. It is important to remember that before the Church had the New Testament it nonetheless worshiped and prayed to God in the name of Jesus of Nazareth. In effect, the worship of the Church created Scripture, though, once formed, Scripture governs the Church's worship.[60]

It is true that Frei emphasized the scriptural narrative as the *fons et origo* ("fount and origin") of the Christian world of discourse. And this appears to implicate him in asserting the priority of Scripture to the church. Of course, there are crucial distinctions to be drawn at this point. Frei recognized that both Scripture and the practices constitutive of the church presuppose the person and work of Christ. And on this point, in particular, Frei was indebted to Barth.

Central to Barth's account of Scripture is the concept of *Geschichte*—a word that can be translated as "story," "narrative" or "history." Barth applied this term to both the form and content of the Gospels' witness to the life, death, and resurrection of Christ. Along these lines Frei had written that "in the Gospels Jesus *is* nothing other than his story, and that this both is the story of God with him and all mankind."[61] He clarified:

> Jesus *is* his story. (Karl Barth makes the same point when he says that Jesus *is* reconciliation and not simply the Reconciler who would then, in a separable action or sequence, enact reconciliation). Now that story is only in one sense finished; in another sense it is part of a larger story, an aspect of which came before this part of the story, another aspect of which succeeds it and is not yet finished. What is important is not simply Jesus, but the circumstance interwoven with him: The triumphant coming of God's reign.[62]

As Barth conceived it, the *Geschichte* conception of narrative/history is prior to a notion of Scripture construed as the set of writings designated as such in the "closing of the canon." More specifically, *Geschichte* of Christ—and the Easter *Geschichte* in particular—is, for Barth, the *sine qua non* of Christian Scripture. "[W]hile we could imagine a New Testament containing only the history of Easter and its message, we could not possibly imagine a New Testament without it," Barth wrote. "For the history and message of Easter contains everything else, while without it everything else would be left in the air as a mere abstraction. Everything else in the New Testament contains and presupposes the resurrection. It is the key to the whole."[63] The Easter *Geschichte* is pivotal in this way because it presents the climax of the whole of Christ's story. Barth describes it as the *prism* that refracts the other parts of his story, and through which the rest of the New Testament can be understood.[64]

Frei has in mind the *Geschichte* sense of history and narrative when he invokes the history-like accounts that the gospel narratives depictively render, and in particular, their accounts of Jesus' death and resurrection.[65] The evangelical narration witnesses uniquely in its depiction of the events of Christ's passion, death, and resurrection, for these events are unique in kind. In and through them the Word of God came to humankind. If the rest of the depictions of Jesus' teachings and sayings are to have any Christological significance, they must be expressions of the Person whose identity is portrayed in and through the climax of this story.[66] The gospel narratives are the written and canonized evangelical narration of Christ's story/history. Christ's *Geschichte* is revealed, proclaimed, and written prior to becoming canonized by the tradition as "Scripture" proper. It is a feature of this text that it is written in light of Christ's resurrection.[67]

Hauerwas identifies the practices of prayer and worship in the prescriptural Christian community as two of the practices that frame the liturgical context. The community's worship within this liturgical context makes Scripture out of the evangelical narration rather than merely text, "for without the liturgy the text of Scripture remains just that—text," he writes. Hauerwas then adds, rightly, that what made just these practices constitutive of the liturgical context is that they occurred "in the name of Jesus of Nazareth." However, the latter claim effectively affirms the insights that Frei shares with Barth on this point rather than identifies a deficiency in them.

To say that "Jesus is his story" is, in effect, to recognize that the "name" of Jesus Christ occurs in the unity of Christ's person and Christ's work. Christ's person cannot be abstracted from his work, nor his work from his person. The person and work occur in the continuous sequence of the "life acts" of Jesus' life, and thus, his story—his *Geschichte*.[68] Hence, insofar as the liturgical and ecclesial practices have the *name* of Jesus as the condition of their possibility, they have as their "inalienable presupposition" Christ's *story* in precisely the *Geschichte* sense. This sense of the story—the evangelical narration—is, as Barth puts it, "the inalienable presupposition of apostolic proclamation."[69] In other words, Christ's *Geschichte* is the condition for the possibility of the community's worship, just as that *Geschichte* is the center of each of the parts of the scriptural text. Preaching, worship, liturgical reenactment all presuppose these accounts of Jesus' life, death, and resurrection.[70] Hence, while necessary, it is insufficient simply to say that the scriptural text presupposes liturgical context and practice. Scripture, liturgy, practice all presuppose the Word.[71]

The biblical witness forms the community of faith in two distinct ways. It witnesses to the identity of Christ in the form of unrepeatable events that happened "once-for-all," and are unique in kind.[72] At the same time, in the coincidence of God's act of revelation with these accounts, through the work of the Holy Spirit, Christ manifests himself in and through this witness "again and again." The Holy Spirit joins believers to Christ by engrafting them as members of his body. The community's telling and retelling of this storied witness, what Frei called its *reenactment*, is a central constituent of what that community is and does. The storied witness is, thus, simultaneously *presupposition* and *constituent* of its worship and liturgy. In other words, liturgical context is inseparable from the "hermeneutical bases" that Frei identified in the narrative/history (*Geschichte*) of Christ. It is, as a result, not simply the community's decision to use just this text within a liturgical context that makes these stories "Scripture."[73] What makes them Scripture is, finally, that in and through the evangelical narration God witnesses to and makes manifest the Person of Christ, not that a community *takes them* to do so, even as part of its act of worship.[74]

And yet, to use such claims as an occasion to enter into interminable debates about "which came first, Scripture or the church" misplaces Frei's concern. Frei is concerned to order properly evangelical witness and apostolic proclamation, without diminishing the inextricability of each from the other. In fact, the scriptural witness cannot be abstracted from liturgical context and ecclesial implications. There is evidence that Frei intended to avoid the temptation to abstract or misorder these dimensions in *Identity*. In particular, Frei's choice to conclude the book with a "A Meditation for the Week of Good Friday and Easter" reflects Frei's ecclesial and liturgical purposes.

Frei wrote the meditation that concludes *Identity* in 1974 and added to the published version at the behest of some of his students. To view it as an afterthought to the chapters that precede it, in my judgment, severely underestimates its significance. In light of the exegetical approach that Frei explicated in the preceding chapters of the book, I think we have grounds to view that meditation as one of the culminating moments of the argument that precedes it.[75] The result is intended to inform the practices of Christian communities and should not be abstracted from their public implications. After all, Frei wrote the chapters leading up to this meditation with lay practitioners as his intended audience.

Frei described the approach to Scripture he articulated in *Identity* as *reenactment* of the Easter story. It is a reenactment, and not simply a reading, in virtue of its interwovenness with the liturgical practices (in particular, the sacraments) that fill out the times and places in which Christian communities read this story. "The passion story and the Lord's Supper belong together," Frei wrote. "Together they render present the original; each is hobbled when it is separated from the other."[76] To abstract the one from the other renders both incomplete. With these claims Frei began to sketch an account of how the accounts of Jesus' death and resurrection, and the embodied practices which they initiate and orient, incorporate believers into what he would come to call the biblical "world of discourse." In particular, he reflected on Christ's call to "Follow thou me!" turning to a particular passage from Romans:

It does not say there 'follow him,' but in 6:4 Paul tells us that whereas being baptized means being buried with Christ, Christ's being raised means that our feet are set on a new path of life. And again in verses 12–14 he suggests that the embodiment of the Easter story's pattern in our lives means no mysterious archetypal consciousness of it, but a new way of governing our bodies. That is how we are in touch with the story. . . . To know this story is to adopt a way of life consequent upon hearing it and being shaped by it.[77]

In other words, Christ's witness draws those who hear it and follow into acknowledgment of its truth by, as Frei put it, "hammering out a shape of life pattern after its own shape."[78] Those dwelling in scripturally oriented communities may come to recognize themselves as *figures* within this story. However partially, through this reenactment "our lives reflect the story as in a glass darkly. The shape of the story being mirrored in the shape of our life is the condition of this being meaningful for us."[79]

These claims in *Identity* highlight distinct glimmerings of Frei's concern for ecclesial context and liturgical practice. Here Christ's presence—not to be abstracted from his identity depictively rendered in Scripture—serves as a hinge for Christian community, sacramental practice, and incorporating believers' lives into a life of discipleship through his calling and empowering them.[80] And if we read these passages with sensitivity to Barth's influence, Frei's focus on Jesus' identity and presence, in fact, echoes Barth's claims about the Holy Spirit's role in making Christ present. Read carefully, the Spirit is never more than an inference away.[81] I must digress for a moment, if only to answer what may be creeping suspicions of Christo*monism* that some readers are likely to register at this point.[82]

Barth claimed that Christ makes himself "absolutely temporally present" in and through the coincidence of God's revelation with the indissolubility of the evangelical narration and apostolic proclamation. This is Christ's "real presence." Christ is not present in abstraction from the work of the Holy Spirit. "[I]n and with the witness continually to be proclaimed and heard by them, [Christ] has given them His Spirit, the Holy Spirit. But where the Spirit is, there is more than a mere tradition or recollection of Jesus." Here Barth highlighted the fact that, in isolation from the activity of the Holy Spirit, the *Geschichte* of Christ, however liturgically received or reenacted, is a "mere tradition" or "recollection." Again, Scripture is not Scripture merely because a community treats it as such. Rather, Christ's *Geschichte* occurs fully in and through the working of the Spirit. These stories of Christ and his work constitute more than textual "tradition" and "recollection" because, where the Spirit is at work, Christ makes himself present to the community of believers in and through them. Barth explained:

[Jesus] becomes and is their Contemporary. As a result of this, His past life, death and resurrection can and must and actually do have at all times the significance and force of an event which has taken place in time but is decisive for their present existence. Hence they can and must and actually do understand their present existence as a life of direct discipleship as their "being in Christ"; as being done to death with Him at Golgotha, renewed in the garden of Joseph of Arimathea, and on the Mount of Olives (or wherever the ascension took place) entering into the concealment of the heavenly world, or rather into the concealment of God.[83]

At this point, Barth conveys the startling character of the figuration in which Christ, through the Spirit, engrafts believers as disciples onto the community of the faithful. "Being in Christ" occurs in Christ's real presence to believers in and through the Holy Spirit. Moreover, these "events" relativize both ecclesial context and liturgical practice, as well as even the apparently most self-evident of certainties. "Note that if there is anything doubtful for Christians here, it is not His presence but their own," Barth wrote. "And if there is anything axiomatically certain, it is not their presence but His." He continued:

There is obviously no baptism or Lord's supper without His real presence as very God and very Man, both body and soul. But this presence cannot be regarded as restricted to what were later called the 'sacraments.' For these are only a symbolic expression of the fact that in its worship the community is gathered directly around Jesus Himself, and lives by and with Him, but that through faith He rules over the hearts and lives of all even apart from worship. Hence the gifts of prophecy, teaching, leadership and service, and hence also miracles in the community. Hence, too, the royal freedom of the children of God, but hence also in Christ's stead the apostolic word of witness, the word of knowledge, direction and exhortation. All of these are possible because "Christians" have the Spirit and are led by Him.[84]

In other words, it is in the Spirit's work that the community lives and moves and has its being as *Gemeinde*—insofar as it is "gathered directly around Jesus Himself." The Spirit works in and through the "liturgical reenactment" of that story, namely (though, clearly, not exclusively or exhaustively), in the sacraments.

Frei made clear that faith presupposes the name of Christ. And the name of Christ occurs in the unity of his person and work—in Christ's *Geschichte*.

Again, this is not "simply Jesus," Frei cautions, but it is "the circumstances interwoven with him: The triumphant coming of God's reign," God with Christ and with all humankind.[85] Moreover, for Frei as well, none of this can be abstracted from the activity of the Spirit. The Spirit makes possible the indirect presence of Christ in the present—analogically manifest, inviting acknowledgment and enabling affirmation—which takes the public and communal form of the gathering under the Word.[86] "Of themselves and separately, the one (Sacrament or Word) is simply religious ritual and the other humane ideology, and the two have very little in common," Frei wrote. "The Church is founded on and sets forth the unity of both only through the presence of Jesus Christ." Moreover, this unity entails the activity of the Spirit.[87] Frei clarified:

> By analogy the feeble, often naive and simple word of written Scripture— and even its usually pathetic, clumsy interpretation in the spoken word—becomes a true witness, yet more than a witness. The Word does indeed witness to that which it is not, the presence of God in Jesus Christ. But far more important is the fact that indirectly (rather than directly, as in the case of Jesus Christ) God witnesses to it, that he makes himself present to it so that the Word may become the temporal basis of the Spirit who is the presence of God in Jesus Christ. The witness of Scripture to God is sure, not of itself, but because the witness of God to Scripture is faithful and constant.[88]

What is evident here is that, as far back as *Identity*, Frei held together God's witness in and through the *Geschichte* of Christ, the presence of the Spirit to the community of the faithful, and liturgical practice, giving priority to the first of these. Frei considered the public and practical implications of this view to be fairly profound. He concluded:

> [T]he Church must be a follower rather than a complete reiteration of its Lord. "To enact the good of men on their behalf" has already been done once for all. The Church has no need to play the role of "Christ figure." Rather, it is called upon to be a collective disciple, to follow at a distance the pattern of exchange, serving rather than being served, and accepting (as the disciple, as differentiated from his Lord) the enrichment given to him by his neighbor. In the Church's case, that neighbor is the human world at large, to which the Church must be open in gratitude without forsaking its own mission and testimony.[89]

Of course, in the preface to *The Identity of Jesus Christ*, Frei reflected on this account nearly eight years after writing it. "[I]n the end it all came to the claim that the specifically Christian affirmation of the presence of God-in-Christ for the world involves nothing philosophically more high-flown than a doctrine of the Spirit, focused on the Church, the Word, and the Sacrament, and the conviction of a dread yet hopeful cutting edge and providential pattern to mankind's political odyssey."[90] From the vantage point of hindsight, Frei also expressed significant reservations about having applied the category of "presence" as a technical category. He feared that such use of the term brought him "within hailing distance" of (neoorthodox) accounts of revelation that intellectualized God's relation to humanity by "riveting it to the phenomenon of consciousness."[91] On such accounts God's presence was either exclusively cognitive, unproblematically direct, construed as "a 'non-propositional' personal encounter," or some combination of the three. Frei found each of these conceptions too heavily infested by "the vagaries and dogmas of its Idealist parentage."[92] Even "hailing distance" of such claims was closer than Frei preferred to be if he had a choice.[93] It is right and good to speak of "God's presence" or "Christ's presence," and to think of such presence in terms no more philosophically high flown than the practices of Word and Sacrament.[94] These caveats aside, Frei thought that both the substance and form of his earlier project held, as did his uses of the "intention-action" pattern.[95] He sought to expand this element of his account by exploring the "formal analytical devices" used by various sociologists of knowledge to understand "individual personhood" and "contextual social structures."[96]

Conclusion

This chapter has traced the continuities in the development of Frei's theology. I have argued that his uses of explicitly "cultural-linguistic" resources and insights in the 1980s do not mark a turn or break in Frei's thinking. In fact, many of these resources are operative in his work of the 1960s. Their much more explicit and refined roles in Frei's final decade represent the material unfolding, development, and enrichment of Frei's applications of those insights. I have argued as well that Frei's ecclesial concerns are not novel to the last decade of his work either. In my judgment, readers with an interest in further developing Frei's work must first move beyond both of these typical characterizations of his work. This is required if the confining categories of the "early" and the "later" Hans Frei are to be overcome. Clearly, Frei's work developed over the course of his career. In fact, this development contributes to why his work is, at once, so intriguing and yet so challenging to grasp accurately. There is coherence to be found here. It is crucial that we take the time to find it.

Despite initial appearances, Frei's claims above about the relation of the world "depictively rendered" in and through Scripture and "the true world in which we live" do not unequivocally implicate him in George Lindbeck's more robust assertions of roughly ten years later that an "intratextual" approach to Christian Scripture will "absorb" the world of believers.[97] This is one of the most elusive distinctions in all of Frei's writing. For he does put forth a claim wholly consistent with Barth's above—that the primacy of Jesus means that believers become figures in a reality oriented by Jesus; they are participants in Christ's story. Frei wrote:

> It is as though we, ordinary human beings, were living in a world in which the true reality is one that we only grasp in this life as if it were for us a figure. Yes—but it is we who are the figures and it is that reality embodied by the resurrection that is the true reality of which we were only figures. It is as though our sense of reality were to be turned about; it is what is depicted—the world, the one world, God's and man's, depicted in the Bible—which is real, and this ordinary world history which is a parable, a figure of that reality. And that is the mystery it seems to me of our life in which the story and the facts fit together.[98]

This central feature of Frei's work raises difficult questions. At precisely this point his position is frequently identified with Lindbeck's claim that Scripture "absorbs" the world of believers. Moreover, Frei's constant struggle to make clear his ideas about the relation of scriptural text and interpretive context, in conjunction with the deep mutual appreciation that Frei and Lindbeck expressed for each other's work in helping them think through these matters, leads many to equate their projects.

This identification is complicated by Frei's apparent endorsement of Lindbeck's description of theology's "intratextual" task in the final paragraphs of his essay on the "literal reading" of Scripture.[99] There he suggested that the *sensus literalis* presented the primary reference point for interpretation of an "intratextual" type within the Christian tradition.

In the chapter that follows I argue that even the important affinities that Frei identified between his and Lindbeck's claims he utilized in *ad hoc* ways and for his specific redescriptive purposes. I make the case that there are crucial (if subtle) distinctions to be drawn between Lindbeck and Frei on a number of points. This is the task I take up in the following chapter.

3

Absorption and Embrace

Worlds of Discourse in Lindbeck and Frei

Frei's decreased reliance upon the genre "realistic narrative" as a technical category for the Gospel narratives accompanied his increasingly explicit articulation of the church as a social organism. He elucidated these insights by borrowing conceptual tools from Ryle, Geertz, and Wittgenstein and identified a comparable framework for understanding the church in Barth's theology. Later, Frei would attempt to read Schleiermacher in a similar fashion.[1] "It is striking," Frei wrote, "that theologians as divergent as Friedrich Schleiermacher and Karl Barth are agreed that Christianity, precisely as a community, is language forming. Not purely, of course, but sufficiently so that that language as embodied in its institutions, practice, doctrines, and so on, is a distinctive and irreducible social fact."[2] As Frei put it, the social practices constitutive of Christian communities formed "a world of discourse."

Frei endorsed Barth's claim that the world of discourse precipitating from the discursive practices of Christian communities was anchored by the biblical narratives. Barth had claimed that the biblical point of origin for this world of discourse was indirectly one with the Word of God. Scripture's unity was to be found in the consistency of its witness to a Name—the identity of Jesus Christ. As such, it possessed a unique integrity. This world of discourse was for Barth, Frei explained, irreducible.[3] As Frei read it, this meant that this "discursive world" has "its own linguistic integrity, much as a literary art work is a consistent world in its own right, one that we can have only under a depiction, under its own particular depiction and not any other, and certainly not in pre-linguistic immediacy or in experience without depiction."[4] The Christian world of discourse is unique. At the same time, Frei endorsed another of Barth's claims—that "unlike any other depicted world it is the one common world in which we all live and move and have our being."[5]

What does it mean for discourse to "form a world"? And how are we to understand the claim that the Christian world of discourse is the "same" world in which we all live? How best to think about this world as the world in which we live our daily lives? At certain points, Frei's attempts to answer these questions brought his work to its closest approximation of his colleague George Lindbeck's work. Frei and Lindbeck posed answers that were clearly compatible at numerous points, and subtly different at others. Any engagement of Frei's work at the level of detail must treat his similarities to Lindbeck delicately, for these present the points that invite the lumping of their projects together into a single postliberal theological program. In the following pages I unpack their respective notions of "worlds of discourse" and how we might make sense of what each means when he claims that Scripture "absorbs the world."[6] I make the case that, in spite of their congruities, the differences between Frei and Lindbeck on these points outweigh their similarities.

I. Absorption and Embrace in Textual Practices

What Lindbeck described as "the normative explication of the meaning a religion has for its adherents," Frei understood as a theological analogue to thickly descriptive reflexive ethnography.[7] The "intratextual" understanding of Scripture to which Lindbeck referred with this phrase claims that, insofar as a community recognizes Scripture as the basic source of norms for its living and speaking, it will pervade and govern the cultural and linguistic sense-making social practices—the "comprehensive interpretive scheme"—through which experience and propositional assertion are possible. Theology based upon this conception of Scripture is "intratextual" because it "redescribes reality within the scriptural rather than translating Scripture into extrascriptural categories. It is the text so to speak, which absorbs the world, rather than the world the text."[8]

Lindbeck's trope of scripture "absorbing" the world of believers has proven rhetorically unfortunate. Moreover, his efforts to clarify it in recent years frequently get overlooked by those eager to exploit its awkwardness.[9] The biblical text "absorbs the world," he clarifies, insofar as it is "followable" or "habitable." A text is "habitable" insofar as it supplies "directions for coherent patterns of life in new situations," and is "construable in such a way as to provide guidance for society, in the one case, and for individual life, in the other."[10] Such a text "must in some fashion be construable as a guide to thought and action in the encounter with changing circumstances. It must supply followable directions for coherent patterns of life in new situations."[11] Lindbeck's account of how Christian scripture "absorbs the world" was influenced by, and shares important similarities with, Clifford Geertz's account of religions as cultural systems, and can be helpfully elucidated by briefly bringing these similarities to light.

In "Religion as a Cultural System," Geertz claimed that a group's *worldview*—"the picture they have of the way things in sheer actuality are, their most comprehensive ideas of order"—at once generates and coheres symbiotically with the *ethos* of that group, ethos understood as "the tone, character, and quality of their life, its moral and aesthetic style and mood." This worldview/ ethos complex provides both a "model *of*" reality, as well as a "model *for*" how members of the group ought to make their way within reality so constituted and situated. What a group of people believe to be true about the character of the world in which they find themselves shapes, collectively and individually, their social, moral, and political life, what they value, what they consider to be possible or desirable ways of living, and thus, their manners, mores, and laws. As a "model *of*" reality, a worldview makes a way of life seem natural and even necessary. It frames the resulting ethos as a way of being in the world that accords with "the way things really are."[12] Much like a map, it orients the group's basic self-understanding and the social practices that embody and express that understanding, offering guidelines and directions for making their way in a reality so constituted.

Geertz used the worldview/ethos complex to articulate a conception of "culture" understood in terms of socially instituted sets of practices and institutions in which human beings find themselves caught up in virtue of the very acculturation and socialization that makes them human beings. These cultural frames disclose the world in particular ways. They open up "ways of seeing" and thus situate the ways that the world "shows up" in virtue of the social roles, languages, public meanings, attitudes and dispositions, projects and equipment into which one finds oneself acculturated.[13] So understood, a worldview is not first a set of beliefs to which one consciously subscribes, which thus inform one's living and which one can take or leave at whim. One is *acquired by* a worldview as surely as one comes to speak some particular language at some particular time and place, as surely as one is nurtured by some particular set of caregivers and learns to get around in, practically distinguish, cope, and deal with the world. One finds oneself caught up in and confronted by the questions of meaning and significance that suffuse the sense-making practices and shared understandings that prevail in some historical and social context.[14] On this reading, a worldview/ethos complex is a species of social practices. They are embodied means of making sense of and coping with one's environment, perceiving and understanding that one comes to in virtue of one's acculturation into a socially and practically embodied "form of life."[15]

Lindbeck's account of comprehensive interpretive schemes bears marks of Geertz's influence. "Like a culture or a language," wrote Lindbeck, "[a comprehensive interpretive scheme] is a communal phenomenon that shapes the subjectivities of individuals rather than being primarily a manifestation of those subjectivities." It works after the fashion of a socially instituted Kantian a priori— "an acquired set of skills that could have been different."[16] Religious comprehensive schemes are those concerned with "the maximally important" and "usually embodied in myths or narratives and heavily ritualized, which structure human experience and understanding of self and world."[17]

The practices constitutive of Christian forms of life, for example, coalesce and take shape around the distinctive claims made by God's revelation in Scripture. The world portrayed in the Bible both makes claims about what the world is really like (a model *of*) as well as claims about how Christians ought to go about being in such a world (a model *for*). Scripture supplies both the framework within which, and the resources by which, one deals and copes in the face of reality. These stories make sense of the things that happen to believers by providing "spectacles, the lens, through which faith views all reality."[18] The scriptural world is one in which God is the primary character, a history in which God is the beginning and the end, and one that gives rise to a form of life in which the stories of those who have gone before us assist, guide, and aid in making our own way through this world. Acculturation into the form of life for which Scripture provides the orienting framework uniquely discloses the world for believers in the first place.

Frei and Lindbeck share several of the above ideas. Frei's *The Eclipse of Biblical Narrative* influenced Lindbeck's formulation of intratextuality. And Frei remarked on one occasion that Lindbeck's account of "intratextuality" illustrated how the *sensus literalis* became the "plain sense of Scripture" for the Christian textual tradition. Frei went so far as to identify the literal sense as "the paradigmatic form of such intratextual interpretation in the Christian community's use of Scripture."[19] And yet while Frei himself identified this crucial point of overlap between his and Lindbeck's projects, their differences at this juncture are both subtle and crucial. My aim in the following sections is to tease out what is really at stake in Lindbeck's trope of "absorption" and elucidate the extent to which Frei's conception of the plain sense may or may not cohere with it.

II. When Worldviews Collide: Untranslatability, Figuration, and Assimilative Success

Lindbeck fashions his account of the specifically Christian, scripturally oriented "comprehensive interpretive scheme" in accord with his cultural-linguistic theory of religions. The "semiotic comprehensiveness" he ascribes to the Christian interpretive scheme, in fact, presents one instance of a broader set of family resemblances that are shared by most major world religions and many nonreligious worldviews.[20] Worldviews generally make comprehensive truth claims about the way the world ultimately is. Confucianism, Hinduism, Buddhism, Islam, etc., along with "secular" worldviews, such as Marxism, Atheism, Liberalism, among others, either explicitly propose or imply some account or basic claims about the nature of reality, personhood, and social life. Logically speaking, only one such comprehensive set of claims can be true. It is possible that none of them are.[21]

Lindbeck explicitly positions this account of comprehensive interpretive schemes against prevailing pluralist trends in twentieth-century Christian theology of religions and comparative religious thought. As he frames the account, a distinctively modern conception of salvation caused many Christians to focus upon conversion of non-Christians as a central mandate of their faith. Within this framework "believers" were generally construed as discrete individuals whose "believing" hinged upon cognitive ascent to the propositionally articulated contents of the Christian faith. The conception of "conversion" implied by this framework became a central impetus for engaging non-Christians. The anxieties that ensued among non-Christians, and the guilt that many Christians felt for the hegemonic and often culturally imperialistic sins committed in the name of "converting the heathen," inspired many Christians to soften the apparent mandate for the outright conversion of nonbelievers.[22]

Christians who resisted such "conversionist" designs often reframed interreligious engagement in ecumenical terms of mutually edifying dialogue. This approach finally refused to assert the kinds of truth claims that would negate opposing claims to truth registered by non-Christian conversation partners. Responses of this sort took one of several possible forms. "Pluralists" maintained that the apparently particular truth claims made by all religions, in fact, reduce to deeper insights or basic religious experiences from which all particular faith traditions derive. Different religious worldviews convey certain fundamental truths, they claimed. Moreover, the various languages in which they articulate those truths can finally be translated into a basic idiom of human religiosity.[23] "Inclusivist" alternatives attempted, by contrast, to retain some degree of the exclusiveness of Christian truth. They acknowledged that other religions contain much that is beneficial, and even true. However, any such elements overlap and agree with, or point toward, the claims of the one true religion.[24]

These counterefforts retained the basic concern with salvation that their exclusivist counterparts exhibited, though they inverted the implications of that emphasis.[25] Pluralists and many inclusivists opposed sorting the "saved" from "damned" on the basis of acceptance or rejection of a specific set of propositional truth claims. However, in either softening or erasing altogether such claims, they tended to subvert their stated goal of mutually edifying dialogue. The various partners to such dialogues, it turned out, basically had been saying the same things all along. That is, parties to interreligious dialogue were making claims that either could be translated into terms that were, in effect, identical or enough in accord to neutralize any ultimate disagreement. Pluralist solutions, in particular, made it impossible for any religious conceptual scheme to assert truth claims that would positively exclude the truth of other schemes. The result was a form of antihegemonic hegemony. In a well-intentioned effort to jettison exclusivist claims, the alternatives installed the default truth claim that apparently exclusivist truth claims were finally commensurable. On this basis the very possibility of asserting "exclusivist" truth claims was severely constrained, if not excluded altogether.[26]

Lindbeck's "cultural-linguistic" alternative, by contrast, trained its attention upon the irreducible differences between different interpretive comprehensive schemes, and thus, the unavoidability of exclusive truth claims. Such schemes make sense of reality and offer an account of the way the world is that is reasonable and true.[27] Some do this more successfully than others. Lindbeck proposed a means of adjudicating between these schemes, writing:

> The reasonableness of a religion is largely a function of its assimilative powers, of its ability to provide an intelligible interpretation on its own terms of the various situations and realities adherents encounter. The religions we call primitive regularly fail this test when confronted with major changes, while the world religions have developed greater resources with this vicissitude. Thus, although a religion is not susceptible to decisive disproof, it is subject, as Basil Mitchell argues, to rational testing procedures not wholly unlike those which apply to general scientific theories or paradigms (for which, unlike hypotheses, there are no crucial experiments). Confirmation or disconfirmation occurs through an accumulation of successes or failures in making practically and cognitively coherent sense of relevant data, and the process does not

conclude, in the case of religions, until the disappearance of the last communities of believers or, if the faith survives, until the end of history.[28]

Thus does a conception of "assimilative success" provide a basic test for adjudicating the reasonableness and plausibility and for confirming a comprehensive interpretive scheme on Lindbeck's account.[29] But this implies not only the *irreconcilability* of different religious worldviews (if one claim is true, then the other is false), but that such conceptual schemes are *mutually untranslatable*.[30] That is, they cannot be translated into some more basic, mythical, or primordial set of truths or universal religious experience, or into each other's terms, without suffering a significant loss of meaning.

Christian scriptural practices have evinced a unique form of untranslatability, according to Lindbeck. Namely, that "every humanly conceivable reality can be translated (or redescribed) in the biblical universe of discourse with a gain rather than a loss of truth or significance whereas, second, nothing can be translated out of this idiom into some supposedly independent communicative system without perversion, diminution or incoherence of meaning."[31] With this claim the full scope and force of Lindbeck's project begins to come into focus. The scriptural universe's "absorption" of the world exerts the full gravitas with which Erich Auerbach described the narratives in the Hebrew Scriptures as bent on overcoming its readers' realities. "The world of the Scripture stories is not satisfied with claiming to be a historically true reality, it insists that it is the only real world, is destined for autocracy," Auerbach famously wrote. "All other scenes, issues, and ordinances have no right to appear independently of it, and it is promised that all of them, the history of all mankind, will be given their due place within its frame, will be subordinated to it."[32] Taken without qualification, the gravitas of such claims suggests an imperialism of the Christian comprehensive interpretive scheme.[33] The reasonableness, plausibility, and continued confirmation of that scheme depend upon its success in encompassing all discourses within its scriptural world. This invests theology with a task that is at once urgent and exceedingly ambitious, arguably along the lines of Atlas shouldering the world.

A central concern raised by Lindbeck's account is the extent to which the theory of religion that frames his account exerts a normative sway in determining how the Christian comprehensive interpretive scheme ought to function and be assessed.[34] Lindbeck recognized the risk of positioning Christianity as a particular instance of a general account, and attempted to sidestep this trap by referring to the fairly general features of worldviews as a range of family resemblances that exert little explanatory power.[35] Comprehensive schemes tend to exhibit the features he identifies, but not necessarily. Clearly, Lindbeck hopes to avoid overly essentialized claims about the generic features of comprehensive interpretive schemes. He underscores that the similarities with which sacred texts mediate reality in various world religious and philosophical traditions are analogical. "Confucianism, Hinduism, and Buddhism, for example, as well as the western philosophical tradition"—these are *like* Christianity in "having diversified canons which are read as having some sort of unity deriving from a common source (e.g., philosophical reason or Buddhist enlightenment), subject matter and aim."[36] And yet, in ascending to the level of generality required to apply his account of comprehensive interpretive schemes, some of the claims that he strives to curtail start to become unruly.

Lindbeck claims, for instance, that "[t]he framing of every comprehensive outlook, furthermore, is arguably a narrative one even when time is cyclical and the story is that of eternal return." A few lines further, readers discover that the importance that classical biblical hermeneutics invested in the notion of narrative (and, in particular, a realistic narrative framework that would figurally embrace all reality without similarly being embraced) is a feature shared by "any *Weltanschauung* which seeks to encompass rather than replace the world of ordinary experience." As it turns out, for any scheme that seeks to interpret reality through a text, figural interpretation "cannot be escaped." Lindbeck explains:

> Much as Jews and Christians read the universe through their scriptural canons, so the Greeks saw themselves through Homeric eyes (sometimes in astonishing detail and with world-transforming import if Robin Lane Fox is to be trusted on Alexander the Great). Similarly, mechanistic materialists of a now defunct kind interpreted all reality through the lens of Newton's physics.[37]

Lindbeck cautions that the content of figural interpretation will differ on a scheme-by-scheme basis, which makes the similarity a formal one. From the uniformity in interpretive approach that such schemes evince, Lindbeck draws the modest conclusion that "classical biblical hermeneutics is not formally unique."[38] Certainly, Frei would appreciate this effort to curtail the strength of the conclusion in which such claims implicate his account. And yet, these implications appear to be far more encompassing than Lindbeck might intend or prefer. As features of textually derived interpretive schemes, realistic narrative and figuration exert substantial explanatory power about the nature of those schemes and how they function generally. Figuration is a feature shared by the members of a class that are identified in virtue of Lindbeck's prior account of the nature and basis of comprehensive interpretive schemes. It is the primary means by which adherents of such schemes use texts to "construct communities (or cultures, civilizations or, in ideological employment, political states or parties) with cosmic legitimation."[39] At this point it becomes difficult to see how his general account of what comprehensive schemes are, and how they organize reality, does not control the identification and explanation of the regional instances he treats (Lindbeck's protests to the contrary notwithstanding). It is Lindbeck's general theory about comprehensive interpretive schemes that provides the normative frame within which Christianity appears as a particular instance, is correlated with, and assessed.

Nicholas Wolterstorff directs incisive criticisms at the claim that the scriptural narrative "absorbs the world" in which believers live. He points out that the historically specific and culturally local contexts in which readers engage Scripture may resist the claims rendered by the intratextual world that Scripture opens and around which the Christian world of discourse coalesces. "The 'you' and 'I' who seek to conform our lives to, and guide our interpretations by, the biblical story, are twentieth-century inhabitants of the Modern West, shaped by our society and culture," writes Wolterstorff. He continues:

> [A]s such, we experience a great many points of collision when we come up against the biblical narrative. At many of these points of collision, our modern western mentality ought to bend and give; otherwise the notion of biblical authority is vapid. But not at all these points. We ought not bend before the social patriarchalism so pervasive in the biblical narrative, nor before the cosmology and natural history presupposed in the biblical narrative. . . . It's too simplistic, then, to say: conform your life to the biblical story. At what points are we to conform? And given some point at which we are not obligated to conform, what are we to make of the fact that at this point conformation is not obligatory?[40]

Here the historicist character of social practice appears to stand in tension with the authoritative role of Scripture. Indeed, the cultural and social contexts in which Christians live and move and have their being resist many elements of the world narrated in Scripture as surely as Luther excoriated Copernicus' *De Revolutionibus Orbium* for its blatant contradiction of the geocentric cosmology to which Holy Scripture testified, that "Joshua bade the sun to stand still, not the earth!"

Wolterstorff's criticisms bring us to a juncture in how we might make sense of Frei's claim that the Christian "world of discourse" is "the one common world in which we all live and move and have our being."[41] One option would be to take up a restricted conception of what we mean by "the world narrated by

Scripture" in tandem with an ambitious sense of "absorption," and then devise criteria for when the believer ought to give way to the world's contradiction of Scripture. A second response is to relax the notion of Scripture as a "world of discourse," as well as how we construe the relationship between "text" and "world." I will explain why I think Frei's position is best described in terms of the latter option.

Long before Lindbeck, Frei identified Auerbach's account of figural interpretation to exemplify the approach to biblical narratives characteristic of Christian communities' respect for the primacy of the literal sense.[42] Frei employed Auerbach to cast into relief the kind of *distinctiveness* and *priority* he thought the biblical narratives required. And while this characterization is roughly consistent with Lindbeck's account, there are grounds to draw an important distinction between the strength of their respective claims. Frei cautiously avoids claiming that the world narrated therein would wholly absorb or subsume other possible orientations within the world in order to assert and maintain that priority. He appropriated Auerbach asymmetrically by qualifying the excessiveness of some of his claims and thus making room for the unpredictability of what may happen when one engages—when one is engaged by—the strange new world within the Bible. This specific world would be sure to subvert its readers' expectations from time to time in virtue of the freedom and sovereignty of the One whose world it depictively renders.[43]

"[A]llowing oneself to be shaped by the biblical narrative is only one facet of a complex picture," Wolterstorff presses. "The shaping . . . has to be a *discriminating* shaping. Unidirectionality is not a tenable stance."[44] Frei, in my judgment, would be inclined to agree that shaping by the biblical narratives must be discriminating. But if so, then how should we understand his claim to redescribe "the world of Christian discourse" as part of "allowing oneself to be shaped by the biblical narrative"? Answering this question will require that we explicate the Barthian background of Frei's claim that Christian discourse forms a world.

Barth viewed Holy Scripture as a central and irreducible point on an inferentially articulated network of discursive practices. On this view the "Christian world of discourse" outstrips just the Bible, though the scriptural witness is its point of origin and orientation. "[T]hose inferences that are consistent with its text join the text with equal weight and authority," Barth wrote, along with the pronouncements of the councils and other authorities.[45] "In short, there now emerges the Church either as a virtual second source alongside Holy Scripture, or simply as a norm for the interpretation of Scripture."[46] Wolterstorff antici-pates such a response:

It is indeed helpful to think of the declarations of the various
ecumenical councils, and of the creeds and confessions of the various
non-ecumenical assemblies, as establishing a sense of faith for all the
Church or some segment thereof. But the councils were not
infallible, the non-ecumenical creeds and confessions are at many
points in conflict, and not even the creed of any particular
confessional tradition settles all the troublesome issues of tensions.
To the issue of interpretation which Galileo so famously raised, no
council had spoken.[47]

Again, fair enough. However, fallibility and internal contradiction present
problems only if one makes forceful claims for Scripture's absorption of the
world. *Unidirectionality* invests Scripture with a kind of inflexibility that risks
becoming an idolatrous displacement of the Word. It construes Scripture as a
comprehensive scheme that will always and already position all other discourses and worldviews in its own terms. As a result, reconciling Scripture
with events, information that does not derive directly from it, conflict with it, or
reject subsumption by Scripture's witness cannot but appear to compromise
with, or give ground to, nonscriptural worldviews or schemes that stand over
against it. If, by contrast, we recognize Scripture as an historically immanent
means in and through which God's Word indirectly, but nevertheless authentically and realistically, manifests God, then the very notion of Scripture and the
"Christian world of discourse" acquire a certain flexibility and, perhaps more
importantly, unpredictability. In my judgment, this trajectory of development is
a primary point at which Frei's thinking bears out Barth's influence in a way
that Lindbeck's does not.

Barth had claimed that the scriptural narratives exert an authority in this
inferential world of discourse by virtue of the Person to whom they witness
and manifest. At the same time, he also recognized the possibility (even inevitability) of revising received interpretations of the stories and doctrines
derived therefrom, as well as "great latitude for the adoption of further
necessary elements of faith that are still outside formulated dogma."[48] Frei
highlighted the inescapably interpretive component of figural interpretation
in the Christian tradition. The same stories that sought to "overcome reality"
had been "constantly adapted to new situations and ways of thinking, [and]
underwent ceaseless revision," Frei explained, even as they continued to orient
the one real and inclusive world in which believers lived and moved and had
their being.[49] Here Frei's position converged with Lindbeck's on the claim that
Scripture presents a perspicuous, coherent, and "followable world." They
diverged, however, in Frei's agreement with Barth that it would be a mistake

to derive from its followability anything as systematic or as final as a "biblical point of view."[50]

Ultimately, if "the sole basis and intention of theology must be God's sovereignty and freedom in this grace and revelation," then God's freedom is even over Scripture as the medium by which God manifests the person of Christ to believers.[51] Just so, God's sovereignty includes freedom over "the recipient mode of revelation"—faith.[52] Hence, a move to relativize the witness of Scripture in light of God's radical freedom parallels Barth's move to relativize faith in light of that freedom. If the believer's primary concern is faithfulness to God in light of God's radical freedom and sovereignty, then she need not (in fact, dare not) fashion fixed preconceptions that conceptual translation occurs always and in every case in a single direction—from the world into the Bible.

The Christian "world of discourse," as Frei put it, "could only be described in a piecemeal fashion."[53] As Barth stated the basic claim, "'[T]he Gospel is what it is in the divine-human person available to us only by the way of a miraculous history, as Jesus Christ himself. And this person does not permit himself to be translated into a proposition."[54] George Hunsinger helpfully expands the point, "the explication of revelation will thus always be 'less a system than the report of an event' (I/1, 280), and the event concerned will have to be understood under a diversified variety of concepts rather than a unified conceptual scheme."[55] He continues:

> The quest for a "system" would be the quest for a general conceptual
> scheme capable of encompassing the totality of relevant terms and of
> explaining more or less exhaustively their underlying formal unity.
> The whole and its parts (the unity of the totality) would thus be
> subject to rational apperception, explanation, and formalization. But
> (if anything) only concepts and principles, not persons and histories,
> could be systematized in this way, to say nothing of a mysterious
> person available to us only by way of a miraculous history, as Jesus
> Christ is affirmed to be by faith. The name of Jesus Christ, wrote
> Barth, "is not a system representing a unified experience or a unified
> thought; it is the Word of God itself" (I/1, 181).[56]

Barth's distaste for systems was especially apparent in his contention with Rudolf Bultmann over the very notion of "worldviews." Bultmann had expressed deep anxieties about the mythic Christian worldview, due to its allegedly irreconcilable discrepancies with the modern scientific worldview. "It is impossible to use electric lights and the wireless and avail ourselves of modern medical and surgical discoveries, and at the same time to believe in the New Testament world of demons and spirits," he wrote. Barth read this claim as exemplifying the reading of Kant he and Bultmann encountered during their studies at the University of Marburg at the feet of the "Marburg Kantians"—"with its absolute lack of any sense of humour and its rigorous insistence on the honesty which does not allow any liberties in this respect." He wrote:

> [W]hat if the modern world-view is not so final as all that? What if
> modern thought is not so uniform as our Marburg Kantians
> would have us believe? Is there any criticism of the New Testament
> which is inescapably posed by the 'situation of modern man'?
> And above all, what if our radio-listeners recognize a duty of honesty
> which, for all this respect for the discoveries of modern science, is
> even more compelling than that of accepting without question the
> promptings of common sense? What if they felt themselves in a
> position to give a free and glad and quite factual assent not to a *fides*
> *implicita* in a world of spirits and demons but to faith in the
> resurrection of Jesus Christ from the dead? What if they have no
> alternative but to do this?[57]

Surely Barth's appeal to this "duty of honesty" to assent to the claims of faith without, first, formally reconciling and assimilating the promptings of "common sense" that the "modern world-view" presented cannot but sound of conversation-stopping fideism to those who identify rational viability with "assimilative success." However, Barth makes no merely noncognitive appeal to an arbitrary starting point for faith. Rather, faith brings its own reasons which it cannot posit as *unintelligible* or *untranslatable* in principle. Faith occurs, in part, in the historically extended, socially situated practices of critical self-reflection and explication. And though at times rendering them intelligible is difficult, they cannot be set off from redescription, analysis, and assessment. In fact, says Barth, faith is compelled to understand and seek increasing explicitness about the reasoning intrinsic to itself. That is what it means for faith to "seek understanding." Moreover, this "search for understanding" is not a separable, tangential, or peripheral task that occurs only when some challenging "external" circumstance presents itself or a "piece of the system" seems not to be in good working order. It is central to faith's vocational identity. Neither is faith incapable of expressing itself to, and giving and asking for reasons with, those who do not share its basic presuppositions.

Stephen Fowl gestures importantly toward this insight, pointing out that "If Christians are to manifest the commitment to reach out to the outsider and the stranger, which was so characteristic of the life and ministry of Jesus, this emphasis on the barriers to translation ought to be balanced by the position that translation is always possible."[58] While I am persuaded by Fowl, I think the point reaches further. Christians are called to become self-reflective and practiced at the range of tasks that translation entails. This is not merely instruction in welcoming the stranger from without. At the same time, a believer may find herself, time and again, a fellow traveler among strangers. It is impossible to know antecedently what the form or occasion, or to what ends, Christians will need to engage non-Christians.[59] The ad hoc and piecemeal character of the engagement with non-Christian viewpoints and claims permits casting into relief the world of discourse that is oriented around scriptural practices by both distancing and approximating that world to other linguistic domains. It permits redescribing (though not *reducing*) the scriptural in nonscriptural terms for ad hoc purposes. Thus the theologian formally can employ any and all technical philosophical concepts and conceptual schemes with the proviso, as Frei put it, that "one must remain *agnostic* about all their material claims to be describing the 'real' world." Frei expounded the point, writing:

> In order not to become trapped by his philosophy, it is best for a theologian to be philosophically eclectic, in any given case employing the particular "conceptuality" or conceptualities (to put it in the German mode) that serve best to cast into relief the particular theological subject matter under consideration. The subject matter governs concepts as well as method, not vice versa.[60]

The subject matter is a person whose coming is an event, not a system. This subject matter constrains how we appropriate other tools, as well as how we think about and frame that subject matter itself.[61]

So, for instance, Barth described the Easter history as the *prism* through which the entirety of the New Testament is to be viewed. At the same time, he warned that it should not be thought of as an a priori category such as would be needed for an interpretive scheme.[62] In other words, to fashion from the gospel narrative and the situated practices that flow therefrom a formal scheme that makes sense of the content provided by reality, and then to justify that scheme in virtue of its capacity to outnarrate competitors, risks reducing the witness of Christ to a system. Barth was averse to the systematization entailed by fashioning an a priori and its *schematic* implications, even an a priori understood as socially constructed. "After all," he wrote, "is it our job as Christians to accept or reject world-views? Have not Christians always been eclectic in their world-views—and this for very good reasons?"[63]

Barth's proviso does not stipulate a rule about the direction of translation in every case, nor untranslatability, but rather *priority*. Frei understood this to mean that the "world" depictively rendered by the literal sense is *irreducible*. It is, thus, prior in the sense that no other description of the world can function as a "'pre-description' for the world of Christian discourse which is also this common world." But this priority makes it neither discrete nor an autonomous world unto itself nor (in principle) unintelligible to nonbelievers. Neither would it indicate either "untranslatability" or unidirectionality of translation. Scripture's *embrace* of our world occurs in virtue of God's catching up believers in a set of discursive practices—the world of discourse that is oriented by the biblical witness. This socially and practically embodied world of discourse thereby implicates them in certain necessary conceptual and practical relations that nonbelievers either do not acknowledge or do not recognize as binding on them. These conceptual and practical relations hold ambiguously for the pilgrim on the way from nonbelief to belief, or perhaps vice versa.[64] Christians make the truth claim that this is the "one, real world" in which we all live and move and have our being. Even so, they claim this with attention to the important ambiguities, deep nuances, and revisability unavoidable in human speaking and conceptualization. Along precisely these lines, Frei spoke of the world of scriptural practices as exerting a *regional* grasp. "We may inhabit other worlds also," he wrote.[65] This is not a claim that people can live in somehow conceptually incommensurable, and thus discretely different, realities. There are important, even radical and irreconcilable, differences between competing truth claims and ways of living in the world. But these differences are recognized and appreciated for their full depth against a background of agreement or comparability.[66] Precisely how this point bears upon the differences between Frei and Lindbeck might be helpfully clarified with a bit of philosophical redescription.

Lindbeck understands his use of the term "untranslatability" to side-step Donald Davidson's argument "that the very notion of incommensurable or untranslatable conceptual frameworks or languages is incoherent because some common measure or idiom, some ability to translate, is necessary in order to recognize instances of untranslatability or incommensurability."[67] Instead, he invokes Alasdair MacIntyre's rejoinder to Davidson that the contents of a language or tradition of inquiry that are untranslatable can be recognized as such by some sufficiently adept interpreter. Lindbeck writes:

> Those for whom that tongue is "a second first language" can recognize and flag what is untranslatable in it without falling into the contradiction of supposing (or allowing others to suppose) that they have thereby provided a translation. This seems to me a satisfactory end-run around Davidson's problem, but even if it is not, there may be other ways of meeting the difficulty.[68]

In other words, practitioners of some language or rival belief system that differ radically enough to warrant being called "incommensurable" may have the capacity to understand and represent many of the beliefs of the other language from within their own. What they *cannot* do, according to MacIntyre, is represent those beliefs in ways that *would not be rejected by* native speakers of that language.[69] Moreover, (and this is the point that Lindbeck deploys) what they come to share is the recognition that certain terms can find no substantial—or perhaps even meaningful—translation into the terms of the other. Hence, on the one hand, MacIntyre concedes to a piece of Davidson's argument that "finding common ground is not subsequent to understanding, but a condition of it." He admits that "a creature that cannot in principle be understood in terms of our own beliefs, values and modes of communication is not a creature that may have thoughts radically different from our own: it is a creature without what we mean by thoughts."[70] Nonetheless, MacIntyre stands his ground on what he considers to be a substantive conception of untranslatability. The pivotal idea here is that, while translatability presupposes some amount of agreement, this will always be partial commensurability at most. In fact, the more significant the content, the more likely the translatability will prove intractable in practice. MacIntyre wrote:

> [T]he fact that certain other parts of the two languages may translate quite easily into each other provides no reason at all for skepticism about partial untranslatability. The sentences-in-use that are the untranslatable parts of this type of language-in-use are not in fact capable of being logically derived from, constructed out of, reduced to, or otherwise rendered into the sentences-in-use that comprise the translatable part of the same language-in-use.[71]

As MacIntyre quips later in the essay, "No one ever had any difficulty translating 'Snow is white' from one language to the other."[72]

Fowl administered the full import of Davidson's insight to MacIntyre's position in his article, "Could Horace Talk with the Hebrews?" What Lindbeck takes to represent the "untranslatability" of the Christian conceptual scheme MacIntyre illustrates with the example that the odes to Jupiter composed by the Roman poet Horace could not have been translated in a way that Hebrew readers of his day would not reject. "The Latin is '*Caelo tonantem credidimus Jovem regare: praesens divus habebitur Auustus.*'" Fowl restates the case: "MacIntyre renders this into English as 'We have believed that Jupiter thundering reigns in the sky; Augustus will be held a present divinity,'" adding, "[w]hat Horace said could only have emerged in Hebrew [Aramaic] as at once false and blasphemous."[73] Fowl responds:

One could not expect a faithful Jew contemporaneous with Horace to be committed to Horace's view. That does not, however, mean that such a Jew could not have translated Horace's views into Hebrew or Aramaic. In fact, the only way a Jew could have found such a view blasphemous is because he or she had been able to translate it adequately. Our hypothetical Jew can translate Horace because he or she and Horace share some common beliefs about gods, what it means for them to reign, who is referred to by the name Augustus and many other things. On the other hand, they are irreconcilably divided on the plurality of divinity and about who it is who actually reigns in heaven, Jupiter or Yahweh. If we could actually list all the agreements which make this translation possible, we would probably find that the number of agreements far outnumber the disagreements. The point, however, is that the disagreements are of such significance that, in spite of the fact that translation is possible, the two traditions are not commensurable. That is, although it is possible to translate first century Latin into first century Aramaic, it would not be possible for a single person to hold to the truth both of the tradition represented by Horace and of tradition of Judaism without seriously deforming one or the other in ways that would make it unrecognizable to other followers of that tradition.[74]

"Incommensurable" here is deflated in significance to refer to the sort of disagreement between conflicting viewpoints in which it is impossible for a single person to hold the truth of two conflicting claims simultaneously. Note, however, that the disagreement, while crucial, is made possible by all that the differing interlocutors share in common. With this insight from Davidson in view, we can admit the case specificity and partiality, even the precariousness, of a given act of translation. At the same time we can acknowledge that, with sufficient care and hermeneutical enrichment, beliefs and truth claims from within one belief system might be made intelligible—and perhaps even persuasive—to people who hold different or conflicting beliefs. Central to Davidson's argument is that what is required in a given encounter must be assessed and worked out situationally and in the specific circumstances in which such translation is called for.[75] The practical possibility should not be ruled out in advance. Cultures, groups, or interlocutors develop new ways of talking in encounter with radically different interlocutors, groups, and cultures. To recognize the other as such means that, in principle, the possibility exists.

If Lindbeck's account of comprehensive interpretive schemes has at its heart conflicting truth claims that Fowl portrays above, then we are probably better off to call such an encounter just that—a conflict between truth claims and their various implications. This would be a more modest and more manageable alternative to investing in a theory that stakes claims in the nature and basis of comprehensive interpretive schemes, incommensurability, and untranslatability. Lindbeck might cast his account more persuasively, and perhaps more cogently, if he dropped terms like "comprehensive interpretive schemes" and "absorption" altogether. First, scheme/content dualism appears unnecessary to retain a conception of the particularity, even irreconcilability, of competing truth claims.[76] Second, the notion of a "scheme" or "worldview" adds little in aiding the kind of hermeneutical enrichment and charitable interpretation that conversations across historical, cultural, and linguistic difference frequently require. Moreover, such notions provide little in the way of precision to our efforts to understand, sift, and adjudicate conflicting truth claims, their implications, how they cohere or conflict with other claims, beliefs, and ways of getting around in the world. They do, however, bring in train long-debated philosophical baggage about where one worldview ends and another begins, and how, under what circumstances, and by what criteria some worldview might outnarrate, absorb, or fuse with another.[77]

Frei's position implies that we need not speak as if Christian truth claims presented a unified, internally integrated "comprehensive scheme" which absorbs all that it confronts and eliminates what will not fit. This does not mean that the world of Christian discourse applies only to Christians nor that its truth claims purport to be less than final. It does indicate that prior to the eschaton we "see through a glass darkly" and that our truth claims reflect a revisability and provisionality in the ways that we understand and articulate them here and now. Frei's claims call into question the advisability of invoking theoretical equipment as weighty as "comprehensive schemes" and "worldviews" to talk about Christian truth claims, and how they conflict with some truth claims and perhaps coexist peacefully with others. I think that he saw no need to construe the Christian world of discourse as a comprehensive interpretive framework that must prove its mettle in virtue of successfully absorbing all the rest. In fact, he claimed that some other such points of view will—from time to time—*subvert* the "diachronic world of agency and suffering" wrought in Scripture. Obviously, Frei refused to compromise the finality of Scripture's truth claims. What, then, might he mean?

As a matter of God's freedom, the Spirit moves where it will, and God's Word may make itself known however it pleases. Occasionally, the Word confronts believers in ways that require testing and revising of the received understandings and articulations of the very forms in which their tradition's central insights have come to them. The church should expect to have its practices and self-understandings tested from all sides, and especially from without. The primary norm guiding the Christian's endeavors is faithfulness to the Person who comes through the witness of Scripture and in a freedom and grace that is certain to scramble human (and thus always provisional) categories—even, at times, those categories most apparently "biblically grounded." The scriptural world may subvert itself. Such subversion should be illuminating and, occasionally, necessary. Kathryn Tanner helps to bring this insight clearly to the fore, writing:

> When theological claims are hardened in a way that obstructs obedience to the Word, they too need to be broken and their provisionality revealed. Borrowed materials should not, then, always be subordinated to Christian claims; they should be permitted, instead, to shake them up where necessary. If Christianity's having the upper hand over non-Christian materials is made into a rule, this only encourages the Word's enslavement to the human words of Christians.[78]

Frei's work contains similar cautions against fashioning systems and schemes from the gospel accounts. Tools drawn from general theory and activities of Christian self-description must be combined unsystematically.[79] In principle, such encounters should not be construed as a "systematic correlation" between equal partners. However, Frei recognizes the implication of God's radical freedom in the theological enterprise and follows that logic out unflinchingly. Hence, even the claim that philosophical tools will be subordinated to the theological task cannot be hardened into rule that is immune from subversion. Frei's approach requires a case-specific sensitivity in which prayerful attention to the ways the Word may be moving and speaking will always take priority. Of course, the term *subversion* suggests a momentary overturning of something already in place and already holding sway. For Frei this entails returning, again and again, to the person and work of Christ rendered in the Gospels.

The insight guiding Frei's divergence from Lindbeck is that believers' recognition of Scripture's grasp here and now is authentic at the same time that human articulation of it is unavoidably provisional. Their adequate reference must be God's doing. Thus, the theologian's claims about the Christian world of discourse as the one true world must be administered in the present with, as Frei put it, an "eschatological edge."[80] The eschatological edge with which Frei tempered his claims for the Christian world of discourse as "the one true world" means that Christians assert the truth of their claims with a sense of flexibility in how they are articulated. "[T]he Christian Church does not speak from out of heaven. It speaks on earth and in an earthly way," as Barth put it. "The meaning and basis of the Christian message and theology, in any case, is, to say it once more, beyond all principles and systems, all world-views and morality, not messianism, but rather the Messiah, the Christ of Israel."[81] The difference between this and the claim that the Christian comprehensive interpretive scheme, now and continuously, must absorb everything else at the risk of jeopardizing its rational viability may be, largely, a matter of interpretive humility. This is humility not for fear of the audacity of making truth claims. This interpretive humility cannot but be inscribed within the conviction that the person of Christ is, and will remain, "the light which will burn the longest," whatever the particular ways he will work in particular circumstances.[82] Such interpretive humility is required of any attempt to follow faithfully a living God who loves in freedom.

It is telling that in Frei's published writings and circulating archival papers the trope of "absorption" appears once. He used it to redescribe the way that the literal sense "reshapes extratextual language" in fashioning a typological relation to the stories in which the Christian tradition has its existence.[83] In the opening pages of *Eclipse*—again, well before Lindbeck's book—Frei described in his own words the ways that the world of the biblical narratives figurally or typologically "must in principle *embrace* the experience of any present age and reader." By this he meant that the Christian was to "see his disposition, his actions and passions, the shape of his own life as well as that of his era's events as figures of that storied world."[84] The distinction between Lindbeck's trope of "absorbing the world" and Frei's invocation of Scripture's "embrace [of] the experience of any present age and reader" is a subtle but salient one I think. Frei's position permits an openness and underdetermination of the specific results. This calls us back to a more modest claim about how Scripture orients the Christian world of discourse. Insofar as one might find it necessary to rehabilitate the terms "worldview" and "absorption," William Placher provides a helpful perspective on the matter:

> A good worldview leaves many particulars underdetermined. Neither "the modern scientific worldview" nor Marxism nor postliberal Christianity has much to tell us about which baseball team to root for, or whether to prefer Brahms or the blues, or about many other aspects of our lives. Visions of the world that try to dictate every detail quickly collapse under their own weight. But if the biblical world absorbs our world, then we will try a) not to hold views incompatible with what we take to be its central claims, and b) regularly to consider whether its categories might be unexpectedly helpful in understanding any aspects of our lives.[85]

Placher's account reflects a modesty that is, in my judgment, far more plausible, potentially persuasive, and true to the spirit of Frei's work.

Of course, Wolterstorff might press his criticisms further. He might ask for criteria for making decisions about when the world of Scripture can give way to the world, and when it is okay not to subordinate the work-a-day world to the world of the biblical story. Otherwise, he writes, we confront "once again the threat of the Bible's becoming a wax nose which we mold to suit whatever convictions we bring to it."[86] If we respond from the vantage point from which Frei addressed the issue, Wolterstorff will get no such criteria except, that is, for an appeal to the continuing task of dogmatics itself.[87] However, the refusal to pre-set criteria or fixed set of principles under which to subsume novel cases does not mean that we make such decisions arbitrarily, and thus fashion from Scripture a wax nose.[88] As we will see, it positions the reading and interpretive processes as a complex, object-directed tradition of inquiry—"faith seeking understanding."

Conclusion

Frei and Lindbeck shared a lively friendship, mutual theological interests, and influenced each other in important ways. The similarities shared by their projects are genuine and call to be sorted through concretely. Their similarities have tended to get overemphasized. I have argued that it is a mistake to equate their work or to view them as variations of a single project. When they are lumped together, it is Frei's work that tends to suffer. Its nuances and deep background—usually frustratingly articulated to begin with—too easily get washed out by the bright provocativeness of Lindbeck's project.

The resources they share present another challenge to detecting the consequence of their divergences. I demonstrated that Frei used these resources with a much lighter touch than Lindbeck has—uses not freighted by Lindbeck's theory of religion. Moreover, Frei worked more directly under the influence of Barth's thinking. Taking these differences seriously should challenge customary applications of the "postliberal" moniker that so often obscure more than they illuminate. At least it eases the tendency of that term to pigeonhole and caricature. Each of their projects will have to be taken on its own merits at the level of detail.

Frei appealed to a set of traditional Scriptural practices in which every engagement with Scripture, whether in reading, critical reflection, or in application (*explicatio, meditatio, applicatio*) further enriches the interpreter's understanding of Scripture as the fount and origin of the Christian world of discourse.[89] This gave biblical reading a flexibility and provisionality that all such historically situated social practices have. At the same time, the practice in question is object directed. What these procedures are, and how they enable believers to justify and hold each other accountable for their discriminations and judgments, is the substance of the chapters that follow. How can such scriptural practices differ between "discriminating conformation and guidance," on the one hand, and "ignoring the authority of Scripture and going one's own way," on the other?

Of course, even if Frei's theological approach is uniquely scripturally centered, this conception of scripture is criticized for allegedly closing its eyes to questions of reference. In effect, such an account collapses both revelational and historical forms of reference into a self-contained, literary construal of the scriptural accounts. At the same time, Frei's uses of Barth—which spell a crucial difference between his and Lindbeck's projects—may also present a terminal deficiency in his project. Such powerful and persistent concerns provide the focus of the chapter that follows.

4

But Did It *Really* Happen?

Frei and the Challenges of Critical Realism and Historical Reference

Criticisms of "postliberal theology" are as wide-ranging as the resemblances that constitute it. Evangelical critics have charged that in refusing to work at historically verifying the events reported in Scripture, postliberal theology forgoes all concern for history or "what really happened," devoting itself to the supposedly autonomous world inside the biblical text. On one hand, such critics claim, postliberal theologians lack faith in the historical reliability of the scriptural witness. On the other hand, and perhaps more importantly, they stand in dereliction of their apologetical duties by refusing to meet historians on their own grounds. In part I of this chapter, I examine perhaps the most famous encounter between a postliberal and an evangelical theologian on the question of historical reference—the exchange between Carl Henry and Hans Frei at Yale in 1985.[1] This particular exchange warrants careful consideration and analysis as a model for what a detailed encounter might look like. At the same time, it also affords an opportunity to clarify Frei's position on what may be the most nagging concern about his theology—the question of historical reference.

The difficulty that "reference" poses for Frei's thinking does not stop with the question of history. In fact, reference poses a double-edged concern. If some evangelicals are especially concerned about historical reference, various Barth scholars are equally worried about Frei's position on a different form of extratextual reference. The latter ask how Frei can posit Scripture as the Word of God manifest linguistically in the way that he does without giving up the *realism* of Scripture's claims about God. How, for instance, are we to make sense of Frei's claim that "for the Christian interpretive tradition truth is what is written, not something separable and translinguistic that is written 'about'"?[2] Does this give up the claim that God's revelation in Scripture actually corresponds to the reality of God outside of the text? Once a realist account of theological reference is compromised, it becomes difficult to see how Frei can avoid slipping into a "linguistically idealist" account of revelation in which the text itself becomes the "linguistic presence" of God.[3] Moreover, motivated by such antirealist suspicions, some critics claim that Frei's work diverges from Karl Barth's at a fundamental level, and in a way that Frei appears neither to have been aware of nor understood.

These charges concerning historical and theological reference are closely related. Both raise worries about construing the biblical text as a self-contained "world unto itself" or affirming, in the words of Jacques Derrida, that "there is nothing outside the text."[4] In the following chapter I work through these difficulties for Frei's treatment of Scripture, moving first through the challenge of historical reference and then through theological reference. Based upon close examination of the full range of resources available in Frei's work, I argue that he makes available means by which both of these challenges can be navigated, even if Frei himself never managed to articulate such means with sufficient clarity. I demonstrate that, while there are important differences, Frei's theology is far more consistent than it is inconsistent with what scholars have come to refer to as Barth's "critical realism."[5]

I. Frei, Henry, and the Challenge of Historical Reference

Carl Henry began his critical analysis of Frei by gesturing toward the significant agreements they shared. They shared, for instance, the conviction that "Scripture is a harmonious unity, that historical criticism has not invalidated the relevance of Scripture, that the biblical world is the real world which illuminates all else and that Jesus is the indispensable Savior."[6] Even so, as Henry saw it, Frei's averse reaction to the modern uses of the Bible as a historical source, in effect, dismissed the reality "behind the text" as either theologically unnecessary or fortunately unavailable from an historical perspective. Frei either bracketed or sidestepped altogether questions about the Bible's reference to historical reality. In fact, at times he appeared to reduce the biblical reports to literature. Henry countered, "The notion that the narrative simply as narrative adequately nurtures faith independently of all objective historical concerns sponsors a split in the relationships of faith to reason and to history that would in principle encourage skepticism and cloud historical referents into obscurity."[7] Henry thought this entirely unacceptable. He wanted to know, quite simply, did Jesus come back to life or did he not? Was he resurrected and did he leave his tomb empty, or not?

Frei's immediate response to such questions sounded equivocal. "Well, yes," he answered. "If I am asked to use the language of factuality, then I would say, yes, in those terms, I have to speak of an empty tomb. In those terms I have to speak of the literal resurrection." Frei quickly interposed a proviso. "But I think those terms are not privileged, theory-neutral, trans-cultural, an ingredient in the structure of the human mind and of reality always and everywhere."[8] Clearly, Frei sought to question the normative assumptions by which some event might be determined historically verified or verifiable. This may sound like he is making a so-called "postmodern" turn away from the very possibility of "objectivity." I contend, however, that this is the wrong way to characterize Frei's reservation.

On one hand, Frei's concern about the "theory-ladenness" of modern historical research derives from the recognition that such forms of investigation have been based upon several philosophically empiricist presuppositions. Such presuppositions include the idea that "the facts" stand independently of, and separable from, the reports that render them, and that accurate correspondence to those facts makes claims or beliefs about them true or false. These presuppositions include, further, that one ought to tailor the strength of one's assertion of factuality or belief in proportion to the reliability of one's evidence and the public testability of one's claim. At the same time, however, Frei's reservations about historical investigation of the gospel accounts reflect his belief that the particular subject matter he has in view is unique in kind. It is this latter concern, in my judgment, that provides Frei's primary motivation for treating questions about Scripture's historical reference as he does.

As Frei saw it, the uniqueness of the biblical subject matter resists the tendency of modern historical investigation to confine the biblical witness to the status of a factual report. This subject matter does not altogether *preclude* historical concerns. However, it refuses to be circumscribed by the limits of historical understanding alone. Frei continued:

> Even if I say that history is first of all the facts—and I do have a
> healthy respect for evidence—I come across something else. Is Jesus
> Christ (and here I come across the problem of miracle) a "fact" like
> other historical facts? Should I really say that the eternal Word made
> flesh, that is, made fact indeed, is a fact like any other? I can talk

about "Jesus" in that way, but can I talk about the eternal Word made flesh in him that way? I don't think so.[9]

These are not words of one who "brackets" questions of history or suspends "questions of reality reference," as is occasionally charged. In fact, in sorting through these difficulties Frei identified two distinct senses of reference operative in the biblical witness. The first he referred to as "old-fashioned historical reference," and the second he called "textual reference."[10]

"Old-fashioned historical reference" is central to Frei's project under the proviso that there can be no "systematic correlation" between God's revelation in Scripture and human procedures of historical investigation. George Hunsinger characterizes this way of relating historical investigation and the gospel narratives as "ad hoc minimalism." This position is "ad hoc" because, while it incorporates historical investigation, it refuses to reduce or ultimately constrain the integrity and efficacy of the biblical witness to the criterion of historical verifiability. It is "minimalist" because "Faith needs no more from modern historical criticism . . . than two very minimal assurances," Hunsinger explains, citing Frei. "First, that Christ's resurrection has not been historically disconfirmed; and second, 'that a man, Jesus of Nazareth, who proclaimed the Kingdom of God's nearness, did exist and was finally executed.'"[11]

While minimal, the role that historical reference plays in Frei's account is anything but negligible. In fact, in some circumstances, it could prove to be decisive. While Frei believed that the resurrection could not be proven historically, he thought that it could be historically *disconfirmed*. Historical *disconfirmation* would indicate that the claim that Christ's resurrection had happened had been a false claim all along. On this scenario, accordingly, the alleged resurrection would be just another piece of falsifiable *Historie* for which historical investigation was both necessary and entirely sufficient. If, however, Jesus is who the Bible portrays him to be, then we are dealing with an event that happened in time, but for which probability or evidence is woefully insufficient. "[I]f the resurrection is true, it is unique, but if false, it is like any other fact that has been proved false: there is nothing unique about it in that case," Frei explained.[12]

What Frei called "textual reference" enters into the account at this point, first of all, because there can be no access to the events that happened "then and there" apart from some terms of description. The "facts of the matter" do not stand by neutrally, awaiting historians to take up a "view from nowhere" in order to access them in unadulterated objectivity. Any account will be relative to some frame of reference, terms of depiction, and investigative interests and purposes. When taken purely on historical-critical terms, the gospel accounts are troublingly fragmentary. So far, empirical evidence for or against "what really happened" has been insufficient to generate sustained scholarly consensus. Frei sought to sidestep intractably speculative debates played out on the field of "historical factuality" (such as the nearly self-parodying sequence of quests for the historical Jesus). He began, instead, with a simple assumption about what happened then and there. Frei wrote:

> I plead guilty to a kind of fall-back on common sense, to which someone may say I have no right. I am assuming that somebody roughly fitting Jesus of Nazareth as described in the Gospels really did live. If and when it is shown that this assumption is unwarranted and the person invented, I will no longer want to be a Christian. Until then, I plan to go on being one and saying, "We know him only under a description, viz., that of the Gospel accounts, and they say that the point at which possibly but not necessarily fictional depiction and factual reality are seen to be fully one is the resurrection. In abstraction from the full connection between them at the point of the depiction, the relation between every description of individual incident and putative factual assertion corresponding to it is simply more or less probable."[13]

The gospel accounts of Christ's life, death, and resurrection provide the indispensable description for two reasons. First, they concretely render the person and work of Christ as fully unsubstitutable and unique in kind. The events they render cannot be grasped in their full significance in abstraction from what the Gospels depict and how they depict it. As Frei put the point, "'The Word was made flesh and dwelt among us, full of grace and truth'—is something that we don't understand except as a sequence enacted in the life, death and resurrection of Jesus."[14] The full consequence of that to which these accounts attest eludes a "neutral and detached" perspective. This subject matter makes a claim upon the lives of its readers. This is not a claim about intelligibility; it does not mean, in other words, that the claim that Jesus is the crucified and risen Savior can be *intelligible* only to those for whom this claim becomes self-involving. It means, rather, that when grasped by the full significance of these stories, readers no longer recognize Jesus merely as "the one of whom it is said 'on the third day he rose again from the dead.'" They recognize him as the one who on the third day rose again from the dead. The latter case is uniquely self-involving because, in Frei's words, "unlike other cases of factual assertion, the resurrection of Christ shapes a new life."[15]

The second and decisive reason that the gospel accounts of Jesus death and resurrection are indispensable for Frei is that they uniquely orient the divine authority of Scripture. The events portrayed by the accounts of Jesus' death and resurrection claim to entail the entrance of Eternity into time, the Infinite into the finite. As such, readers should neither expect to comprehend them exhaustively nor to maintain control over the terms by which they make themselves available. In fact, to presume that the finite terms in which humans live and move and have our being could comprehensively contain this Infinite, and that we could have these at our disposal to know and do with as we see fit, would only speak against the credibility of such an account. A claim on behalf of the Infinite that could be submitted wholly and entirely to the finite would testify against itself. It would cease to be Infinite. Moreover, the pretense of human beings to do so would amount to a form of idolatry—an account of God's revelation fashioned after humanity's image. Hence, if the gospel accounts indeed portray the uniquely unsubstitutable Savior as they claim to, then the only descriptions finally adequate to this subject matter are those that God used—and uses—to convey it. Ultimately, it is God's use of them that makes them adequate. As the means by which God reveals God's self, these accounts are indispensable for that knowledge and encounter. Frei explained:

> The truth to which we refer we cannot state apart from the biblical
> language which we employ to do so. And belief in the divine
> authority of Scripture is for me simply that we do not need more.
> The narrative description there is adequate. "God was in Christ
> reconciling the world to himself" is an adequate statement for what
> we refer to, though we cannot say univocally how we refer to it.[16]

Notice in this passage that, for Frei, the adequacy of the gospel accounts is not merely a matter of *how* they depict what they depict (though that is crucial, as we saw in chapter 1) nor merely the fact that they give their readers "enough to go on" regarding what happened then and there (though, again, as we saw in Frei's "fall-back on common sense" above, this is important as well). Their adequacy is, most basically for Frei, a matter of the divine authority of Scripture.

Where does this leave historical reference? It means that the positive contribution historical reference makes to the *kerygmatic* efficacy of these accounts, while necessary, is secondary and dependent. The order of this relation led Frei to add that "the text is witness to the Word of God, whether it is historical or not."[17] Frei's point with this claim is that, whether or not each detail happened as described in the gospel accounts, these accounts nonetheless convey the identity of Jesus Christ by portraying what he was like and what he has accomplished.[18]

Of course, when it came to discussing how ideas of "reference" fit into this complex equation, Frei frequently became sparing—if not squeamish—in his explanatory terminology. He exerted great caution to avoid either systematic or even overly cogent explanation (e.g., an attempt to cover every explanatory detail so completely as to drain all flexibility and mystery from the account) or speculation abstracted from the central claims and features of the text. Hence, on one hand he asserted that "belief in Jesus' resurrection is more nearly a belief in something like the inspired quality of the accounts than in the theory that they reflect what 'actually took place.'"[19] And yet, this claim can be abstracted from his further stipulations only upon pain of misunderstanding Frei's position. He added:

> [A]t one point a judgment of faith concerning the inspiration of the descriptive contents and a judgment of faith affirming their central factual claim would have to coincide for the believer. He would have to affirm that the New Testament authors were right in insisting that it is more nearly correct to think of Jesus as factually raised, bodily if you will, than not to think of him in this manner. (But the qualification "more nearly . . . than not" is important in order to guard against speculative explanations of the resurrection from theories of immortality, possibilities of visionary or auditory experience, possibilities of resuscitating dead bodies, miracle in general, etc.)[20]

Later in his career Frei described this approach to the gospel accounts:

> [Readers] read the accounts as meaning what they say, so that their subject is indeed the bodily resurrected Jesus. They also believe that a miracle—the miracle of the resurrection in particular—is a real event; however, it is one to which human depiction and conception are inadequate, even though the literal description is the best that can be offered, not to be supplanted or replaced by any other and therefore itself not simply metaphorical in character. In this view text and reality are adequate, indeed, indispensable to each other but not identical. Inadequate by itself, the literal account of the text is adequate to the reality of the events by divine grace. The text is not a photographic depiction of reality, for not only are the accounts fragmentary and confusing, but they depict a series of miraculous events that are in the nature of the case unique, incomparable, and impenetrable—in short, the abiding mystery of the union of the divine with the historical, for our salvation from sin and death.[21]

Read in tandem, the foregoing passages provide as close to a stereoscopic sense of Frei's understanding of the status of historical reference in Scripture as may be available. The first passage demonstrates how Frei thought that

Scripture's witness to, and proclamation of, the person and work of Christ retains an element of *Historie* as a nonfungible ingredient.[22] It clarifies, moreover, that this ingredient (historical reference) is secondary to, and dependent upon, the Gospels' depictive rendering of their subject matter (sense).

The second passage makes clear that, ultimately, even the adequacy of the sense of the text depends upon God's self-revelatory activity. For, while the "literal description" is "the best that can be offered" in the way of human conception and depiction of what happened then and there, on its own it remains inadequate to the nature of the case. Ultimately, it is "by divine grace" that these descriptions can be "adequate to the reality of the events."[23] Frei amplified this point in his response to Carl Henry:

> Once again, yes, "Jesus" refers, as does any ordinary name, but 'Jesus Christ' in scriptural witness does not refer ordinarily; or rather, it refers ordinarily only by the miracle of grace. And that means that I do not know the manner in which it refers, only that the ordinary language in which it is cast will miraculously suffice.[24]

Notice here that Scripture's witness to, and proclamation of, the person and work of Christ occurs both in virtue of what happened there and then *and* what God does here and now. It is thanks to the miracle that God wrought once for all (there and then) to which the gospel witnesses attest, *and* the miracle God continues to enact again and again (here and now) in and through that attestation, that we have what we need in the way of access to the reality of God. This convergence of factors entails factual claims. But any such claims are uniquely conditioned by the subject matter. Because this subject matter is unique in kind, in the final analysis "[t]he witness of Scripture to God is sure, not of itself, but because the witness of God to Scripture is faithful and constant."[25]

Of course, Frei's account of "textual reference" assuaged Carl Henry's misgivings no more than did his position on "historical reference." Henry persisted in his claim that Frei had exchanged a notion of reference to something outside the text (what he called "text-transcendent reference") for the "literary presence" of the Word of God.[26] Clearly, Frei struggled to articulate his ideas about reference throughout his career. And indeed, in his latest work, pieced together and published after his death, some passages occasionally sound like Frei thinks that the presence of God is purely literary or linguistic. For instance, he wrote:

> [W]e don't have more than our concepts of God. We don't have a separate intuition, a preconceptual or prelinguistic apprehension or

grasp of God in his reality. . . . But we don't need it either; for the reality of God is given in, with, and under the concept and not separably, and that is adequate for us.[27]

Here we have an awkwardly phrased point that will strike some as flatly antirealist (that "we have the reality [of God] . . . only linguistically"). However, what at first may appear as a most egregious form of linguistic idealism in his understanding of revelation may appear differently when situated within the trajectory and development of Frei's body of work. If we situate it with sufficient care, I think we will find that what Frei means here is that the possibility of God's self-revelation in and through human concepts and language is predicated on the actuality of God conscripting, breaking, and utilizing those concepts for the purposes of God's self-revelation. Hunsinger points out that this makes Frei's understanding of the mode of reference of these concepts doubly analogical. "They refer not only to Jesus in his earthly life (whether we can verify that factuality by modern methods or not) but also and at the same time to the risen Jesus Christ who lives to all eternity, and who attests to us through those narratives here and now."[28]

Frei's claims on this point reflect a contention that he reiterated again and again throughout his writings—the claim that the content of God's miracle of grace makes revelation *inseparable from*, yet *not identical to*, its form. Frei arrived at this position largely as a result of his extended engagement with Barth and the Protestant Reformers on the nature and character of the scriptural witness. He wrote:

> The odd, philosophically ambiguous status of "reference" in this
> tradition, for which literal and historical, word and thing were
> congruent in a semiotic rather than epistemological representational
> way meant that the text did not communicate—as though by way of a
> channel of absence—the presence of God. The text did not refer to, it
> was the linguistic presence of God, the fit embodiment of one who
> was himself "Word," and thus it was analogous to, though not
> identical with, Incarnation.[29]

If we read such claims as more or less consistent with Barth's account (which I believe we have grounds to, as I argue in what follows), then the miracle of grace that makes "textual reference" possible is God's taking up human conceptual practices—words, concepts, and the claims and assertions they constitute—and breaking and transforming them for God's self-revelatory purposes. And yet at the same time, God's revealing activity leaves the human character of those concepts, claims, and assertions intact.

Charges arise that Frei's treatment of "textual reference" and his reliance upon an *analogical* mode of reality reference, in particular, results in a nondialectical account of revelation. This overlooks God's continuing activity in revelation. If correct, such charges drive a deep wedge between Frei and Barth. Bruce McCormack has argued that Frei's claim that we have God's revelation "in, with, and under" our concepts works to "dangerously flatten out" the dialectical relation of God's being and the language that witnesses to Him. If this deficiency in Frei's thinking is not terminal in itself, it at least indicates a point at which Frei not only departed from Barth but risked positively distorting his theology.[30]

As McCormack sees it, Frei's account of Barth is indicative of a misunderstanding of the development of Barth's thought "that has dominated the Anglo-American reception of Barth's thought in fundamental ways."[31] It is rooted in the account of Barth's theology provided by Hans Urs von Balthasar in 1951, claiming that Barth's 1931 book on Anselm of Canterbury represents his turn to the use of analogical thought form—"the point at which Barth abandons his dialectical method and adopts a more 'objective' and 'positivistic' approach to theology."[32] This account is fundamentally flawed, McCormack argues. By centering his treatment of Barth upon it, Frei's theology replicates those flaws. McCormack explains:

> What is missing from the Anselm book, from the point of view of the *Church Dogmatics*, is an adequate emphasis on the network of dogmatic assumptions which would prevent the theological "science" described in [*Anselm*] from becoming just one more complacent, bourgeois discipline: viz: 1) attention to the fact that theology can only succeed in its task of speaking adequately of God if God does something, and 2) the comprehension of this realistic emphasis on divine action in terms of a *Realdialektik* of veiling and unveiling, which would locate the reality of God in a realm beyond that accessible by means of direct intuition and, thereby, make clear the fact that the reality of God cannot simply be grasped, controlled, manipulated. It is this set of dogmatic presuppositions which would forever make theology, for Barth a human impossibility. It is a divine possibility, or it is not possible at all. Not for Karl Barth a definition of theology in terms of the learning of a linguistic skill! Frei seems to have understood all this with regard to the early Barth or the second edition of Romans. . . . But Frei believed that the Anselm book constituted a methodological "revolution" in Barth's thought.[33]

Insofar as Frei split apart dialectic and analogy, his reading of Barth resulted in a "positivistic Biblicism"—so great an emphasis upon "the given-ness of

God in revelation (e.g., through collapsing revelation into the text of the biblical witness) that Barth is made into a revelational positivist."[34] McCormack explains that the dialectical dimension of Barth's account means, by contrast, that "God makes the language of the biblical witness conform to Himself and, in that He does so, we do indeed grasp God in His reality."[35] McCormack positions Frei as having committed such a fallacy in his dissertation on Barth's doctrine of revelation and then transmitting that fallacy to many so-called "American neo-Barthians." In the pages that remain, I conduct a bit of textual excavation of Frei's earliest writings in order to demonstrate that positioning his account of Barth in this way overlooks the nuance and complexity of Frei's account of analogy and dialectic and results in a fairly schizophrenic view of his theology.

II. Frei, Barth, and Analogy

In his doctoral dissertation of 1956 Frei described Barth's 1931 book on St. Anselm of Canterbury as "absolutely indispensable for a knowledge of the revolution in his thought between the two editions of the *The Doctrine of the Word of God*."[36] The "revolution" in question was Barth's movement from an earlier reliance upon a dialectical theological method to an analogical thought form. This term that Frei uses—"revolution"—is today portrayed as representative of his understanding of the development of Barth's thought. It conveys the "revolutionary" difference between Barth's adoption of an analogical mode of reference in the *Church Dogmatics* and his earlier, "dialectical" period.[37]

To be clear, Frei did convey the distinct impression that his position on these points can be adequately characterized in terms of a "revolution" or "radical transformation" in Barth's thinking.[38] On one hand, Frei wrote:

> It remains true for him that God is always *Subject-in-Act*. But now
> [after his turn to analogical thought form] Barth affirms that in grace,
> in Jesus Christ, this God, who is subject and nothing else, gives
> himself as object to us. God remains mysterious, but in this mystery
> it is He that is revealed. He that is hidden, reveals himself in
> hiddenness. He who becomes God for us is nothing and no less than
> God himself. The living God gives himself as object, thereby
> affirming and not denying his living freedom.[39]

Frei continued by expanding upon the significance of this development in Barth's thinking. He added:

> Hence, then, there is—not identity but correspondence and congruity, radical congruity between Creator and creature, grace and nature, but on the basis of grace and revelation alone. Barth has turned to a doctrine of analogy. . . . the analogy between our words, concepts, intuitions and their object, God, through the self-giving of God in his Word. This is the *analogia fidei*.[40]

In the context of Frei's dissertation one can detect in these particular passages almost celebratory tones. As Frei sees it, Barth's "turn" to the *analogia fidei* from dialectical thought form succeeded in breaking through barriers erected between humanity and God by Kant and Schleiermacher.[41] "Barth no longer has to insist that in his radical realism, the knowledge of God is simply *ac-knowledgement* of myself as being known: in knowledge, as in existence, Barth seems now to say, I am actually and meaningfully confronted by the One who is the lord of grace."[42] The result is that theology becomes a human possibility. This is because, and solely because, God confronts humans in the miraculous activity of self-revelation.

As Frei understood the unfolding of Barth's thinking, while "dialectic" came to be no longer "as necessary," neither was it dispensable. Even amidst his effusiveness about the breakthrough that Frei takes Barth to have achieved, Frei never entirely jettisoned "dialectic" from his account of Barth's theology. Hence, after the "turn" to the *analogia fidei*, it remains the case that "all theological theses are inadequate to their object" and "there is no identity between the *Credo* and its *res*."[43] Perhaps more tellingly, Frei characterized Barth's "turn from dialectic to analogy" as a *de-emphasis* rather than a complete rejection of dialectic.[44] He added, "It is not so necessary now (since Barth thinks that he has drawn sufficient attention to the fact) to affirm that we cannot, of ourselves, predicate any qualities of God, that he is the unpredicable or unintuitable center between positive and negative attributions and judgments."[45] Frei reiterated that "similarity of predicability" occurs in virtue of God's own act of "making himself similar to the creature, and yet remaining identical with himself in this act." And this is where Frei stood at roughly the 200-page mark of his nearly 600-page dissertation. Indeed, these are fairly distinct claims about the movement in Barth's thinking from dialectical to analogical thought form using such words as "turn" or "revolution."

And yet, to limit our understanding of Frei's account of dialectic and analogy in Barth's thinking to dramatic and revolutionary terms turns out to be woefully inadequate. For in the final chapter of Frei's dissertation, a markedly different picture of the relationship between analogy and dialectic in the development of Barth's thought emerges. What Frei earlier characterized as Barth's *turn* from dialectic to analogy is assessed under a different aspect. There Frei characterizes this as a *gradual development* in Barth's thinking that had occurred steadily over the course of the decade of the 1920s. Clearly, Frei still writes in terms of two "stages" in Barth's thinking. However, his guiding concern in the later chapter is to highlight, clarify, and account for the *continuity* between these stages. Somewhat startlingly, in that final chapter Frei traces Barth's use of an analogical thought form as far back in his thinking as the 1922 edition of *The Epistle to the Romans*.

Here Frei portrays dialectic as an indirect *giving* by which God reveals God's self without "erecting a corresponding magnitude of response on a creaturely level." As such, he wrote, "faith must negate itself, point away from itself; yet not in such a way as to dissolve the reality of the creaturely action that it is, since it is human, not divine activity." Frei continued:

> But dialectic, if it succeeds in this negative, indirect task of pointing
> away from faith itself to the actuality of faith in revelation alone, fails
> thereby to indicate that this actuality in revelation which takes place
> in faith is nevertheless an undissolved, untranscended human act,
> i.e., that a miracle takes place and not a sublation of the created spirit
> into the Holy Spirit. In order to indicate this miraculous fact Barth
> even at this early and thoroughly dialectical stage of his thinking has
> to draw upon some sort of doctrine or [*sic*] analogy. It is pale and
> vague indeed; nevertheless it is there, precisely in conjunction with
> the understanding of faith. In some concrete way he must indicate
> the relation of this wholly divinely—actualized fact of faith, this sheer
> gift of revelation, to its natural setting. He does so within the context
> of dialectical negation and movement; nevertheless he does so.[46]

As these lines indicate, on Frei's reading the dialectical character of the miracle of God's revelation does not eliminate human agency. This is because a faint but nonetheless emerging conception of analogy promises to mediate the radical otherness of God's agency and its relative likeness in human agency. In the miracle of faith (as the recipient mode of God's act of revelation) human agency becomes "a pointer to the absolute." However, while quite real, the human element remains "relative, the witness, the parable."[47] Frei read this "positive valuation of 'parable'" by Barth as an early glimmering of analogy within a predominately dialectical framework. He took Barth's use of "parable" here to, at once, mediate an apparent contradiction and yet permit the full stringency of that contradiction to remain intact. Thus, while humanity could never speak directly of God, nonetheless, God's miracle of grace enabled human words and capacities to adequately witness to God.

Frei read this use of parable and witness as an important, early movement in what he characterized as "Barth's steady shift toward a doctrine of analogy."[48] Of course, Frei pointed out that any such early glimmerings of analogy at that point in Barth's work occurred "wholly within and on the basis of dialectic." At that earlier point in Barth's development, Frei wrote. "It [analogy] has no independent position of its own." Nevertheless, Frei identified Barth's use of analogical thought form as present and effective even at the height of what he refers to as Barth's "dialectical period."[49]

What made "analogy" such a promising insight for Frei's concerns? In Barth's hands, analogy became a tool by which to conceptualize the "correspondence in predicable qualities between him [God] and his creatures." At the same time, it kept in view the guiding insight that "it is of his [God's] own grace that this is so, through the historical miracle that he has wrought."[50] Frei stressed the historical character of this miracle as a miracle that occurred in the concrete particularity of Christ's person and work (his *Geschichte*). Christ's incarnation makes possible the indirect, but nevertheless authentic, correlation between "our [human] words, concepts, intuitions and their object"—God.[51] Thus, Frei wrote, God affects a "correspondence and congruity, radical congruity between Creator and creature, grace and nature, but on the basis of grace and revelation alone."[52] In no way does this congruity rely upon an ontologically inscribed point of intersection between the creature and the Creator. Rather, it occurs in God's free act of revelation, and, for the creature, in the recipient mode of that act—faith. This "correspondence and congruity" takes the form of the *analogia fidei*—analogical intersection given in and to faith. Christ gives himself to believers in a way that "enables us to know him as object in the act and decision of faith," Frei wrote.[53] And yet, though this knowing belongs to the creature, faith's comprehension of Christ cannot reduce him to an *object* to be known like any other. "We are recognized, we can only acknowledge, and yet therein we know him and know him genuinely."[54]

How might believers be said to "genuinely know" this object that is unlike any other? And how can it be a believer's positive act of knowing if such knowledge is available only in virtue of God's miracle? "[O]ur reliance for this similarity is upon his [God's] own act in making himself similar to the creature," Frei explained. In other words, in virtue of God's miracle within history, the Creator authentically takes up and uses the creature's concepts and basic form. "[A]nd yet," Frei countered, "[God remains] identical with himself in this act" that brings about a radical congruity. In other words, in this act God remains qualitatively distinct from humanity and the human concepts God uses retain their social and practical identities. There is no "higher synthesis" in the relation; no confusion or change in the parts. Moreover, God's activity in the person of Christ uniquely orders the whole. "In all this, one need hardly add, the customary understanding of analogy is turned about," Frei wrote. "In the relation of faith, it is God who is the analogue and man who is the analogate. In faith and to faith the creature and not the Creator stands in need of explanation, of clarification by analogy."[55]

At the same time, Frei made quite clear that Barth's increasingly explicit use of an analogical thought form did not mean that he eliminated dialectic from his thinking. He was well aware that Barth had openly expressed concern about his increasingly explicit emphasis upon the possibility of positive speech about God in his lectures on the first volume of the *Church Dogmatics* (1931–32). Clearly, Barth had worried about producing "an all too knowledgeable, 'undialectical posterity.'" He had worried that his students might become "'far too positive' in their enthusiasm over the rediscovery of the 'great concepts of God, Word, Spirit, revelation, faith, church, sacrament, and so on'" as though "'we speak *of* them because we know how to speak *about* them with such relative freedom,'" Eberhard Busch recounted.[56]

Nonetheless, viewed through the lens of these latter claims, it becomes increasingly difficult to maintain that Frei positioned Barth's Anselm text as a discrete "revolution" in Barth's thought *in abstraction from* the broader development of his thinking over the preceding decade. Clearly, Frei (following Barth's recollection well after the fact[57]) saw the Anselm book as the point at which Barth perhaps most powerfully and succinctly explicated a movement in his thinking that Frei believed to have been completed sometime between the first and second editions of the *The Doctrine of the Word of God*. Even so, when read in light of the full breadth of Frei's claims in his dissertation, it is apparent that Frei saw the position that Barth described in the book on Anselm as a culmination of "a steady shift toward a doctrine of analogy."[58] This shift was not an abrupt occurrence. Frei saw distinct reason to think that it had been occurring in Barth's thought over the preceding decade.

Contrary to how they may appear at first, the apparently opposing characterizations with which Frei accounts for this shift—"gradual" and "revolutionary"—do not present a simple contradiction. In fact, they fit together complementarily in the scheme of his dissertation. Which characterization Frei stresses at a given point depends upon his mode of analysis at that time. When laying out the specific milestones of the development in Barth's thought, Frei defers to Barth's personal recollections published in the "How My Mind has Changed" articles. In those moments, he gestures to the Anselm text as a point of "revolutionary" importance in the development of Barth's thought. However, when Frei descends to the level of close textual analysis and criticism of Barth's use of dialectic in the second edition of *Romans* in the final hundred pages of his dissertation, Barth's incipient use of analogy—and the gradual development of those uses in his work throughout the 1920s—become both apparent and important.[59] What is clear is that Frei had a distinct sense that analogy and dialectic coexisted in Barth's thinking throughout the 1920s. Analogy did not appear on the scene in the Anselm book as a distinctively novel element.

Now, even if my excavation of Frei's dissertation brings new insight into his early reading of Barth's development, so what? Aside from a more precise appreciation of the nuances of Frei's thinking on the matter, the fact that he continued to attach considerable importance to Barth's book on Anselm makes even this revised version just another variation on the basically flawed Balthasarian account, does it not?[60] If Frei had a clear sense at this point of the dialectical character of Barth's use of analogical thought form, then where did it go in the work that followed? Did Frei simply forget about it? I submit that he did not. In fact, it is evident throughout his ensuing engagements with Barth's work.

Frei remained attentive to the indirectness entailed in Barth's description of the analogical relation between God's act of revelation and human concepts throughout his career.[61] Scripture and the Church speak authentically of God in Himself in virtue of God's miracle wrought in the *analogia fidei*. And yet, that peculiar human speech remains never without qualification. Frei found this "partial correspondence" quite difficult to articulate. Nevertheless, it was on this basis that Frei clearly identifies Barth's reliance upon dialectical thought form reaching well into the *Church Dogmatics*. Explicating a seminal passage in Barth's account of the *analogia fidei* in the *Church Dogmatics* he wrote:

> [T]he fact that God veils himself in his revelation excludes the notion of equality or identity (*Gleichheit*) between God and faith. The fact that he unveils himself in his revelation excludes the notion of total non-correspondence (*Ungleichheit*). Now this mysterious act of veiling and unveiling is not a quantitative balance (as the terms "immanence" and "transcendence" of God are sometimes taken to imply) between two magnitudes in God and (*per analogiam*) in man. "Partial correspondence" means no quantitative division in God or man. The act of veiling and unveiling himself in revelation is a unitary act of the unitary God to unitary man, *though it may only be grasped dialectically. But even the dialectic is teleologically ordered, for the gracious will of God to reveal himself is basic to his veiling as well as his unveiling of himself.* The word 'partial' must be introduced then not for reasons of quantitative division in the relation between God and

man but in order to grasp that our genuine apprehension and the conformity that takes place in it meet their limit in the very same act of God which enables them to come about in the first place. So the conformity or correspondence of faith-apprehension with its indirect object, God, remains partial.[62]

As these lines demonstrate, Frei understands the indispensability of dialectic to become situated within, and oriented by, the analogical form of God's act of revelation. Frei understands Barth's account of analogy's relation to dialectic as ordered by "the gracious will of God to reveal himself" and the actuality of his having done so in Jesus the Christ. He takes Barth to have resituated dialectic within an emphasis upon analogy. The miraculous possibility of adequate speech about God comes to take normative priority to the unqualified need of the creature to negate every human affirmation about God, and follow each denial with an affirmation. And yet, at no point does either work in abstraction from the other.

Frei's claims about the relation of dialectic and analogy in the passage above present a mirror image of his characterization of their relation at the height of Barth's dialectical period. In his dissertation, Frei pointed out that analogy occurred entirely on the basis of dialectic in the second edition of his *The Epistle to the Romans*. As Barth's thinking progressed, this relation became, in effect, reversed—the indispensability of dialectic comes to be oriented by the priority of analogy. However, at no point does either work in abstraction from the other, even into and throughout the *Church Dogmatics*. As such, it is incorrect to ascribe to Frei "the great weakness of the Balthasarian account"[63] after all, that is, the inability to account for the fact that Barth was a dialectical theologian even into the *Church Dogmatics*. In fact, as the above passage indicates, just the opposite is the case. Frei maintained a keen sense of the dialectical character of Barth's theology in the *Dogmatics*.

Time and again Frei refers to the "indirect identity" of God's revelation in biblical witness in virtue of the fact that God "did *and does* relate himself to us," as Frei wrote in his 1968 essay commemorating Barth's death.[64] Notice that Frei here suggests that God's self-revelational activity is not simply once for all (there and then). Clearly, relegating God's activity to the miraculous events then and there and Scripture's reports of those events would indeed collapse revelation into the biblical text and thus turn theology into biblical positivism and yet another "bourgeois discipline." However, Frei understands God to continue to relate God's self to believers (again and again, here and now).

Roughly a decade further on, Frei's review of Eberhard Busch's biography of Karl Barth undoubtedly favored the Anselm text. Indeed, he there identified it as instrumental for understanding Barth's full-fledged use of analogy as a formal "analytical, technical category" in contrast to Barth's "earlier" use of "dialectic." And yet, the relation remains complex. Dialectic remains "an important subordinate device (and formal category) in the service of 'analogy.'"[65] Far more interesting is the fact that Frei orients both of these "devices" by the concrete accounts of Jesus' death and resurrection. He understands both dialectic and analogy to be tools in need of proper ordering—each to the other, and both by the narratively rendered identity of Jesus Christ. In my judgment, this indicates how, for Frei, Christ orients not only his predicates but also any tools by which we describe and redescribe God's activity in making him present.

Does this turn engagement with the text into yet another positive science about God's revelatory activity? I do not see how it can. And this for the same reason that Frei's account of historical reference cannot reduce the gospel accounts of Jesus resurrection to a piece of history or to a literary world inside the text. As we saw in his exchange with Henry, Frei appealed unequivocally to God's miraculous activity in the present, making scriptural accounts adequate for God's revelatory purposes. "Once again, yes, 'Jesus' refers, as does any ordinary name," he wrote. "But 'Jesus Christ' in scriptural witness does not refer ordinarily; or rather, it refers ordinarily only by the miracle of grace. And that means that I do not know the manner in which it refers, only that the ordinary language in which it is cast will miraculously suffice."[66] Further on in his Alexander Thompson Lecture of 1986, Frei framed these claims positively (again, drawing upon Barth's work), writing:

> What is written is the Word of God. The divine touch on it is not that extravagance by means of which what is written, the word, might be transformed into that about which it is written. Christians do have to speak of the referent of the text. They have to speak historically and ontologically, but in each case it must be the notion of truth or reference that must be re-shaped extravagantly, not the reading of the literal text. . . . The textual world as witness to the Word of God is not identical with the latter, and yet, by the Spirit's grace, it is "sufficient" for the witnessing.[67]

The text is incapable of capturing, once for all, God's revelation. As Frei put it, "the message and miracle of faith are accounted for by the very character, and therefore a function of, Jesus' being and his resurrection from the dead; and so Jesus and faith, as well as reality and text, belong together as the miracle of resurrection."[68] For Frei, this miracle occurs again and again, here and now. Christ's "full self-identification with us is perpetual and not temporary."[69]

Conclusion

From the foregoing it should now be clear that Frei's accounts of historical reference and textual reference, while perhaps cryptic, are coherent. I have argued that these are pivotal to his project, even if they remain two points on which his work is most misunderstood. He neither reduced the scriptural witness to God's "literary presence" nor did he forgo God's revelatory activity in and through the scriptural witness. On both points Frei's thinking reflects Barth's influence. Nonetheless, central claims about the grace-given adequacy of the Church's language about God and the accountability of Christian discourse to God frequently get overlooked in Frei's thinking.[70] When recognized, they are taken to be quizzical or curious, more or less accurate yet woefully underdeveloped.[71] At worst, they are seen as vestiges of a radically different body of work composed, in effect, by someone else called "the early Frei."[72]

When viewed in concert with Frei's career-long engagement with Barth and in conjunction with his own account of the literal sense up to the end of his career, the theologically realist claims that appear in his posthumously collected and published fragments cease to be anomalous. Moreover, as my parsing Frei's response to Carl Henry should make clear, they are consistent with his views on the nature of scriptural authority—that "by the miracle of grace . . . the ordinary language in which [scriptural witness] is cast will miraculously suffice."[73] It should be clear that, for Frei, the Word of God comes not as a "biblically positivist" single act of analogy but indirectly, again and again. We will see in the next chapter that the recovery and elucidation of these dimensions of critical realism and reference in Frei's project lift a considerable burden from Frei's construal of theology as "communal self-description." The latter becomes an ecclesially situated and embodied activity that is at once predicated upon and accountable to God's self-revelatory activity in and through Scripture. So I will argue in the chapter that follows.

5

The Rationality Intrinsic to Faith

If Frei's theological approach does not founder upon questions of historical and textual reference, it may do so nonetheless in virtue of his use of nonfoundational philosophical insights for his theological purposes and his concomitant characterization of the theological task as the explication and redescription of the Christian "form of life." Here again, Bruce McCormack articulates concerns that are shared by many others. With Frei's treatment of Barth in *Types of Christian Theology* in his sights, McCormack conveys the concern that Frei restrains "reality-reference," focusing instead upon "the internal logic of theological statements." "Indeed, the door has even been opened to making an appeal to Barth for a view which would seek the norm(s) governing the Christian language-game in the language itself rather than in the presence of God to the Church in Jesus Christ."[1]

Criticisms like this one appear to gain traction against Frei for several reasons. First, indeed, Frei came to describe the historically situated and socially located practices that constitute the Christian world of discourse as fraught with all the internal tensions, discrepancies, and provisionality characteristic of historical and social processes and culturally situated interpretations. And largely in light of this recognition, he came to liken the theologian's task to a sort of "reflexive ethnography" charged with the task of reflecting descriptively and critically upon these practices and understandings.

At the same time, contrary to what several of his critics claim, Frei never relinquished the claim that the biblical text is a central normative criterion by which to assess the practices and institutions that constitute this "Christian world of discourse." Neither, however, did he think it possible to describe the Christian world of discourse as anchored in a static set of representations conveyed in Scripture to which all understanding must conform. Rather, he thought that the claims and patterns conveyed in Scripture are caught up in the continuing set of cultural and historical practices and second-order scrutiny (which they continue to orient). Moreover, the tasks of critical reflection upon scriptural understanding are themselves caught up in that search for understanding into which faith impels the believer. These precipitate the development, revision, and self-correction of believers' understandings of Scripture as well as their grasp of the implications that extend from it. That Frei came to construe the Christian world of discourse in terms of a set of linguistic and inferential cultural practices proves to be central to how this scripturally derived world retains its christological orientation and theological irreducibility without forgoing historical and cultural flexibility. This chapter executes a careful examination of these claims and the criticisms to which they give rise.

The Rationality Intrinsic to Faith

George Hunsinger refers to the form of the cognitive content of faith "Anselmian coherentism." According to this view, while the criteria of justification for doctrinal beliefs are internal to faith, this means anything but a lack of concern for making them explicit and elucidating explanatory support for them. Barth, and Frei after him, identified the testing, ordering, critical scrutiny, and revision of doctrinal beliefs as essential to the theological enterprise. In fact, this is a considerable part of what it means for faith to seek understanding.[2] Barth modeled such an exercise of self-examination at the points in his work where, much like Anselm, he suspended the validity of a given doctrine in order to test and explore its cohesion with the network of beliefs in which it inheres.[3] Faith is axiomatic in this set of conceptual and practical relations. And yet, it is insufficient to label it an uncontestable "given" and leave it at that. Faith is not an epistemic "foundation," as traditionally understood. For, while the basic conviction of faith is *formally* axiomatic, it is not incorrigibly so. The axiomatic status of faith born of, oriented, and continually reoriented by the witness of Scripture does not make it immune from contestation, revision (some would say "reformation"), or even renunciation.

Can scrutiny of this axiomatic status ever be more than hypothetical? Does it ever really permit alterations in this world of discourse? While the suspension of a doctrine's truth may prove useful to the theologian in her coming to a clearer self-understanding and redescription of her faith, is there any *genuine* possibility that the tested convictions will be found mistaken and in need of being replaced? An objector might claim that even if the rationality of faith was not in principle "foundational" due to the corrigibility of its axioms, insofar as these axioms are beyond revision in practice, faith functions as a foundation. Making a mere show of testing the nodes and strands of the Christian web of belief is certainly a temptation with regard to axiomatic beliefs—those beliefs and practices that are "so definitive of the identity of a community and its members that these beliefs cannot be given up without decisive change in communal self-understanding."[4] Is it possible (even in principle) to jettison or revise the background belief that Jesus Christ is at once fully human and fully God?

Ronald Thiemann has made the case that while axiomatic faith convictions do not require explicit justification, they are neither indefeasible nor is explanatory support and clarification of them unnecessary. In fact, such explication and elucidation are two central procedures in faith's search for understanding.[5] In other words, the contestation and possible revision of doctrines—axiomatic and otherwise—is quite genuine. Moreover, while certain beliefs are so axiomatic that without them Christian faith and practice would indeed cease to be *Christian* faith and practice, even these background beliefs are subject to interpretive contestation among different Christian communities. It is not the case, then, that axiomatic beliefs are beyond the pale of testing and revision, and better or worse forms of explication and justification. A belief's status as "axiomatic" does not mitigate the necessity of examining that belief, contesting proposed understanding of it, and possibly revising or jettisoning it.

One procedure for testing a belief is through the critical practice of "retrospective justification."[6] In the case of "Anselmian coherentism," retrospective justification begins from the specific understandings or doctrines derived from the "essential underlying conceptual patterns in Scripture interpreted as a whole" as well as the social practices within the church that they, in part, norm. It then argues from the doctrine in question to a particular understanding or interpretation of the axiomatic belief that they presume. By this procedure one can test and contest the viability of competing interpretations of even axiomatic convictions.[7]

A scriptural component of the testing, revision, and reinterpretation of doctrines and beliefs—axiomatic and otherwise—occurs through a "doctrinal-hermeneutical feedback loop" in which "doctrines arise from and point back to the interpretation of Scripture. Scripture as a whole is interpreted to bring out its essential underlying conceptual patterns as they converge upon and are clarified by the name and narrative of Jesus Christ."[8] These are, as Frei's subtitle to *The Identity of Jesus Christ* portends, the hermeneutical bases of dogmatic theology, according to which "the meaning of the doctrine is the story rather than the meaning of the story being the doctrine."[9] Of course, mention of the "essential underlying conceptual patterns" and their interwovenness with "the name and narrative of Jesus Christ" may suggest "textual essentialism" when those patterns are construed as inherent in the narrative, and self-identifying regardless of interpretive circumstance.

The centrality that Frei ascribed to the biblical witness does not construe Scripture as "self-interpreting," as if it were a neutral, self-evident, or universally accessible object. Again, doctrinal formulations and interpretive claims derive from the patterns identified in the interpretation of Scripture. Those doctrines then, in turn, participate in and bear upon the continuing formulation and revision of doctrines and further interpretation of Scripture.[10] These interpretive processes do not occur "once for all." Continuing interpretation of Scripture further inflects, informs, and enriches the doctrines themselves. Doctrines so enriched then further inflect the reading, understanding, and reenactment of Scripture in new ways. As such, the scriptural witness is always and already caught up in a continuing interpretive process that engages the conceptual patterns that direct the general direction of the continuing process in which those patterns participate. The general interpretive direction of this process will be normed by the witness of Christ as the central actor in these narratives. Beyond that, however, there is considerable flexibility in how the patterns of the narrative appear. The "patterns of meaning" available in the Christ narratives can accommodate different emphases and inflections. Frei, for instance, was quick to point out that for the gospel narratives there are a number of possible "formal ordering schemes" by which to illuminate the patterns presented in Scripture. And some of these possibilities may conflict with others.

As we saw in chapter 1, in *Identity* Frei devised a "formal ordering scheme" with the help of Gilbert Ryle's "intention-action" and "self-manifestation" descriptions. There he highlighted the meaning patterns of "1) Jesus's obedience, 2) the coexistence of power and powerlessness, 3) the transition from one to the other, and 4) the interrelation of Jesus' and God's intention and action."[11] At the same time, he pointed to Barth's account of "The Judge Judged in Our Place" as an alternative pattern that was "profoundly perceptive and quite different" from his own.[12] In another important sense, then, the interpretive process is both "once for all" and "again and again." These narratives recount events that happened "once for all" in Jesus's life, death, and resurrection. The patterns that the narratives portray are, at once, uniquely identified and clarified in light of the specific content of those narratives and reflect back upon them. Insofar as the testing and contesting of those patterns on the basis of various "formal ordering schemes," doctrinal derivations, and their implications for practice, the interpretive processes occur "again and again." To treat any one of the multiple features of this complex process in isolation from its counterparts is to assess something less than Frei's full views on the interpretive dimensions of engaging Scripture's witness.

At the formally theological level, reflexive conceptual redescriptions intend to facilitate the believing community's understanding of what it means for believers to discriminately conform and guide their lives in light of Scripture's witness. They do this, first, by locating Scripture's role in the broader world of discourse that it orients. They then "seek understanding" of that world through procedures such as scriptural interpretation, deriving, testing, and justifying doctrines on the basis of Scripture. These procedures facilitate a flexibility and revisability to that world of discourse that has Scripture as its point of origin and orientation. Faith is rational in that it continually seeks understanding within a setting of reasons afforded by revelation. Scripture's centrality within that setting of reasons is born of God's grace. As we saw in chapter 4, Frei took this to mean that Scripture witnesses to the life, death, and resurrection of Christ both through the accounts, the conceptual patterns therein, and God's use of those patterns in the present.

Of course, this description of the hermeneutical basis of the theological task opens the way for several possible criticisms. And, in fact, Frei's account incurs criticisms at this point from two distinct directions. Practice-minded critics charge that characterizing theology as second-order reflection upon and redescription of the norms implicit in Christian practices projects an overly integrated and too-coherent picture of on-the-ground Christian practices and institutions. Such critics charge that this approach cannot account for the range of diversity that exists among Christian communities. Others claim that construing the theological task as akin to reflexive ethnography does away with accountability to norms outside of communal practices. As a result, there are no criteria by which to identify and correct Christian "malpractice."

Kathryn Tanner levels the charge that construing the theological task as a second-order explication, elucidation, or redescription of first-order practices is problematic. "The language of reflection and of first order/second order suggests that the academic theologian simply follows the dictates of the object studied as he or she goes about clarifying and ordering beliefs and values that circulate in Christian practice."[13] She continues:

> Most of the time . . . postliberal talk of describing the internal logic of
> first-order practices strongly suggests that second-order theology does
> nothing more than uncover a logic internal to those practices
> themselves; the task of second-order theology is simply to make
> explicit what is already present there in an implicit, unformulized
> manner. Presumably only one logic is implicit in the practices, to
> which the second-order theologian is merely to conform. The critical
> or normative capacities of the second-order theologian are therefore
> not exercised in the process of articulating the logic of Christian
> practice; he or she criticizes and recommends changes in only those
> particular Christian practices that deviate from "the" logic or grammar
> of the faith, a logic or grammar that second-order theology seems
> simply to be tracing according to its already-established outlines.[14]

Tanner cites Frei as the object of these remarks.[15] However, this characterization does a disservice both to Frei and to the particular insights he drew from
Barth in order to formulate his ideas. Clearly, Frei accounts for some of the
second-order tasks of theology in terms of conceptual redescription of communal practices. Nowhere does Frei claim that a single logic is implicit in the
practices nor that a theologian does no more than descriptively uncover a logic
implicit in practices. In fact, careful attention to the passages that Tanner cites,
in conjunction with the full breadth of Frei's reflections on the second-order
tasks of theology, indicates quite the opposite.

It is important to keep in mind, first, that Frei took himself to be extrapolating from Barth's account of theology as redescription of the practices that
constitute the church. "As a theological discipline dogmatics is the scientific
test to which the Christian Church puts herself regarding the language about
God which is peculiar to her."[16] Frei understood this to mean that the redescriptive task is, at one level, aimed at elucidation, explication, and critical evaluation
of the normative proprieties implicit in practices. In Barth's case, these practices are to a great extent *linguistic* (more broadly construed, *conceptual*). Insofar
as this is the case, articulation of the "grammar" of those practices is an apt
metaphor. But there are no essentialist claims here. The practice of redescription of the "implicit logic" is contextual. It is true that normative proprieties
constitute practices. However, how those proprieties might be redescribed is
underdetermined and certainly a matter to be contested on a case-by-case basis.
And this is an insight that recurs throughout Frei's work. He writes, for
instance, "There is, it seems to me, a variety of descriptions for any given
linguistic phenomenon, and hence, above all, no ontological superdescription
or explanation. Furthermore, the 'grammar' (use according to rules of such a

construct) is more readily exhibited or set forth than stated in the abstract."[17] It is on precisely this basis, moreover, that Frei makes the case that the *sensus literalis* stretches to accommodate a range of inflections of its "grammar." This "grammar"—the basic proprieties of the *sensus literalis*—are Frei's fairly mundane observations "that the subject matter of these stories is not something or someone else [than who they portray, namely, Jesus Christ], and that the rest of the canon must in some way or ways, looser or tighter, be related to this subject matter or at least not in contradiction with it."[18]

Here, as with other practices, certain proprieties are constitutive of the respective practice across contexts. However, when compared across contexts, specific instances of the practice may well evince substantial variability. Moreover, agreements on the proprieties basic to the practice will not be determined by consultation of some metarule book. This is what it means to say that what unifies a range of instances of a practice is certain "family resemblances" that they share. These can be determined by the ability of practitioners from different contexts to recognize other participants as engaged in more or less the same practice. Perhaps they can identify some background or presupposition of agreement against which their (sometimes extensive and sustained) disagreements occur. However, the very ability to disagree—and the recognition of subject matter significant enough to warrant investing the effort and time to sort through and/or persist in such disagreements—presupposes a background of significant agreement.

For instance, the scriptural practices of a Protestant and an Orthodox Christian are likely to vary drastically, even with regard to some of the texts that they identify as canonical. And yet, their deep disagreements presuppose certain background agreements upon the status of the central character of these canonical texts. They agree, moreover, that all the parts of Scripture are such in virtue of their relation to that central character, however their particular claims or readings of a passage might differ. In each case, the varying degrees of difference interweave with varying degrees of similarity. And these similarities and differences play out in the proprieties constitutive of the practice in question. And yet, the normative recognition of many of the same texts as authoritative, as sacred and revelatory, will exert some constraints similarly. It makes this text, for instance, worth inquiring into and convening conferences about. It warrants—perhaps it compels—all the efforts of critical dialogue and extended argument.

Frei holds up Barth's interpretation of Anselm's ontological argument as exemplary of the context-sensitive conceptual redescription he has in mind. "[A]s Barth saw it, Anselm was saying that the right conceptual description of

God—that than which no greater can be conceived—logically implies God's reality: for if that than which no greater can be conceived does not exist, then a greater can be conceived, which contradicts the description." Frei points out:

> But (1) this case in which we grasp the reality by means of a logical sequence or description is a unique case, because God and his relation to us is absolutely unique; it cannot be recapitulated in any finite instance or case of knowledge of finite reality. (2) This train of thought and its result, that God is present as the object of the intellect only in the concept or the use of the word God, is the meaning of the concept "faith" or "Christian faith" when used in the context of reflection on the *grammar* of the word *God* as it is used in the Christian Church.[19]

Clearly, the inferential constraints exerted by the concept "God" logically implicate the meaning of the concept "faith," or more specifically "Christian faith." This move might appear to substantiate Tanner's charge that Frei's theological approach simply uncovers the single logic implicit in Christian practice. And yet, as it turns out, Frei's central point in this passage is that "Barth does not have a single definition for the term faith; it is various things in various contexts—the only thing they have in common is that 'faith' is defined by the adjective 'Christian' rather than vice versa."[20] Frei's account here reflects his insistence that "ruled uses" should be understood as informal and ad hoc. He added, "It must depend on the specific context in which one speaks; it cannot be context-invariant. I suspect that [Barth] would say that even in regard to intertheological talk—even in theological discourse—it depends on what issues one addresses, whether this distinction should or should not be kept."[21] Elsewhere, Frei offered his own analysis of the word "faith":

> Faith itself is not a single thing to be defined. . . . [Faith] is a knowledge; faith is an obedience; and faith is also a trust: it is a leap; it is a belief; but a belief in the very strongest sense, a belief in the existential sense of total commitment. But faith is not only total commitment; it is not only knowledge; it is not only obedience; and it is not the case that one of these is the root form and the others are derivative. Well—I think not.[22]

Frei continued by extrapolating from these insights with the Wittgensteinian rule of thumb in mind—to look for use rather than ask after meaning—with specific reference to usage in ordinary language.[23] "There are technical languages, you see, in which the concepts—say the concept 'atom'—always means the same thing: it has a fixed, stipulated meaning; and when you deal with a language like that you can ask for the fixed, stipulated concept as a general term which runs by its definition and is always connected to other concepts by its definition." Ordinary language is not so rigid and formulaic as that. Of course, even ordinary language has its own "rules" in the sense of proprieties and customs that organize it as a discursive practice. However, discerning these informal proprieties, explicating them as norms, and perhaps formalizing them as rules is a redescriptive affair that often must be done on a case-by-case basis. As Frei clarified, "it is very difficult, in fact sometimes impossible to state the rules apart from the use; it is the ruled use that gives us the rules, and the rules may be highly various depending on the use to which the concept is put in the context in which it is being used."[24]

In his Greenhoe Lectures of 1976, Frei had already begun to articulate and refine his ideas on this point. "One of the tasks, in fact *the* task of Christian theology is simply to talk about the way Christian language is used by Christians, and to ask if it is being used faithfully," Frei claimed, offering his own restatement of Barth's definition of dogmatics from *CD* 1/1. "The theologian simply examines contemporary use of Christian language to see if it is faithful to what he senses to be the traditional use or the biblical use—usually some combination of the two: the use the Church has made of its source, namely the Bible; that is what theology is about."[25] To speak of the church's language meant ordinary Christian usage of all the embodied, conceptually articulated practices that constituted the church in all its multifarious contexts, shapes, and forms— "Christian language in meditation, in public worship, private prayer, in the obedience of the moral life: Christian language in the public and private use of faith."[26] This language is more or less coherent and "held together by constantly changing, yet enduring, structures, practices, and institutions."[27] Both the community's uses of it and the theologian's second-order criticism of and reflection upon those uses are accountable to the biblical witness.

Here Frei's explication of Barth's position is especially helpful in clearing away those criticisms that misunderstand his position by claiming that he is concerned solely with explicating the single logic internal to theological statements and practices. As Frei described Barth's position:

[Theology] arises because the Church is accountable to God for its discourse about God. To the best of its lights, then, the Church must undertake a critique and correction of her discourse in the light of the norm she sees as the presence of God to the Church, in obedience to God's grace. Expanding the concept of the Church in a manner typical of him, Barth says that the criterion of Christian discourse is the being of the Church, and the being of the Church for him is Jesus Christ, God in his presence or turning to humanity. The question is, *Does Christian discourse come from him and move toward him, and is it in accordance with him?*[28]

It is frequently overlooked that a central point at which Frei distinguished himself from Lindbeck was in his qualified sympathy for a "moderate propositionalist" account of truth—the position that takes "second-order doctrines about the Trinity, atonement, etc., to have the character not only of intra-systematic but ontological truth statements."[29] On this point he was more persuaded by Barth to the effect that:

On the one hand, justification by faith is a doctrine that functions as a rule in, let us say, orthodox Christian discourse. Not only does it function as a rule but it looks as though it were asserting something about how God deals with human beings, and to that extent is a statement that holds true regardless of the attitude of the person or persons articulating it.[30]

So, for instance, Frei held up the Chalcedonian affirmation as an example of a categorical scheme employed both for heuristic and redescriptive purposes, as well as a truth claim by which the church holds itself "accountable to God for its discourse about God."[31] In affirming that Jesus Christ is a particular person in whom two whole and unabridged natures are perfectly joined, the doctrinal affirmation does two things. First, it asserts the truth claim that "this is so," which—in part, because of its central role in the larger web of belief and practice—serves as a critical norm for assessing other beliefs, claims, and practices. When deployed in its second-order heuristic capacity, it explicates a pattern in the narratives about Jesus and presents that pattern as a normative criterion by which to critically assess Christian claims and practices. As a result, Frei explains:

Any statement that would deny the full humanity, full divinity, or full unity of Jesus Christ is unacceptable. In the form of a rule, the statement is negative, setting the limits beyond which no such identifying statement can go. But we can put the same second-level function more positively. The formula is a conceptual redescription of a synthesis of the gospel stories understood as the narratives identifying Jesus Christ. It is taken for granted that in that story he, the protagonist, is a unitary agent, so that, whatever the relation generally between the categories "person" and "nature," in this case they both function logically as descriptions of the unitary subject to whom they are ascribed.[32]

Here we can see that Frei takes the Chalcedonian formula to elucidate a pattern in the narratives of Jesus, namely, "that the subject to whom predicates are to be ascribed, the unitary ascriptive subject, has a certain priority over the descriptive characteristics that he embodies. They are *his*; he holds them and is himself as each of them singly and both together."[33] The unity of Christ's two natures takes priority over their abiding duality and logical distinctness.

Frei emphasizes this aspect of "logic" and "rules" even in his account of the Chalcedonian pattern as a redescriptive and heuristic pattern that I pointed out just above. He writes:

> [T]he internal logic is inherent in, perhaps even limited to, the case; no statement is being put forth here as to the general conditions of intelligibility that would make this statement possible. The statement of the formula's logic is not of a transcendental, at least not of a strongly transcendental, kind. Nor does the formula affirm that Christology must be thought about in ousia/hypostasis categories. *What is at stake is the proper identification of the agent under a categorical scheme, not the correctness or indispensability of the scheme*: the meaning of the doctrine is the story rather than the meaning of the story being the doctrine.[34]

In other words, Frei's primary concern is the proper identification of Jesus Christ. The scheme which facilitates this identification is secondary. There are multiple possibilities for the latter, depending on the need, use, and context of use. Which scheme is helpful heuristically and redescriptively depends largely upon how well they enrich or expand upon the content of the biblical narratives at the same time that they ultimately point readers back to the biblical narratives. A motivating insight throughout Frei's entire career was that a primary concern for the church ought to be the person and work of Jesus as portrayed in the biblical witness. This is the object at which all of the categories, schemes, and tools are directed, and which they must be oriented by. Where does this leave the concerns about Frei's alleged attempt to ascertain a single logic internal to Christian practice?

Frei's account of the second-order theological redescription is highly contextual and interpretively nonreductive. This character of his approach made Clifford Geertz's development of thick descriptive ethnography a handy set of tools for Frei's own redescriptive purposes.[35] Recall that precisely when Geertz was most Rylean in his account of thick description, he also cautiously warned his readers against mistaking the occasionally positivist tones of his terminology for the irreducibly interpretive affair of thick description. "[S]orting out the structures of signification—what Ryle called established codes, [is] a somewhat misleading expression, for it makes the enterprise sound too much like that of the cipher clerk when it is much more like that of the literary critic."[36] And elsewhere, "[W]hat we call our data are really our own constructions of other people's constructions of what they and their compatriots are up to—[and this fact] is obscured because most of what we need to comprehend a particular event, ritual, custom, idea, or whatever is insinuated as background information before the thing itself is directly examined."[37]

"Thick description" is not a matter of simply abstracting one's self from the currency of exchange of daily living in order to articulate conceptually the single logic therein.[38] Interpretive analysis can occur across a range of possible redescriptions. It is intentionally nonreductive. It is like trying to "construct a reading of a manuscript—foreign, faded, full of ellipses, incoherencies, suspicious emendations, and tendentious commentaries."[39] Insofar as Tanner construes the task of redescription as uncovering a single "logic implicit in practice," she positions it as an explanatory practice in the reductive sense of the word "explanation." Frei quite explicitly concerned himself with the kind of nonreductive analysis that he referred to as a "hermeneutics of restoration"—"an interpretation that does not operate with an explanatory hypothesis to nearly the same sweeping degree as the hermeneutics of suspicion does," Frei wrote. "[R]ather than explaining the culture that one looks at, one tries to describe it."[40] These descriptions were to be context sensitive, flexible, underdetermined in their terms of description, and most importantly of all, part of continuing argument about which of these descriptions were more or less adequate in light of God's faithfulness in and through the person and work of Jesus Christ.

A primary point is that "Christian" analysis depends extensively upon the context and the ethnographer. Frei thought Geertz's concern for meaning (figuring out, in other words, "what the devil these people think they're up to") was a helpful example of what a nonreductive "hermeneutics of restoration" might look like. This approach was not concerned to make explicit a single logic of the social transactions in which meaning inheres and for which any good explanation must account. That would make the affair decidedly positivist. Rather, discerning and deciphering "meaning" is a continuing process of negotiation, interpretations upon interpretations. "In short, anthropological writings are themselves interpretations, and second and third order ones to boot. (By definition, only a 'native' makes first order ones: it's his culture)," Geertz reminded his readers. "They are, thus, fictions; fictions, in the sense that they are 'something made,' 'something fashioned'—the original meaning of *fictio*—not that they are false, unfactual, or merely 'as if' experiments." Frei found this a helpful way of characterizing theology as a biblically oriented, redescriptive investigation of the Christian world of meaning. He wrote:

"Meaning" in a cultural-linguistic and intratextual interpretive frame is the skill that allows ethnographer and native to meet in mutual respect; if they happen to be the same person, it is the bridge over which (s)he must pass from one shore to the other and undertake the return journey; if they are natives from different tribes, it is the common ground that is established as they learn each other's languages, rather than a known precondition for doing so.[41]

This is not merely a claim about the relation of "insiders" to "outsiders." Notice here that, on Frei's account, the ethnographer may simultaneously be the native. Moreover, she may be studying some tribal locality of people who are, more or less, fellow natives in virtue of certain family resemblances or basic commitments they share. In other words, the distinction between observer and participant was not as clear for Frei as it was for Geertz. Nonetheless, Geertz's account of the goal of ethnographic redescription remains more or less consistent with Frei's appropriations of it for his own christological purposes. Frei's account resonates with Geertz's claim that "What recommends [a particular description], or disrecommends them if they are ill-constructed, is the further figures that issue from them: their capacity to lead on to extended accounts which, intersecting other accounts of other matters, widen their implications and deepen their hold."[42] As far as it goes, this is an adequate gloss on the redescriptive spinning out of the inferences and implications of the scriptural world that embraces and orients believers' work-a-day existence. Clearly, the kind of redescriptive prolixity Frei thought best modeled by Barth widened the implications of the scriptural witness and deepened its hold.

And yet, there is far more at stake for Frei in this account, and herein lies the import of the normative, critical edge of the theologian's redescriptive task. For the theologian's criteria of assessment reach far beyond questions like "Is this redescription interesting?" "What do you say in saying that?" and "Where does it get you?"[43] The redescriptive task is, at the same time, the substance of a living tradition—a set of essentially contestatory, embodied social practices extended over time. Again, the primary impetus for the theologian's redescriptive undertaking and its ultimate aim is an answer to the question "Does Christian discourse come from him [God] and move toward him, and is it in accordance with him?"[44]

Far from foreclosing on the meanings that Christian practices might demonstrate, thus making the theologian's task more that of a cipher clerk than a literary critic, the redescriptive task might further enrich the practice it redescribes (just as it can further enrich the practice of redescription itself). It might expand upon, shed new light, cast into relief particular elements of the practice, problematize, critically challenge, propose correction, perhaps resolve previous points of contestation as it gives rise to new ones. But it does this in light of the norms of faithfulness to the One who comes to believers in the witness of Scripture. In other words, the Christian practices of engaging Scripture does not simply seek to modify those texts in order to fit or comply with prevailing theological opinion or whatever practices or "language games" happen to hold sway at the time within Christian contexts. Engaging Scripture tests theological truth claims, proclamation, and even prophetic words against theological exegesis of those Scriptures.[45]

It is inadequate, then, to conclude that redescription is *essentially* interpretive and to assert, for example, that there is no set of normative constraints constitutive of the object being described that constrain the describer. Of course there are. But this kind of objectivity is characteristic of the normative features of theological exegesis as Frei understood it. Moreover, the "object" of the "object-directed" scriptural practices in question does not make for just any "facts of the matter." For in this case the subject matter—God's revelatory activity in and through these narratives—norms any procedures and redescriptive tools brought to bear.

Conclusion

This chapter has argued that it is not the case that in allegedly "mimicking" certain anthropological procedures, "postliberal" theology—in the present case, Frei's theology—"projects onto the object it studies what its own procedures of investigation requires—a coherent whole."[46] Nor, moreover, does Frei's approach "validate the conclusions of the theologian while disqualifying the people and practices it studies from posing a challenge to these conclusions."[47] I have stressed, moreover, that Frei's portrayal of the theological task in terms of reflexively ethnographic redescription does not forgo concern for propositional truth claims. Quite the opposite in fact. And this presents yet another point at which Frei recognized himself diverging from Lindbeck's rule theory of doctrine.

So understood, the theologian is more nearly like a "reflexive ethnographer" who should recognize herself as but one among many fellow practitioners engaging in but one among many of the practices that constitute the life of Christian communities. Such practices are constituted by (initially unformulated) proprieties implicit in them. Frei insisted that these regularities must, more often than not, be discerned in particular and embodied instances of the practices in question. This insight inoculates the charge that he "fetishizes rules."[48]

The accusation that Frei takes as his object some clear, distinct, and stable set of shared rules purportedly underpinning all the material differences in Christian practices that appear across contexts and awaiting to be discerned and catalogued turns out to be less than persuasive upon closer examination.[49] However, they can be articulated in second-order fashion using logical vocabulary, doctrinal or aesthetic vocabulary, or a number of possible terms of redescription. Frei's insight was that any such redescription must remain delicate and contextually sensitive. Hence, while there is much problematic about theology as conceptual redescription as Tanner characterizes it, her characterization does not fit Frei's theological approach.

Of course, Frei's appeals to the "givenness" of revelation—the claim, for instance, that all doctrines or theological assertions are directly or indirectly grounded in faith, or that faith is rational in that it seeks understanding within a set of reasons afforded by God's revelatory activity in Scripture— incur charges of "revelational foundationalism." Such charges persist in spite of recent efforts by many of Frei's former students to dispel them. Without straying too far from my treatment of Frei, I employ recent treatments of foundationalism in order to show that what these have in common can help to dispel this charge of "crypto-foundationalism." I conclude by answering the frequent charge that talk of "rationality intrinsic to faith" implicates Frei's thought in a type of fideism.

6

And Not Antifoundationalism Either

In its epistemological sense, the term "foundationalism" refers to a theory of knowledge that says that a claim counts as knowledge insofar as it directly rests upon, or can be traced back to, self-justifying epistemic grounds. In his book, *Revelation and Theology*, Ronald Thiemann set forth a helpfully succinct explanation of the position, writing:

> Knowledge is justified true belief, and justification consists in tracing the pattern of inference supporting the belief in question until we find those true beliefs on which the questioned belief rests. If we accept those beliefs to be true, and if the pattern of inference is valid, then we can assert the belief in question to be a justified true belief. But, the foundationalist adds, we are not *theoretically* justified in bringing our inquiry to an end until we have discovered a self-evident, non-inferential belief, i.e., a belief that must be *universally* accepted as true.[1]

Attempts to identify such self-evident foundations for knowledge—either as incorrigibly given in the immediacy of perception or in clear and distinct ideas—proliferated throughout the European Enlightenment and persisted well into the twentieth century, largely in effort to sidestep appeals to the seemingly arbitrary authority of religious traditions.[2]

Criticisms of epistemic foundationalism are now widespread. The problem with foundationalism, at least in part, is that the search for self-evidently true beliefs supposes unmediated access to "the given" antecedent to interpretation, presupposition, and in abstraction from other concepts. But to have any single concept is to have, through inferential relations, multiple concepts.[3] The upshot is that one cannot have a grasp of any single piece of knowledge without already knowing many other things. In order to sidestep the long-held belief that the true object of knowledge is the immutable and self-certain thing as accessed through unhindered sensory experience, John Dewey made helpful use of Werner Heisenberg's principle of indeterminacy—to know any-thing through observation is to alter the thing under observation by one's very act of observing it. "What is known is seen to be a product in which the act of observation plays a necessary role," Dewey explained. "Knowing is seen to be a participant in what is finally known."[4] Insofar as it was presumed necessary for theological purposes, philosophical foundationalism held theological knowledge claims captive to supposedly universal, generically human criteria for knowledge.[5]

"Nonfoundationalism" or "antifoundationalism" refers to a range of philo-sophical positions claiming that foundationalism is not philosophically defen-sible. It has described knowledge as a historically immanent and inextricably linguistic, engaged, and self-correcting process, configured much more like a boat traversing open seas than a pyramid set upon a self-justifying groundwork. John Thiel recalls this nautical image that W. V. O. Quine borrowed from Otto Neurath to illustrate this position.[6] On this account knowledge consists in a set of "relative claims, at best coherent, floating on the ever-moving currents of time and culture rather than as certain truths timelessly fixed in never-shifting sands."[7]

Postliberal thinkers generally agree in rejecting philosophical foundation-alism in the strong sense described above by Thiemann. At a high-enough level of generality, the term "nonfoundationalist" is more or less adequate for describing their rejection of the foundationalist position. Applied incautiously, however, "nonfoundationalism" quickly becomes insufficient as a descriptor of the philosophical resources employed by this range of thinkers, interests, and projects. Applied incautiously, the term obscures more than it illuminates.

Many postliberal thinkers whose work gets lumped under the moniker "nonfoundationalist" are, in fact, not concerned to be "nonfoundational" in their epistemic commitments. They are concerned to be faithful in light of the radical ingression of God's revelation in the person and work of Jesus Christ. If various "nonfoundational" insights are helpful in the search for understanding this rev-elation, then so much the better for those insights. "[T]heology cannot even invest so much in the foundational/anti-foundational debate as to come out (qua theology) in principle on the anti-foundational side," Frei put the point.[8] He appealed to nonfoundational insights on an ad hoc basis. As we have seen, this reflected his thinking generally about the relation of philosophy and theology.

At the same time, somewhat ironically, "postliberal theology" appears to invite charges that its appeals to the centrality of God's self-revelation terminate in some version of scriptural foundationalism—that it takes the scriptural witness as a "given." In this chapter, I sort through such claims with the help of a little ad hoc redescription Drawing upon various nonfoundational philosophical insights might help deflect such misplaced charges. One of the convictions motivating the current project is that there are materials available that can help dissolve these apparent conundrums. Moreover, one of the central tasks that Frei took up was identifying and developing the kind of connections that were needed in order to utilize such resources.[9]

In the spirit of Frei, in the following pages I elucidate certain of the conceptual parallels shared by recent pragmatist thought, Reformed epistemology and the Anselmian coherentism of 'postliberal' theology. With these comparisons I intend to demonstrate that Frei's account of God's self-revelation implicates him neither in a classically foundationalist position nor simply its opposite, non- or antifoundationalism. I propose, rather, to explicate Frei's thinking on these matters in terms of a certain understanding of conceptual inferentialism. On this account, the dichotomy between foundationalism and nonfoundationalism turns out to be a false one. I articulate this insight by conceptually redescribing Anselmian coherentism in terms made available in recent pragmatist philosophical thought and Reformed epistemology.

The resources upon which I draw in this chapter have their peculiar distinctions and do not reduce to some essential claim or set of claims. Each is motivated by varying concerns, aims at various audiences, and draws out a range of different implications from its claims. And yet, these resources may prove helpfully compatible in some of their claims about the justification of belief. They overlap helpfully in their respective rejections of "foundationalism" in its "classical guise." Moreover, each subscribes to some form of the claim that noninferential moves that are caught up in essentially inferential practices of concept use and application make judgment, experience, and reason giving possible in the first place. And this should permit "immediacy" or "noninferential moves" in inferential practices without implicating the accounts in question in "foundationalism."

I. Specters of Foundationalism

"Anselmian coherentism" resists the charge that it opposes all positive relationships to "rational inquiry," at least in part, in virtue of its affinities with Wilfrid Sellars's claim that inquiry is rational "not because it has a *foundation* but because it is a self-correcting enterprise which can put *any* claim in jeopardy, though not *all* at once."[10] At the same time, Anselmian coherentism is not "pure" coherentism. Hunsinger explains:

> [D]octrinal beliefs are not thought to be justified merely because they are members of a coherent set (the view of pure coherentism). They are rather thought to be justified also and primarily because they are suitably grounded in revelation as normatively attested in Scripture. For Barth, like foundationalism and unlike coherentism, some beliefs are basic such that other beliefs may be reliably derived from them.[11]

But does this description not simply smuggle back in a kind of foundationalism if certain revelatory beliefs are basic? Drawing upon Sellars' work, and certain points at which it parallels basic insights in Reformed epistemology, we can gather a sense in which a belief can be "basic" or "noninferential" and yet not "foundationalist" in an untenable sense of that term.

The charge of "nonfoundationalism" it is not entirely accurate as a positive description of Sellars' account of inferential holism in his classic text *Empiricism and the Philosophy of Mind*. That is, in rejecting this notion of epistemic foundations, Sellars does not then impale himself on the nonfoundational horn of a foundationalist/nonfoundationalist dilemma. In fact, he mediates that dilemma in a way that renders it obsolete. One of Sellars's most distinctive philosophical contributions was in drawing the appeal to noninferential perceptions (so dear to the heart of the classical foundationalist) into the ambit of his inferential-holist account.[12]

For Sellars, noninferential moves such as observing and acting upon one's environment (what Sellars called "language entry" and "language exit" moves) place actors in direct interaction with her environment and with all the physical objects therein. Through processes of acculturation into and development of reliable responses and dispositions, interacting with one's environment comes to be direct and immediate (engagement in which one draws no deliberate inferences). While this position entails a particular conception of "noninferentiality," its crucial difference from classical foundationalism is that direct or immediate perceptions are never "indubitably self-evident to all rational perceivers."[13] In fact, Sellars extricates his position from the "foundationalist/nonfoundationalist" dilemma by moving beyond the kind of "pure" inferential holism that cuts itself off from the objects that populate the actor's environment, thereby "losing the world" and all possibility of immediacy or noninferential epistemic access with it.

Sellars' account retains the "objective" or "object-directed" epistemic access to the world, while rejecting the classically foundational appeal to the knower's being set upon by "the given"—self-evident, incorrigible sense perception in abstraction from the use of inferential faculties. For, though the noninferential moves into and out of language that Sellars describes are quite obviously not themselves inferences, they are moves in an encompassing activity that is basically inferential and for which the capacity to draw inferences is required. It is adequate to describe Sellars' position as "nonfoundational." However, the category becomes detrimental once it begins to obscure the capacity of his account to mediate the apparent deadlock between foundationalist and nonfoundationalist concerns.

What Sellars calls noninferential transitions in the game of giving and asking for reasons (in his case, "language-entry" transitions like observation and "language-exit" transitions like acting) share important similarities to what Alvin Plantinga has called "properly basic beliefs."[14] In particular, Plantinga's primary examples of "properly basic beliefs" might be redescribed as propositionally articulated claims that serve as noninferential entry points for inferential reasoning. The important point for my present purposes is that such properly basic beliefs can be recognized "noninferentially" or "immediately." So construed, they serve as noninferential moves into a conceptual practice that is more broadly inferential. These noninferential moves are made possible in virtue of the inferential nature of the discursive practices of which they are parts.[15]

A salient feature of Plantinga's account of "properly basic belief" is that the believer can *be justified* in holding it without *being able to justify it*. In his essay entitled "Can Belief in God be Properly Basic?" Plantinga answers his title question in the affirmative, if by "belief in God" we mean appeals to noninferential, propositionally articulated assertions as:

"God is speaking to me"

"God has created all this"

"God disapproves of what I have done"

"God forgives me"

"God is to be thanked and praised"

Plantinga goes to great analytical lengths to show how believers could be justified in asserting these as noninferential or immediate reports. Taken in abstraction, any one of these claims might appear to implicate him in a revelational foundationalism similar to the kind with which Barth is charged. Plantinga goes on to add—and this will turn out to be another crucial parallel to Sellars—that the fact that these claims could be properly basic "is not to deny that there are *justifying conditions* for these beliefs, or conditions that confer justification on one who accepts them as basic. They are therefore not ground-less or gratuitous."[16] Neither, moreover, are they simply accidental or arbitrary.

There is an important distinction to be drawn here between the status of *being justified* in holding a belief and the activity of *justifying* that belief. Being justified, for Plantinga, is a contextually specific status in which many "obvious," "commonsensical," or commonly shared beliefs are granted prima facie epistemic justification in virtue of the time-tested practices of a given epistemic context or community. Such beliefs are treated as "innocent until proven guilty." Heaving the burden of proof onto a would-be skeptical challenger, Plantinga writes, "[I]t would be irrational to take as basic the denial of a proposition that seems self-evident to you":

> [S]uppose it seems to you that you see a tree; you would then be irrational in taking as basic the proposition that you don't see a tree, or that there aren't any trees. In the same way, even if I don't know of some illuminating criterion of meaning, I can quite properly declare. . . . ['Twas brillig and the slithy toves did gyre and gimble in the wabe] meaningless.[17]

For Plantinga, noninferential reports can be explicitly inferentially examined, justified, and extrapolated from. These moves are possible because the condition for the possibility of a noninferential claim is the justifying conditions, which entail the capacities to noninferentially grasp (be grasped by) and apply concepts. In epistemic terms, this "being grasped by" is as simple as finding the appropriate belief formed in one. Plantinga explains:

> [I]n the typical case we do not decide to hold or form the belief in question but simply find ourselves with it. Upon considering an instance of *modus ponens*, I find myself believing its corresponding conditional; upon being appeared to in the familiar way I find myself holding the belief that there is a large tree before me; upon being asked what I had for breakfast, I reflect for a moment and then find myself with the belief that what I had was eggs on toast. In these and other cases I do not decide what to believe; I don't total up the evidence (I'm being appeared to redly; on most occasions when thus appeared to I am in the presence of something red; so most probably in this case I am) and make a decision as to what seems best supported; I simply find myself believing. Of course, in some cases I go through such a procedure.[18]

Sellars makes a comparable set of claims. On his account, a competent concept user is one whose training in concept use entails the cultivation of dispositions to respond reliably (and thus, noninferentially) to, say, the physical state of affairs appropriately responded to with application of the word (the concept) "tree." This appropriate response may take the form of an assertion like "That is a tree," or "there is a tree outside the window." This response is "appropriate" in the sense that it is a socially conferred status. This is to say that it results from not *merely* a certain physical state of affairs existing between the speaker's retina and a corporeal body. It certainly entails response to a physical state of affairs, but not only this. There are certain physical conditions necessary for the possibility of being able to participate in this social practice, in this case, to "appropriately" make such a claim. However, this is a physical state of affairs inseparably caught up in a network of social and practical, conceptually articulated practices. And some of these states of affairs participate in the relevant "justifying conditions."

One way we might distinguish between the *apprehension* of this physical state of affairs (the tree outside the window) and *comprehension* of it (in the form of my assertion "the tree outside my window is losing its leaves") is in our distinction between *seeing* and *perceiving*.[19] Hence, the newborn baby strapped into her stroller so that a tree stands in her line of sight is not recognized as having *perceived* a "tree," though we would surely say that she *sees* it (assuming her eyesight is healthy). Neither do we attribute to her the social status of having perceived the tree. We consider her neither entitled to, nor accountable for, making whatever inferences might be valid from such a noninferential ("properly basic") move into the game of giving and asking for reasons. In fact, the infant requires a great deal of acculturation into and much practice at the concept applications that constitute cognitive judgment and experience. These shared processes of acculturation into the relevant social practices of concept application contribute to the "justifying conditions" of which Plantinga writes—"conditions that confer justification on one who accepts [the beliefs in question] as basic."[20]

Given such *justifying conditions*, the wholly acceptable response on behalf of such a properly basic belief is to respond to the skeptic's challenge "But how do you know that is a tree?" with "Because I know a tree when I see one." The philosopher, or perhaps the reflexive ethnographer, might translate this response "Because, under conditions favorable to accurate perception (and without any reason to think that I am hallucinating) I am generally correct in my reporting that I see a tree. And, clearly, *that* is a tree." The ordinary language user need not make such a response. She would still *be justified* in taking up the commitment that she sees a tree, though she may well not be able to justify her commitment to the inquiring skeptic.

A Wittgensteinian quip to the would-be skeptic's "But how do you know that's a tree?" might run something like "Well, I know how to speak English"—meaning

I know how to and under what circumstances and states of affairs it is correct to apply the concept (to use the word) "tree."[21] On a Sellarsian account, a justified, noninferential response to the physical state of affairs in which a tree stood outside my window is possible only because the reporter is a competent player of a game that is inferentially conceptual. A self-consciously Sellarsian response to the skeptic would exercise inferential capacities to justify a noninferential report. Distinguished from these other roughly similar accounts, the Sellarsian might respond to the skeptic's query "But how do you know that's a tree?" with "Well, it has leaves and branches extending up and outward from its trunk, and is swaying in the breeze outside my window right now," and perhaps add "and I am generally reliable as a reporter of trees." Here the tree perceiver has justified her noninferential assertion that she perceives a tree and demonstrated her reliability as a perceiver of trees, in part, by demonstrating her adeptness in using the concepts inferentially implicated by the concept "tree."[22]

Recent work by the pragmatist philosopher Robert Brandom further explicates the social status and implications of such an exchange. For instance, I sit at my office desk, glancing outside my window across the lawn, and remark to the student sitting across the room from me (just beyond the scope of the window's purview), "That tree is losing its leaves." Under the assumption that I am a reliable reporter of trees (a status for which there is likely not a high threshold of expertise to count as reliable among one's fellow discursive practitioners), my student is entitled to endorse my commitment that there is a tree outside my office window, and thus, to take up that commitment for herself. Thus, the student leaves my office with what Brandom calls an "inferential license." When she walks toward the library and a friend accosts her in order to ask "Where's a quiet spot where I can sit and review my notes in peace prior to class?" my student is justified in drawing the inference and making the ensuing assertion, "There is a tree on the lawn just outside. Perhaps you could sit beneath it." Say the second student proceeds to seek out the tree implicated in my report and discovers that there is, in fact, no tree outside my office window. This would either cast into doubt my reliability as a reporter of trees or perhaps call into question the first student's accuracy in taking my statement ("That tree is losing its leaves") to be a report of a current state of affairs outside my office window.

Anselmian coherentists like Frei claim that God's self-revelation as attested in Scripture, in effect, becomes "properly basic." Another way of putting this is that claims made about God's revelation in Scripture from its recipient mode (faith) can be noninferential.[23] "The status of warranted assertions is ascribed to certain complex beliefs which are themselves derived from scriptural interpretation," Hunsinger clarifies. "That God has engaged in an act of self-revelation, that the Bible is the Word of God, that Jesus Christ is the center and norm of the scriptural witness, that Jesus Christ is at once fully God and fully human, are all examples of beliefs to which warranted assertability is ascribed. Their epistemic justification is understood to be confessional and hermeneutical (and thus, formally speaking, coherentist)."[24] In the context of the present discussion, I think Hunsinger's use of the term "warranted assertability" is compatible with Plantinga's conception of "properly basic." Both statuses result, in part, from the justifying conditions relevant to the epistemic contexts in question.

Plantinga appears to require as little from justifying conditions as that one's perceptual and belief-forming faculties are functioning properly within a cognitive context in which they were designed to function. In other words, so long as I had not recently drunk Kool-Aid laced with some hallucinogenic substance, for instance, my belief that God is speaking directly to me at a given point is ostensibly as properly basic as the belief that I see a tree in front of me.[25]

The Anselmian coherentist differs on this point.[26] She is interested in primarily scriptural instances of the elicitation of noninferential beliefs. Conditions that contribute to rendering such beliefs justified—making them more than arbitrary or accidental—include several possible factors. One such factor might be that the testimony one encounters is that of people who are generally trustworthy and reliable testimony givers (both those first-century followers whose testimony constitutes the evangelical witness and apostolic proclamation in Scripture, and believers of intervening generations whose testimonies witness to the veracity and efficacy of that witness and proclamation). Other conditions might be one's capacity and good faith effort to attend to the accounts and claims set forth in Scripture, to avoid wishful thinking about what those claims are, as well as obstinate refusal of accountability to the text-directed claims of fellow readers, or the normative constraints constitutive of the practices of engaging Scripture.

As we saw earlier, in Frei's case, one justifying condition for the "proper basicality" of Scripture's witness to Christ is that this testimony has not been disconfirmed by means of modern historical investigation.[27] Moreover, Frei would concur with Barth that the condition of the very possibility of appealing to the witness of Scripture and the patterns it gives forth as "properly basic" for Christians is the work of the Holy Spirit making the living Christ present.[28] These are some of the justifying conditions that would make entry into the "world of discourse" at the level of such "properly basic beliefs" prima facie "warranted" and "assertable." Such conditions (or some combination of such conditions) would entitle one to endorse scriptural claims or features of its witness as such. Moreover, one would be entitled to those noninferential beliefs without being able to justify those beliefs (to make explicit arguments as to why one was entitled to them).

And yet, that such scripturally derived beliefs are justified and "properly basic" does not render them indefeasible. Nor are they exempt from object-directed assessment, critical reflection, and interpretive contestation. In fact, these are constitutive features of what it means for faith to seek understanding. Moreover, the fact that critically engaging Scripture participates in such a socially embodied, historically extended range of self-examining textual practices could itself contribute to the justifying conditions in virtue of which scriptural reports are "properly basic."[29]

To say that Anselmian coherentism is not *pure* coherentism means, in part, that it materially entails objects that may noninferentially elicit these beliefs—in this case, the observational reports and testimony to the events portrayed in the biblical narratives. Moreover, the claims and patterns of these texts embrace, interweave with, and intervene upon the world by orienting and framing particular understandings and impelling those who follow to act within and throughout the world in which they live and move and have their being. In other words, the "properly basic" beliefs that Anselmian coherentists identify have a hermeneutical basis—the witness of Scripture as oriented by the person and work of Christ and as illuminated by the testimony of the Holy Spirit.[30] This makes for an instructive point of comparison between such theology and Reformed epistemology.

Nicholas Wolterstorff identifies the projects of Frei and Plantinga as in different ways both predicated on the questions "Who says that we may only reason to our convictions about God, never simply reason from them? If one wants to think along foundational lines, who says that beliefs about God may never be in the foundation?"[31] Elsewhere, Wolterstorff sharpens this point of contact, pushing forward Plantinga's conception of "properly basic beliefs" in direct conversation with Frei's work. Believing the gospel witness will be, in some instances, believing on the "say-so," or testimony, of Scripture. Elsewhere Wolterstorff develops the point at length:

> Frei appears to recognize that such believing-on-say-so is a case of immediate, as opposed to inferential belief: "no matter what the logic of the Christian faith, actual belief in the resurrection is a matter of faith and not of arguments from possibility or evidence" (*Eclipse*, 152). And quite clearly he recognizes that, in tacitly assuming that such immediate belief is (sometimes at least) entitled, he is bumping up against an epistemological tradition which affirms the contrary: "I am well aware of, but not terribly distressed by, the fact that my refusal to speak speculatively or evidentially about the resurrection of Christ, while nevertheless affirming it as an indispensable Christian claim, may involve me in some difficult logical tangles" (*Eclipse*, xiii).

He also recognizes that such immediate believing-on-say-so would not be entitled under all circumstances: "Reliable historical evidence *against* the resurrection would tend to falsify it decisively, and . . . the forthcoming of such evidence is conceivable" ("Theological Reflections," p. 302). Presumably evidence that Jesus did everything possible to elude his captors and evade execution—that his behavior was far from "obedient"—would also remove entitlement.[32]

This latter set of claims about the immediacy of belief, and certain of the justifying conditions that such immediacy presupposes, highlights the similarities of their positions concerning the sense in which belief may be noninferential.[33]

Frei followed Barth at a near distance in his claims about the hermeneutical bases of dogmatic theology. He wanted to clarify and highlight, on one hand, Barth's rejection of the task of "epistemology" as traditionally construed (by which Frei meant, at least in part, the very kind of "Enlightenment rationality" that Wolterstorff and Plantinga have so relentlessly demystified).[34] At the same time, Frei understood Barth to have done anything but forsake such epistemological tasks as elucidating, interrogating, extrapolating, explicating, and applying (many of the practical tasks that "epistemology" pursues) the rational content intrinsic to Christian faith. And this is a feature of Barth's work that appealed to Frei. But, again, these are hermeneutically based, confessionally situated, and ecclesially embodied epistemological practices. They are invited by God's activity in and through the witness of Scripture. They awaken faith as the self-involving, recipient mode of God's self-revelatory activity. They presuppose the accounts of Jesus' life, death, and resurrection as inscribed in Scripture. This is grace-initiated "epistemology"—the search for understanding conducted within the space of reasons afforded by God's revelation.

Barth did not bother attempting to explain to the philosophical community how this was possible. He was not concerned to explain how it was faith's right to recognize itself as the noninferential point of departure. Neither did he attempt to demonstrate that faith's departure from itself in seeking understanding of itself was no more arbitrary than the classical or professional epistemologists' appeal to some threshold of "acceptable empirical evidence" or a "self-justified justifier" on the basis of which one could legitimately assert a claim. Barth simply began explicating and applying the *intellectus fidei*—evolving the discursive world from the cognitive presupposition of, and practical implications internal to, faith as the recipient mode of God's self-revelation. As Frei redescribed Barth's position, the *possibility* of faith's seeking understanding is predicated upon the *actuality* of the Word having become flesh and dwelling among us.[35]

But there is another dimension of Barth's account that Frei emphasized and extended and which made the social and practical dimensions of faith so central to Frei's work. It rests upon Barth's claim that the cognitive implications of the "basic," or "foundational" or "noninferential," freedom of God's self-revelation extended beyond all those procedures constitutive of faith seeking understanding. It is the recognition that faith is not exhausted by such *epistemological* procedures. Faith, as a finally miraculous and mysterious event, could not be wholly theorized or predicted. It is theoretical only insofar as it is also practical, and thus, *self-involving*. Knowledge that takes the forms of acknowledgement and affirmation is one among several "qualitative determinants" of faith—the others being love, trust, and obedience.[36] Faith desires self-understanding. It seeks to make explicit, explore, self-critically reflect upon, and refine all the inferences and implications internal to it. And while this "knowledge as the knowledge of faith" means for Barth "the union of the knower with God," faith only *secondarily* takes the epistemological forms of articulating, exploring, testing, and ordering the "rational content" of that knowledge.[37] *Primarily* it means "that the resurrection of Christ shapes a new life."[38]

"Faith seeking understanding" is no mere formal rehearsal of the logic internal to faith. It is self-involving, and this makes it ecclesial. On this view, the theological enterprise is itself sacramental practice. The proofs are theological occasions only because they are first and foremost acts of prayer and praise.[39] The role of theologian and the theological task cannot be construed in abstraction from the life of the communities of believers nor conducted apart from reflective and prophetic service to church and world.[40] And history bound, as she only can be, the theologian strives in the here and now amid the lived world of discourse that is embodied in the social practices constituting the church to discern and critically reflect upon God's word for the church.

II. Specters of Fideism

Some will view the foregoing noninferentialist redescription as little more than the use of technical jargon to obscure what are, in fact, fideist tendencies of Frei's approach to theology. To speak of Scripture's depictive renderings as a noninferential entryway into the Christian "world of discourse," they might say, in fact promotes a set of concerns and understandings too inwardly focused on the practices of Christian community. And indeed, the self-interrogation and reflectiveness of Frei's theological approach may cast the impression that engagement with cultural forms beyond Christian forms of life is not high on the agenda. In the following section I hope to defuse such criticisms. Careful explication should show that Frei's work cannot be assimilated to some form of theoretical fideism nor a practical isolationism that results in apolitical posture nor an outlook incapable of rendering and receiving criticism.

Frei's reading of the rationality intrinsic to faith, and the relation of assertions grounded in that logic to other discursive norms, may present the most seemingly "isolationist" or "fideistic" tendencies in his thought.[41] As Frei explicates him, Barth ruled out the regnant axioms that would allow theology to qualify as *Wissenschaft*, namely, "(1) the postulate of non-contradiction among and within propositions; (2) internal coherence; (3) testability (revisability of propositions—nondogma); (4) arrangement of all propositions into axioms and theorems, and being susceptible of demonstration on that basis":

> Then Barth says, that's unacceptable to theology. *Even* "the very minimum postulate of freedom from contradiction is acceptable by theology only upon the very limited interpretation, by the scientific theorist upon the scarcely tolerable one, that theology will not assert an irremovability in principle of the 'contradictions' which it is bound to make good."[42]

Many thinkers find Frei's treatment of Barth here unsatisfying, if not simply fideistic. A "logic" internal to faith purports to tie theology to a static and backward-looking traditionalism. It construes Christian forms of life as cultural enclaves separated from broader culture. It isolates and protects the central claims of faith from other modes of analysis.

Sheila Davaney, for instance, situates "postliberal" theology as an authoritarian theological mode irrevocably inward looking and isolationist.[43] "A number of postliberals are responding to this charge by calling for an ad hoc apologetics—unsystematic and occasional conversations with other perspectives around specific shared concerns," she writes. "Yet postliberals have no basis within their approach for entering these conversations, or, once there, for making them much more than show and tell."[44]

As we saw in chapter 5, Frei invoked Clifford Geertz's work to help describe how intelligibility and meaning in Christian communities was like a set of skills into which one is acculturated or socialized. These skills participate in the range of social practices that make up the community or form of life in question— practices that exert normative constraints upon what counts as participation in that form of life and which are themselves constituted by certain normative constraints. Something like this social-practical conception of community grounds the "postliberal" conception of "tradition," which Davaney glosses as "a historical line of development that embodies in an ongoing fashion a set of essential tenets." Such tenets, she points out, function like grammatical rules.

What results is that "theology becomes a descriptive endeavor that seeks to delineate and make clear the normative foundations of a specific tradition."

Davaney is correct to say that "postliberals" see theology as reflection upon, or redescription of, norms internal to the social practices constitutive of Christian communities that extend themselves over time. However, she infers from this that the "central criterion" for such theology "consists in faithfulness to the originating tenets of the tradition and whose reference is almost exclusively to the particular community and its history."[45] And while she acknowledges the "postliberal's" capacity to converse with thinkers outside his or her tradition in an ad hoc and unsystematic fashion, she finds this conception of tradition is too beholden to these very founding tenets for such conversations to amount to substantive exchange and revision of their claims, practices, or beliefs. She thinks that such singular emphasis upon tradition cannot accommodate the multitraditioned quality of existence in today's world. Moreover, it is suspiciously *un*historical by portraying traditions as organized around "basic tenets [that] themselves do not change," and it invests those founding beliefs with the kind of authoritarianism of which we ought to be suspicious. "Our world, [postliberals] claim, should allow itself to be absorbed by the world of our traditions, and where contemporary values or commitments or beliefs conflict with those of these regulative tenets, it is the present that must yield."[46] Insofar as she would include him as a target for these criticisms, Davaney underestimates the capacity for change and innovation available to Frei's account.[47]

First, at a general level, various thinkers have demonstrated at length how normative constraints provide the possibility of innovation.[48] On such an account, social practices develop and change over time like case law. Novel performances of the practice enrich the practice itself and thus enrich, expand, and even transform the practice (at times gradually, at times decisively). Understood in such social-practical terms, theology is not a task of preserving originating tenets or ascertaining a *fixed* grammar. It is rather a thinking through of the development, significance, proper application, and self-correction of those tenets as part of, and in response to, the discernment of God's presence to the church. This is a critical investigation and redescription of the various facets of the tradition specifically with an eye to interpreting and applying them critically in light of the current circumstances and experiences, past applications, and future possibilities that constitute the tradition that such applications unfold. At a general level, Davaney's challenge, and others like it, rest upon a mistaken understanding of the character of this social-practical approach. In particular, they overlook the kind of innovation, improvisation, testing, revision, and rearticulation that the normative constraints constitutive of a socially embodied, historically extended tradition of inquiry makes possible. Moreover, they neglect the resources available to such traditions for overcoming the purported "isolationism."

Frei affirms the unacceptability of the *necessary* submission of theology to the general norms of *Wissenschaft*. Rules such as "the force of the better argument," "the principle of noncontradiction," and rendering one's argument from a position of impartiality that all rational interlocutors could find convincing would tie him to some general criteria of meaning or norm of discourse to which he cannot unequivocally assent. That is, they would require the submission of the norm that guides all of his speech and action—"knowledge of the Lord who is Lord of all"—to a general criterion for participation and success, whether in the guise of public reason or impartiality. And yet, Frei's response to this potential difficulty translates into anything but a radical disengagement of faith from interdisciplinary engagement. Nor does it permit irresponsibility in regards to striving for clarity, cogency, and intelligibility when Christians exchange reasons with non-Christians. Frei highlights a proviso against submission of the logic of faith to any general norm of meaning or discourse. However, this does not rule out altogether overlap between them. Moreover, any ad hoc correlation conducted in virtue of such overlaps must be itself guided by the knowledge of the Lord who is Lord of all.[49]

In public political discussions, for instance, not everything Christians say will make direct reference to convictions deemed "paradoxical" by non-Christians or even need to be couched in explicitly theological or biblical terms. And yet in his refusal to apologize for basic commitments by translating those convictions into terms of a supposed "lowest common denominator" (or, for that matter, terms that any reasonable person could reasonably be expected to accept), Frei's characterization is at once modest and uncompromising. Faith can neither disengage from public political discourse nor compromise its particularity. "Obviously, you don't want to talk nonsense or in flagrant self-contradiction, and, of course, you've got to try to make clear what you're after," Frei cautioned. "But you won't be surprised if there's something incomplete and fragmentary about your reasoning."[50] Incomplete or fragmentary reasoning is anything but uncommon in the ordinary practices in which people live their lives, unless one makes a habit of conversing with professional philosophers.

Moreover, the charge that Frei's position implies "outsider inaccessibility" as a sort of "protective strategy" that sets faith off from critical assessment by an outsider overlooks the possibility—and perhaps the necessity—of immanent criticism to Christian convictions and practices. One deploys immanent criticism from outside a given community by assuming the interlocutor's premises and demonstrating that they are in some way problematical, perhaps incoherent or unable to succeed on the basis of its own presuppositions. Put positively, the critic assumes her interlocutor's premises and attempts to show how his own claims function as plausible and persuasive conclusions on the basis of the assumed premises—"it makes their reasoning move towards him."[51] This is one critical form that acknowledges the viability of external criticism of the Christian community in this immanent form.

Heeding such criticism rendered by external critics may be a God-given obligation.[52] After all, even the church's most faithful moments of witness are riddled with imperfections. The church can be wrong, its witness unfaithful. Believers falter; theologians lose the faith. The point is that it is God who is constantly at work in ever new and surprising ways to reconcile and to teach with a sense of humor that takes the "doubt, denial and derision" of believer and unbeliever alike with far less seriousness than they could ever take them themselves.[53]

Quite clearly, Christian churches have much about which to be corrected. Such lessons may be administered immanently, according to which a non-member of a community or cultural setting studies the languages, practices, and stories that underpin their self-understanding(s) with the care and precision of a cultural ethnographer.[54] Barth is clear that a Christian who does not speak publicly and beyond the confines of the Christian community risks irrelevance. But irrelevance is a negligible result of a cloistered witness. *Unfaithfulness* is the true and serious risk. That is, a disciple of Christ "loses his soul, and hazards his eternal salvation, if he will not accept the *public* responsibility which he assumes when he becomes a disciple of Jesus."[55]

Of course, an unapologetic character to one's witnessing, and perhaps an air of peculiarity which the Christian's speech and actions may take on from time to time, is part of faithfully responding to God's vocational call. However, the reasons afforded by revelation do not lead the Christian to sequester her witness from the Christian community without regard for involvement in inter-communal or interdisciplinary concerns, or to restrict her public involvement to an anonymous use of reasons and language all parties will find palatable and convincing—reasons and language allegedly able to be shared by everyone because peculiar to none. Neither does this advocate, in principle, Christian anonymity in the public realm. In fact, faith entails a positive obligation requiring Christians actively to participate with and among people unaffiliated with Christian communities in matters public and political. Disengagement from public concerns is a true and serious risk for the Christian.

Christians, then, are not just prohibited from sequestering themselves into the Christian community proper, as if the world around them did not exist or was solely a source of Christian resentment. They are positively obligated by

God's call to engage actively in matters public with the occasional peculiarity of their Christian convictions. Such an obligation means that Christians should be prepared to converse with those unaffiliated with Christian communities, unfamiliar with Christian convictions, *as well as* in and through all the differences that exist between multiform Christian communities themselves. They must, therefore, seek an intimate understanding of the people with whom they live in order to identify overlapping points of commonality from which discourse might begin, always prepared to give account of the hope that is within them by way of self-description and practical application of their convictions and beliefs.

As we saw in the above explication of Frei's position, faith is not *incapable* of engaging other disciplines, discourses, modes of argument, or styles of reasoning. Alliances between theology and "other intellectual resources of our culture" are possible—even necessary—on an ad hoc basis. The upshot here is that ad hoc apologetics is a complex and multifaceted affair. It has multiple forms and is likely better understood as a genre of engagements—a range of ways of relating—rather than a single procedure.

Such ad hoc relationships are far more complex than simple friendly alliances, and far more significant than "show and tell." In fact, there are several other equally crucial characteristics of ad hoc engagements, such as the *seriousness* afforded one's nontheological interlocutor (as either ally or antagonist—and sometimes as both), the *risk* internal to serious engagement, perhaps of being persuaded by the claims of one's interlocutors, the ultimate *relativization* of that other (however benevolent their relation may be) once that other is positioned in reference to God's revelation in Christ; and an enhanced and altered *self-understanding* that comes as the result of engagement with an other in and through whom God may well be at work. "Ad hoc apologetics," then, actually entails quite a bit, including the bricoleur's borrowing of tools and materials in order to cobble together useful arguments and descriptions in the course of investigation, understanding, confrontation, and instruction, among others.

III. "Adorning Ourselves with Their Feathers"

Some will respond that I make ad hoc apologetics a far too friendly enterprise, that what I advertise as concrete and situation specific in fact boils down to the rigorous *subordination* of implements "external" to dogmatics and even more specifically, to the scriptural witness. It is true that Frei employs the term "subordination" to describe Barth's account theology's engagement with nontheological resources. And yet, Frei is well aware that what Barth means by "subordination" is complex and situation specific. As Frei points out, the term itself must be held provisionally in order to be consistent with Barth's own position.[56] What results is anything but the elimination of all things "nonscriptural." Quite the opposite, in fact; the inclusion of *any* mode of thinking and exegetical method is possible, so long as it is finally oriented by the witness of Scripture.[57] Notice what has *not* occurred with such a claim. There has *not* occurred an "annihilation and replacement" of insights, resources, or implements that do not originate in Scripture. Clearly, Barth avoids a flatfooted "autonomy and reciprocity" between the object of Scripture and whatever instruments and tools the exegete might bring to bear in his exegesis. Nonetheless, "autonomy" and "reciprocity" remain central to the enterprise in reoriented senses of these terms.

"Imported" modes of thought remain "autonomous" in the sense that they must be recognized as differing from scripture and having their own integrity and normative orientation as such—that is, as modes of thought that differ from the biblical witness. This is well and good and could not be otherwise. In fact, Barth adds that to neglect this original difference risks presuming that some particular method or approach is essential and necessary to this subject matter of the biblical witness. Its uniqueness prohibits this. Here *subordination* eliminates "autonomy" only in the sense of treating a method as absolute or an end in itself—as an object that commandeers the exegete's obedience. And while this rules out any final allegiances to external methods, it makes every methodological implement a potential candidate for the exegete's scriptural purposes. "There is none [i.e., no philosophy or method] which *must* become dangerous [to the scriptural witness], because there is none which we cannot have without positing it absolutely," Barth writes. He continues, "There is none which *cannot* possibly become dangerous, because there is none which we cannot posit absolutely, that is, in disloyalty to Scripture erect its presentation into a principle and an end in itself."[58]

For the purposes of scriptural exegesis, then, whatever tools the exegete brings to bear must finally be oriented by the witness of Scripture. This means that they must be applied in provisional, experimental, and exploratory ways.[59] It is crucial to keep in mind that theology itself must follow obediently the object of the biblical witness. And for precisely this reason orientation by the object of the text does not eliminate *reciprocity* between scriptural and nonscriptural modes of thought. Their engagement may be mutually enriching. Of course, belief in the final truth of the scriptural proclamation means that any reciprocity will ultimately be *asymmetrical*. Even so, loyalty to the object of Scripture means that the theological task may well be corrected from the literary or historical side.[60] Here Barth should speak for himself:

It is not as though we had simply to abandon and forget our ideas, thoughts and convictions. We certainly cannot do that, just as little as we can free ourselves from our own shadow. Nor should we try to do it; for that would be arrogance rather than humility. Subordination does not mean the elimination and annihilation of our own re-sources. Subordination implies that the subordinate is there as such and remains there. It means placing oneself behind, following, complying as subordinate to superior. This is what is required in subordinating our ideas, thoughts and convictions to the witness which confronts us in Scripture. It cannot mean that we have to allow ideas, thoughts and convictions to be supplanted, so to speak, by those of the prophets and apostles, or that we have to begin to speak the language of Canaan instead of our own tongue. In that case we should not have subordinated ourselves to them, but at most adorned ourselves with their feathers. In that case nothing would have been done in the interpretation of their words, for we should merely have repeated them parrot-like.[61]

To his claim about the inevitability of using some approach or philosophical tools, Barth added that "there is no essential reason for preferring one of these schemes to another."[62] Which tools, approach, or mode of thought will be bene-ficial will have to be determined on a case-by-case basis. They must all remain tentative, hypothetical, and exploratory vis-à-vis the freedom of the Word of God. What is particularly helpful in one instance may not be in another. Thus, Frei writes in sum, "The relationship between internal self-description and external description thus remains ad hoc, with freedom for each side, possible family resemblance, and obedience to the criterion of the priority of Christian self-description as the task of the Church."[63]

Conclusion

In this chapter I have proposed that the Anselmian coherentist features of Frei's account can avoid classical foundationalism without implicating itself in "losing the world" in a pure coherentism. I have illuminated these nuances of "Anselmian coherentism" by developing their similarities and compatibilities with insights drawn from the pragmatic inferentialist approaches of Sellars and Brandom and the conception of properly basic beliefs developed in various ways by Plantinga and Wolterstorff. This explication required that I then respond to the charges of fideism and practical isolationism to which Frei's approach to theology, and others like it, have been prone. This chapter presents only the first step in my redescriptive engagement with Frei's work. The tools are now upon the table. In the two remaining chapters I apply these and related redescriptive insights to explicating and clarifying Frei's accounts of the literal and plain senses of Scripture.

7

From Word Alone to Word and Spirit

As his theological project unfolded, Frei expanded his earlier focus upon the structural makeup of the scriptural text in order to account more explicitly for the different ways that scriptural texts are used in various contexts. This increasingly explicit duality of focus upon context and content raises questions about the relativity of interpretation. How, for instance, could Frei follow Wittgenstein's instruction to "look for uses" of the text in specific contexts rather than "ask for their meaning" without reducing the meaning of Scripture to how it is used or the way that it functions within the reading practices of a given community?[1] In other words, can Frei's emphasis upon interpretive context avoid *reducing* itself in a textual "warranted assertability" that treats meaning as "what your peers will let you get away with" or "what fellow readers will agree to"? How, on the other hand, can Frei retain his claim on behalf of Scripture's basically christological content without smuggling in some notion of textual essentialism—positing a particular meaning of the text "in itself"?

Frei is notoriously difficult to pin down in his attempts to answer these questions. At some points he invokes what the Christian tradition of interpretation predominately has taken to be "plain" as justification for his claims about the uniquely christological content of the scriptural text. At other times he claims that the literal sense of the text itself plainly presents this Christ-centered account. In the following pages I aim to demonstrate how Frei can coherently retain both a christocentric account of the biblical text and a context-sensitive conception of the plain sense of Scripture. To accomplish this, I first work through what may be the best account of the *plain sense* of Scripture yet available, demonstrating that its key insights come from a particular reading of Wittgenstein. I then unpack a dense passage of Frei's "The 'Literal Reading' of Scripture" essay in order to display how I think that position should not be read. In the final segment of this chapter I introduce recent philosophical expansions of this reading of Wittgenstein in order to enrich Frei's conceptual tools and thereby clear up some of the apparently paradoxical formulations that obscure his claims for a christologically high plain sense of Scripture. The remainder of my argument for the coherence and plausibility of Frei's dually focused account of the plain sense unfolds in the final chapter.

I. From Text to Text and Context

As we saw at the end of chapter 2, Frei's attention to context had not been entirely absent in *The Identity of Jesus Christ*. However, in his writings of the early 1980s he more explicitly began to attend to the ways that specific contexts and circumstances shape believers' engagements with Scripture. In particular, he accentuated the fact that readers' understandings, interests, and purposes inevitably bear upon their reading. "Understanding" and "meaning," he recognized, are largely products of context-specific reading practices rather than solely a matter of a particular content conveyed in virtue of realistic narrative form. Frei came to describe "understanding a text" as "more nearly an ability to use it appropriately in specific contexts (and the appropriate skill of judgment about whether or not to activate that capacity) than to know the rules for proper 'interpretation.' To construe the text properly is part of learning the requisite conceptual skills. To understand concepts is to have the ability both to explicate and to apply them, without necessarily resorting to a theory that would indicate how to couple the two."[2]

At the same time, Frei acknowledged that his previous appeals to "realistic narrative" had inadvertently privileged a general literary category over the content conveyed in the biblical narratives. He clarified that the *history likeness* of these particular narratives does not result from their standing as a particular instance of an antecedently identified, pretheological category. There is, indeed, coherence between "the real world" and the narrative world that the biblical narratives depictively render, as Frei had earlier claimed. However, this coherence occurs not because the text "narrates a world" as a function of its literary genre. Neither, Frei added, is this coherence between "text and world" due to a more basic narrative constitution of human identity that, thereby, makes the biblical narratives fitting frameworks for daily life.[3] In fact, Frei continued to work with the "realistic" qualities of these narratives but deployed this description in explicitly formal and ad hoc terms. The biblical accounts of Christ's life, death, and resurrection happen to be cast in narrative form. Describe them as "realistic" if it helps.[4]

Increasingly, Frei sought to factor the impact of textual practices and contexts of use into thinking about the narrative form and christological content of the gospel accounts. To do this he primarily relied upon the framework that generally had been used by the Christian churches to characterize the shape of the history likeness that these narratives portray—the *sensus literalis*. The *sensus literalis* provided Frei with a basically theological framework within which to strike a balance between context specificity and normative christological content. The literal sense, Frei wrote, is "a case-specific reading which may or may not find reduced analogues elsewhere"— a reading that "belongs first and foremost into the context of a socio-linguistic community, that is, of the specific religion of which it is part."[5] At the same time, Frei ascribed to the *sensus literalis* a normative status similar to that which he had formerly identified in terms of realistic narrative. Emphasizing "meaning as use," he thought, need not preclude the influence of constraints that the stories themselves exert. In other words, attending to contextual specifics ought not reduce the meaning of the text to whatever its readers take it to mean.

Kathryn Tanner has perhaps most incisively explored the social and practical dimensions of the plain sense and illuminated the challenges raised by Frei's emphasis upon "meaning as use."[6] This sense of the text is "plain" not in virtue of "what the text simply says" regardless of context or what the text means "when the expositor is purely passive" or avoids imposing "extratextual categories."[7] The "plain sense" is, by contrast, "what a participant in the community automatically or naturally takes a text to be saying on its face insofar as he or she has been socialized in a community's conventions for reading that text as Scripture." On this account, a community's conventions of reading and textual use generate what members of a community naturally recognize when they read the text without explicitly reflecting upon—and in some sense without even thinking about—what they are doing. The plain sense is, in other words, what some community comes to recognize as "obvious" about the text— "the immediately apparent sense produced by a habit of reading in which the members of a community engage without thinking about it."[8]

Community members come to recognize the plain sense as they become acculturated into and gradually come to be increasingly skilled participants in the community's conventions and background practices. To refer to such unthematized practices as "what they do without thinking" or "second nature" is not to imply that these are noncognitive or behavioristic.[9] The practices in question are cognitive because they are conceptual and thus norm-laden. Practitioners recognize and hold one another accountable for executing moves of the practice in more or less correct ways, and reflect on and contest why some instance is adequate and another is not. To characterize the engagement of the plain sense as "unthematized" is simply to say that such actions occur as practical discriminations prior to being formally explicated or deliberately reflected upon.

Tanner's account remains true to Frei's attention to the case specificity of the plain sense and his general aversion to grand theories. For descriptive purposes, she points out, the term is as formal as can be. Certain practices of appealing to texts tend to produce normative readings within a given community. The "plain sense" is a formal placeholder for such readings as they are identified from context to context. Any investigator interested in the reading and interpretive practices of a given community ought to be on the lookout for this function of those particular social practices.[10] The plain sense for a given community or congregation need not be construed as stable. And depending on the character of the reading community in question, likely it will not be. Where it occurs, it might be recognized, in part, by the practically normative constraints it exerts in distinguishing a range of more or less proper uses from improper ones. In a community organized around an authoritative text, to recognize (or take for granted) the plain sense—and to recognize others as one's fellows, in part, insofar as they also recognize (or take for granted) that authority—may contribute significantly to what this group of practitioners mean when they say "us."

In order to illuminate these formal, functional strands of Frei's account, Tanner draws upon David Kelsey's work on the subject. According to Kelsey, Scripture speaks as the interests and purposes of the interpreting community give voice to the text in question. In other words, the text's meaning is a function of the community's particular uses of the text. Kelsey pushes this point further to claim that even (and perhaps especially) the *sacred status* of a text is a function of how a community takes or treats the text in question, and thus it is not a property of the text. To call the biblical text "Scripture" is to place it in the context of Christian community. It is to say "that the text is to be used (in some fashion or other) to shape, nurture, and reform the continuing self-identity of the church."[11]

Initially, Kelsey's definition might appear to render the plain sense contextually variant in a problematic way. For insofar as local conventions for reading or consulting a text vary among communities, times, places, and circumstances, so will its meanings. Once one has relativized the meaning of

Scripture in this way, no longer, it would seem, can one propose a christological reading as normative across contexts (as Frei attempted to). Identified as
"an object of communal consensus on the use of texts," the plain sense is
nothing prior to some community's determination of it.[12] This set of claims
appears to open Tanner's account of the plain sense to the same criticism
Ronald Thiemann leveled against Kelsey's and Charles Wood's accounts of
scriptural interpretation.[13]

Positing Wittgenstein's instruction to "look for the use" as a methodological rule and then following it to its apparently logical conclusion, Thiemann
argued, leaves textual meaning so *in*determinate as to open the way for in an
irreducible diversity of meanings.[14] More importantly, it renders the *revelational authority* of the scriptural text a product of the community's decision to
take this text as authoritative, in conjunction with the theologian's imagina-
tive decisions to "organize theological thinking around certain determinate
patterns within Scripture itself."[15] In each case, the text's meaning and significance—including that sense "normally acknowledged as basic [by the
community]"—is a predicate of communal consensus.[16]

Frei's account of the plain sense, I aim to demonstrate in the following
pages, avoids the latter—and, in my judgment, more formidable—of
Thiemann's criticisms. Moreover, careful attention to the particular reading of
Wittgenstein that underpins Tanner's account will help demonstrate this.
The broader upshot of my argument is that a social-practical account of the
plain sense need not leave itself open to Thiemann's charge that *meaning as use*
results in a functionalist view of Scripture and thus indeterminacy of interpretations. Nor, moreover, must such an account attribute the revelatory status of
the biblical text to communal consensus about that text.

II. Plain Reading as a Social Practice

To participate in a social practice is to be responsible to the recognition of the
community of fellow practitioners. It is, at the same time, to be accountable to
the normative constraints of the inferential exigencies of the practice, regardless of what any of one's fellows might take those constraints to be at any given
point. To be acculturated into a set of discursive practices, then—to become a
competent user of concepts and speaker of words, a maker and respecter of
claims—is to become competent in discriminately applying the norms implicit
in those practices (even if only in practical application, and not in explicit articulation of those norms). It is thus to hold one's self and one's fellows accountable to those norms.

Acculturation into embodied sense-making conceptual practices is more than learning to grasp and apply concepts. It also entails *being grasped by* concepts. That is, the normative dimensions of concepts hold sway over the judgments that one *ought* to make.[17] In other words, acculturation into social practice entails being dispositionally socialized to respond in certain ways to the grasp of those concepts. "By (for instance) using certain words, we give concepts a grip on us, place ourselves under their sway," writes Robert Brandom, "implicitly recognize their standards as authoritative for assessments of what we are committed and entitled to."[18] The dispositional aspect of the normative dimension of concept use constrains what concept users *do* as well. Would-be participants "acquire the tendency to make the transition from occupying the position 'I ought now to do A' to the doing of A."[19]

When Tanner characterizes the plain sense as "a consensus reading," she illuminates a normative dimension to social practices similar to the one just described. On Tanner's account, a community's conscious deliberation and explicit agreement does not determine the plain sense of the text. Rather, the plain sense issues from consensus at the level of practice—congruities at the level of social practices that, in part, constitute what it is for something to be "a text," what it is to read a text, and what the text "says," along with what will be recognized as falling more or less within (or outside of) the range of recognized readings. Members of a community may disagree about particular interpretations of the text, but such disagreement is made possible by a background of congruities at the level of their practices. "Communal habits of appealing to texts are what give rise to talk about a plain sense," Tanner writes, "even when such a consensus in practice is not itself what is talked about."[20] The result is that discourse about the meaning of the text becomes accountable to more than just what one's fellows will let one get away with—more, that is, than what they explicitly take the text to say.

The community's claims about textual meaning, as well as claims made by individual community members, are accountable to the normative proprieties implicit in the practices of appealing to texts. Thus, the plain reading is an objective affair in the sense of "objectivity" that Sabina Lovibond identifies in Wittgenstein's later thinking:

> [A]lthough (in Wittgenstein's view) it is an agreement, or
> congruence, in our ways of acting that makes objective discourse
> materially possible, this agreement does not itself "enter into" the
> relevant language-game: when we ask a question about some aspect
> of reality, we are not asking for a report on the state of public
> opinion with regard to that question, we are asking to be told the

truth about it. . . . The idea of rationality as resting upon a consensus, then, does not imply that the *fact* of consensus need carry any weight with us in any particular piece of thinking about the objective world: a point which is demonstrated by the absence of any logical (or "grammatical") objection to statements of the form: "I'm right and everyone else is wrong."[21]

Lovibond here employs a distinction between consensus "at the level of the language game" (consensus upon the particular use, and hence meaning, of a text) and a consensus in our acting that makes the language game possible (that texts are things that are used, that certain actions count as using a text, that uses of the text can be distinguished as more or less plausible vis-à-vis what the text as text says). The point is that the normative constraints implicit in reading practices make it possible for an individual community member to dissent from communal consensus by appealing to the norms constitutive of the practice at hand, the object that orients the practice, and that toward which it is directed. Some such dissenter can claim, as Lovibond points out, "'I'm right and everyone else is wrong'" and demonstrate that this is actually the case.[22] But to be recognizable as a reader in the first place is to be accountable to the normative constraints that constitute the practices of reading and consulting texts and, concomitantly, the constraints composing the object as a text.

Diversity of interpretations presupposes a background of congruities in what participants in the practice do. Particular uses of the text will differ— sometimes drastically—and claims about meanings will vary accordingly but far from irreducibly so. The range of variability is not so *in*determinate as to negate the community's, or community's member's, capacity to refuse to recognize or accept some proposed interpretation or warrant for a claim under the auspices of "what is obvious about the text." This is the sense that Tanner has in mind when she construes the plain sense as a "consensus reading."

This facet of Wittgenstein's account provides normative traction that enables readers—insiders and outsiders to a given community—to appeal to Scripture in order to critique and resist prevailing, yet wrongheaded, uses of the text. In principle, all practitioners are accountable to the proprieties constitutive of the practice in question. Communal consensus about meaning that is explicitly achieved or taken for granted by the community itself is similarly accountable. This means that prevailing consensus or shared habits—what is taken for granted as obvious about the text—can be challenged in virtue of the normative constraints that make the practice possible in the first place.

At the same time, the norm-constituted practices themselves develop and evolve. In principle, every applied instance of the practice can further enrich the

practice as well as the norms constituting it by extending, challenging, and transforming it.[23] Thus, a social-practical account of the plain sense neither reduces
meaning to consensus nor practices to stable phenomena that resist change. And
yet, I do not see how Tanner's account (like the accounts of Wood and Kelsey) can
avoid Thiemann's criticism that this general approach reduces the text's revelational authority to a function of the community, thereby eliminating God's preve-
nient act of self-revelation, invitation to discipleship, Christian community, and
the tasks of theology.[24] Frei's account, by contrast, does avoid this criticism, or so
I argue in the remainder of this chapter and the next.

III. "The Symphony of Scripture": Mediating Text and Tradition

Frei refused to distill the literal or plain sense to a single thing. He sought
nonetheless to retain a strong conception of God's initiative in and through the
person of Christ. In effect, this combination aimed to reconcile context-relative,
interpretive *under*determinateness (as opposed to *in*determinateness) of plain
reading with the kind of christological surface description and plot that he had
articulated in his earlier work.[25] Restraining his reliance upon "realistic narrative" as a general category, he nonetheless preserved a normatively christological sense to the surface of the textual accounts. As such, his work on the plain
sense is not a simple departure from his earlier account of the identity of Jesus
Christ. Rather, it reconciles his earlier claims about the normative and plainly
christological character portrayed by these realistic narratives with his increasingly explicit articulation of the social-practical character of engaging Scripture.
This development takes the form of a conceptual expansion—a broadening of
focus rather than a "turn" from or "break" with his earlier claims—"from Word
to Word and Spirit."[26]

On what basis, then, could Frei justify his seemingly contradictory claims
that the plain sense manifests the person of Christ as its literal subject and yet
simultaneously maintain his emphasis upon its contextual and practical flexibility? The answer to this question lies, in part, in Frei's description of the
literal sense as "not only as use in context but as unity of grammatical/syntac-
tical sense and signified subject."[27] Frei's recognition of "meaning" as precipitating from social practices acknowledges the text as a normative constraint
upon interpretation. He wrote:

> "Literal sense" here applies primarily to the identification of Jesus as
> the *ascriptive* subject of the descriptions or stories told about and in
> relation to him—whether the status of this identification is that of

chief character in a narrative plot, historically factual person, or
reality under an ontological scheme. . . . "[L]iteral" is not referentially
univocal but embraces several possibilities. All other senses of the
quite diverse and changing notion "literal" are secondary to this (to
my mind, basic ascriptive Christological) sense of "literal," that the
subject matter of these stories is not something or someone else, and
that the rest of the canon must in some way or ways, looser or tighter,
be related to this subject matter or at least not in contradiction with
it. That is the minimal agreement of how "literal" reading has
generally been understood in the Western Christian tradition.[28]

As Frei describes it in this passage, the literal sense is a context-variant discursive object. Nevertheless, it depicts Christ grammatically and syntactically in
storied form as its signified subject—inseparably, that is, from what the text as
written is in order to be a written text and, in this instance, a text centrally concerned to witness to the life, death, and resurrection of Christ. To invoke the
grammatical/syntactical character of the text is to assert that insofar as this is a
text—insofar as it participates in the social practices of writing and reading and
consulting texts by virtue of conforming to the constraints of those practices
(the exigencies of language, for instance, submitting to myriads of normative
constraints in order to say anything at all)—a central feature of that text is that
it portrays the person of Jesus as its central signified subject. This permitted
considerable interpretive leeway and room for contestation. At the same time,
its christological orientation has served as an orienting constraint for Christian
readings of Scripture.[29]

At the same time, Frei recognized the constraints exerted by the text's
grammatical/syntactical and signified subject are inextricably interwoven with
the reading practices and interpretive tendencies of the "Western Christian
tradition." He asserted, accordingly, that this tradition has demonstrated consensus in taking Jesus as the unsubstitutable, ascriptive subject of the gospel
narratives. In fact, at some moments in his account, the warrant provided by
contextual consensus appears to take priority to the "literary-literal" character
of those narratives. Indeed, Frei is not entirely clear about how his de-emphasis
of "realistic narrative" fits with his claims about the church traditions' taking
the literal sense as plain. George Hunsinger highlights this ambiguity:

What is important to note is that the primary warrant for seeing
Jesus as the unsubstitutable ascriptive subject of the gospel narratives
is [in and after the 'Literal Reading' essay] said to be a matter of
'traditional consensus' among Christians regarding the 'literal sense'
rather than, as before, a matter of formal literary structure. What

remains perplexing, however, is just how Frei thinks text and
tradition, formal narrative structure and communal *sensus literalis*,
are finally related in the justification of how the church reads
Scripture. (In other words, why does Frei suppose that the traditional
sensus literalis—its ascription of certain predicates to Jesus alone—is
still really justified, and to what extent is this justifiability thought to
depend on a description of the gospels' formal narrative structure?)[30]

This query points to one of the most important, elusive, and persistent concerns throughout Frei's work. Yet we may already be in the vicinity of an
answer to this question if we are cautious not to characterize Frei's construal
of the christological ascriptive reading as solely a product of traditional consensus. Traditional consensus is a factor, to be sure. However, I think we
would be mistaken to emphasize traditional consensus in isolation from, or
even as primary in relation to, Frei's emphasis upon the christological features of the text—as telling the story of, and thereby making certain claims
about, Jesus of Nazareth.

In the "Literal Reading" essay Frei claims that it was not "logically
necessary" that the literal sense took on the role as the plain or obvious
reading. He writes:

Interpretive traditions of religious communities tend to reach a
consensus on certain central texts. We have noted that the literal
reading of the gospel stories was the crucial instance of this
consensus in the early church. What is striking about this is that the
"literal" reading in this fashion became the normative or "plain"
reading of the texts. There is no a priori reason why the "plain" reading
could not have been "spiritual" in contrast to "literal," and certainly the
temptation was strong. The identification of the plain with the literal
sense was not a logically necessary development, but it did begin with
the early Christian community and was perhaps unique to Christianity.
The creed, "rule of faith" or "rule of truth" which governed the
Gospels' use in the church asserted the primacy of their literal sense.
Moreover, it did this right from the beginning in the ascriptive even
more than the descriptive mode. That "Jesus"—not someone else or
nobody in particular—is the subject, the agent, and patient of these
stories is said to be their crucial point, and the description of events,
sayings, personal qualities, and so forth, become literal by being
firmly predicated of him. Not until the Protestant Reformation is the
literal sense understood as authoritative—because perspicuous—in
its own right, without authorization from the interpretive tradition.[31]

Some readers take Frei here to mean that the priority of the literal sense resulted from the habits of reading the community happened to adopt or find themselves caught up in. In my view, such a reading of this passage renders one-dimensional what is, in fact, a multifaceted position that entails the inter- wovenness of several strands of normative constraint (though, admittedly, these separate strands do tend to get tangled or obscured in Frei's writing). Other readers suggest that the above passage reflects the fact that Frei did not engage the details of the process by which the literal sense became primary. On this reading, Frei was not concerned with *why* or *how* the church estab- lished the literal sense as plain, such critics say, but only *that* it did. He was, rather, singly concerned with how the contemporary church should correct its scriptural practices given that some sense has been established.[32] But I do not find this characterization of Frei exactly correct either. In my judgment, Frei's remarkably dense set of claims move beyond the limits of both these charac- terizations. My purpose in the remainder of this section is to unpack and sort through the implications of these claims. This will require, first, brief atten- tion to the complex interrelation of text and tradition out of which the rule of faith emerged.[33]

Frei says that the early identification of the literal sense as plain was not a logically necessary development. At the same time, his appeal to the "ruled reading" of the ancient church in the above passage suggests that he recog- nized that this development was neither arbitrary nor accidental. Identification of the literal reading as plain or obvious emerged, as he says, "right from the beginning" from the type of "ruled use" that was central to the identity of this community—reading that would come to be understood as governed by "the creed, 'rule of faith' or 'rule of truth.'"

Historically, the "rule of faith" emerged as a formal principle for scriptural reading, teaching, and worship near the end of second century with St. Irenaeus (c. 180). It coincided with the formalization of the Christian New Tes- tament, though the writings collected therein were known to Christians prior to the end of the first century.[34] Rowan Greer refers to the rule as an "authori- tative summary" of the apostolic faith (as it was preserved in their authoritative writings and teaching)—"a kind of creed, [that] outlines the theological story that finds its focus in the incarnate Lord."[35] The rule was derived from apostolic proclamation and "prepared the material for the future Apostles' Creed." Ire- naeus described it as the "condensation of Scripture."[36]

To describe the rule of faith as the "condensation of Scripture" is to recog- nize it as emerging from the story of Jesus itself—that is, from the *Geschichte* (history/narrative) of Christ as handed down in the apostolic tradition (writing, teaching, preaching, catechesis, and liturgy).[37] While Irenaeus explicitly formulated the rule as a response to the Gnostic controversies of the second century, its emergence also reflected the positive theological developments of the early church communities. It represented the apostolic tradition coming to terms with the questions and concerns with which it found itself confronted. Rowan Greer explains:

> [F]or the early church the chief question was, who is Christ? At one level, the answer to this question involves the doctrinal development of the early councils and the dogmas of the Trinity and of Christ's person. But at another level, the answer involves what Christ has done. And so the meaning of salvation and its implications for the Christian life were a part of discovering Christ's identity.[38]

The accounts of "what Christ has done"—and thus, who Christ was—were transmitted in and through evangelical witness and apostolic proclamation. In fact, "apostolicity" became the criterion by which writings were included in the New Testament.[39] This criterion was less about what we moderns call the "historical verifiability" of the accounts (though they did not preclude such concerns) than whether or not the writing conformed to "what the church came to regard as a true understanding of Christ."[40] While the rule emerged from the theological life of the church, it was not simply the result of the accruing consensus in that community. The rule derived its authority from the truth of the apostolic witness which accorded with the claims of Scripture.[41]

Where, we should ask, does Frei's discussion of the literal sense stand in relation to this development? In particular, we must ask how his claim that the ancient church's taking the literal sense as plain was not logically necessary or determined on an a priori basis. At one level, Frei's claim is a counterfactual consideration. That is, counterfactually speaking, when it came to the emergence of the church's recognition of the literal sense as plain or obvious—the obvious things about the text from which interpretation and application begin— things might have gone differently. This is as obvious as noting that the practices and understandings unfolded as a sequence of historically contingent developments.[42] "It is no exaggeration to say that Christian attitudes toward Scripture remain obscure and confused until the time of Irenaeus," Greer explains.[43] Childs adds that "Scripture did not fall from heaven, but arose within the bosom of the community of faith, shaped by its usage in worship, preaching, and catechesis."[44] I take Frei's point to acknowledge the historical situatedness of the reading practices of the community of faith.

And yet, at the same time, Frei's discussion indicates his awareness that the normative priority of the literal sense was, as a matter of historical fact, a complex process of emergence. While there was great diversity of views and

contingency in the process of development, the emergence of positive orienting norms was not coincidental in much the same way that the formation of
the scriptural canon was not, as Childs argues, a "haphazard growth."[45] Frei's
claim that this development was not "logically necessary" does not implicate
him in the claim that the primacy of the literal sense resulted by sheer luck or
the community's arbitrary preference to "opt for" one sense over another. In
fact, this complex, historically contingent process was predicated upon object-
oriented theological witness, discernment, and dispute.[46] These disputes
entailed questions about canonicity (which writings ought to be included) and
questions about how the church ought to read and interpret the writings of
Scripture that were incorporated.[47] Writings were included in virtue of telling
truly who Christ is, in part, by witnessing to what Christ has done and said (the
criterion of "apostolicity").

Irenaeus derived the *regula fidei* from the apostolic witness in accordance
with the contents of Scripture. It formally articulates the norms implicit in the
practices constitutive of the community—not just on the basis of what they are
but on the basis of what they should be in virtue of the constraints exerted by
the apostolic witness and the contents of Scripture.[48] Once derived, this formal-
ized rule pointed back to Scripture as a heuristic guide for reading and interpretation, illustrating what Hunsinger calls a "doctrinal feedback loop."
Engaging the biblical stories presents the point of departure (*explicatio*). Faith-
grasped meditation and critical reflection upon those stories (*meditatio*) affords
the occasion to derive second-order articulations from the story—doctrines in
some cases, creedal statements in others. Creedal or doctrinal derivations, in
turn, influence and inform further reading and interpretations of the stories
that first gave rise to them. Again, they can function "regulatively"—as pointers
or heuristic aids for further reading—or "constitutively," "as legitimate exten-
sions and clarifications of the knowledge of faith" and in the form of propositional truth claims.[49] At the same time, faith-grasped meditation upon the
stories issues in various practical implications, impelling believers to act (*applicatio*) in ways that also feed back into their further engagements with scriptural
stories and claims.

Recall that Frei consistently asserted that deriving doctrines and formu-
lating creeds is not a task of distilling the essence or kernel of truth from the
story. As such, the doctrine (or rule, or creed) ought not be taken as the meaning
or moral of the story. It is, rather, the story that is the meaning of the doctrine
(or rule, or creed).[50] In other words, Frei saw the biblical narratives as orienting
both doctrinal and interpretive endeavors.[51] In other words, Frei's account of
the church's recognition of the literal sense as plain—and its institution of this
in the rule of faith—does not alleviate this process of constraints exerted by

what the accounts of Jesus portrayed and how they portrayed it. In fact, Frei indicates quite the opposite.

Specifically, Frei addresses two features of the process by which the literal sense emerged as primary in the ancient church, both of which are consistent with the background that I have set in the preceding paragraphs. First, in distinguishing itself from the rabbinic tradition (for which cultic and moral regulations were "relatively autonomous" from narrative biblical texts), the Christian tradition derived the meaning of any such regulations (Frei mentions "the sacraments, the place of the 'law' in Christian life, the love commandment") "directly from its sacred story," by which he means directly from "the life, teachings, death, and resurrection of Jesus the Messiah." The accounts of Jesus' life, death, and resurrection (around which the tradition coalesced) exerted "a unifying force and a prescriptive character in both the New Testament and the Christian community."[52] What resulted was a "largely but not wholly informal" set of parameters that marked out the spaces within which interpretations could arise and contend. Frei identifies the minimum parameters of the literal sense in the form of three roughly hewn guidelines:

> First, Christian reading of Christian Scriptures must not deny the
> literal ascription to Jesus, and not to any other person, event, time or
> idea, of those occurrences, teachings, personal qualities and religious
> attributes associated with him in the stories in which he plays a part,
> as well as in the other New Testament writings in which his name is
> invoked. . . . Second, no Christian reading may deny either the unity
> of the Old and New Testaments or the congruence (which is not by
> any means the same as literal identity) of that unity with the
> ascriptive literalism of the Gospel narratives. Third, any readings not
> in principle in contradiction with these two rules are permissible,
> and two of the obvious candidates would be the various sorts of
> historical-critical and literary readings.[53]

Frei points out, secondly, that it was because of the centrality of the story of Jesus that the tradition came to assign normative primacy to the literal sense in its scriptural practices. Other senses (tropological, allegorical, and anagogical) acquired their legitimacy because the literal sense had priority. Frei gestured toward the allegorical reading of Jesus' parable of the Good Samaritan (Luke 10:25–37) as an example. This parable (and others) were interpreted allegorically and thus were taken to refer spiritually to various types, and even to Jesus himself. And then Frei adds "but this could only be done because the story of Jesus itself was taken to have a literal or plain meaning: He was the Messiah, and the fourfold storied depiction in the gospels, especially of his passion and resurrection, was the enacted form of his identity as Messiah."[54]

Why did the community take this story in this way? Wolterstorff ascribes to Frei the claim that the literal sense was taken as basic because it was in some way more beneficial for the community than other senses.[55] But Frei does not say this. He says, rather, that "the singular agent enacting the unity of human finitude and divine infinity, Jesus of Nazareth, is taken to be itself the ground, guarantee, and conveyance of the truth of the depicted enactment."[56] In other words, a precondition for the community's consensus that the literal sense ought to be plain was that the text's literal account ascribes the predicates that it does just to the person of Jesus. Because of this, these accounts could be recognized as portraying the truth about Jesus in accord with the apostolic witness. The primacy of the literal sense, Frei wrote elsewhere, recognizes that these stories are adequate to portray this truth. It recognizes "the fitness and congruence of the 'letter' to be the channel of the spirit."[57] So, there is far more at stake here that what the Christian community perceived to be beneficial, useful, or how the community decided to use the biblical text.

IV. The Text as Normative Constraint

Of course, Hunsinger's query above presses the extent to which Frei really let go of "essential underlying conceptual patterns" upon which *meditatio* reflects. This concern is particularly relevant to Frei's account of the literal ascription of certain wholly unique predicates to Jesus of Nazareth. How do such claims on behalf of the narrative structure of the text either cohere with or give way to Frei's claims about the consensus of the community in taking the literal sense as plain? To what extent do "formal narrative structures" warrant predicate ascription to Jesus in his later work?

Well, considerably so in my judgment, though in a sense far less fraught with theoretical baggage than his earlier claims that these stories present instances of "realistic narrative." Scripture does, after all, come to us in the form of texts and, in many instances, as stories. This text and the stories it portrays are normatively constrained and enabled by all the grammatical, syntactical, and literary-literal constructions that constitute being a "text" and, in this case, "story." Moreover, Frei continued in his latest writings to draw the analogy between the plain sense of biblical narratives and the form of realistic novel—what was earlier a full-fledged identification of the Gospels as "realistic narratives." This time he made this comparison without deference to, or invocation of, realistic narrative as characteristic of the "formal literary structure" of which the gospel narratives represent an instance.[58] The relation becomes analogical in his later thinking. Frei wrote:

> There really is an analogy between the Bible and a novel writer who says something like this: I mean what I say. It's as simple as that: the text means what it says. Now that doesn't mean that there aren't metaphors there. It doesn't mean that I take every account literally. But it does mean that I cannot take the biblical story, the gospel story especially, in separation from its being the identification, the literal identification of someone identified as Jesus of Nazareth. It's not about something else, not about somebody else.[59]

Such claims emphasize that the literal ascription of predicates to the person of Christ is warranted not merely in virtue of the community's consensus that these are the predicates belonging to Christ. They are warranted because these predicates of the person are ascribed by the literal sense of the text. This is, among other things, "what the text says." Hence, while the literal sense came to be taken as "plain" for the Christian tradition as a historical matter of fact, it was not the tradition's endorsement of it as such that made the literal sense literal. The literal sense could conduct endorsement of it as the plain sense because of what the literal sense, as such, portrayed, namely, the person and work of Jesus Christ in its full significance.

In encounter with the accounts of Christ's death and resurrection, the believer "discovers the very capacity to subordinate himself to it," Frei wrote. In this way, the witness of Scripture constrained and shaped its readers, the community of all who followed Jesus at a distance, of which it is the fount and origin. "In interpreting conceptually and existentially, we are governed first by the story and, in the second place, by the way it functions in the Christian religion," he wrote.[60] This claim is crucial for understanding Frei's account. We are *first* governed by the story and secondly by the function of that story in the Christian religion. This is a distinct claim of proper order, which gives priority to the stories because they witness to Jesus Christ. And yet, Frei sought to make this claim without smuggling back in a naive conception of "the text in itself" or the claim that the *sensus literalis* manifests an underlying essence (giving rise to the bibliolatry that Frei guarded against).[61] Here we have arrived at some of the most mind-bending claims in all of Frei's corpus.

As confusing as such claims appear, in fact they bear considerable consistency with the scriptural practices of the early church communities and the derivation of the rule of faith as a directive for literal reading as plain. On one hand, Greer points out, Irenaeus is the figure most responsible for formalizing the *regula fidei* as an interpretive key derived from the prevailing normative currents emerging from the apostolic tradition (including, among other things, that the literal sense of Scripture is basic for the church). At the same time, he adds:

> [I]t is in another sense Scripture itself that supplies the categories in which the principle of interpretation is expressed. Text and interpretation are like twin brothers; one can scarcely tell the one from the other. What emerges is an unbroken dialogue of discourse between the letter and the spirit, and between the word and the experience of those hearing it.[62]

The challenge for those of us grappling with these questions on the far side of the story that Frei told in *The Eclipse of Biblical Narrative* is to think of these distinct dimensions seamlessly, yet without simply conflating the two or collapsing one into the other. This tends to be exceedingly difficult to do. We find it natural (if not necessary) to press Frei, as Hunsinger does above, about how precisely "text and tradition, formal narrative structure and communal *sensus literalis*, are finally related in the justification of how the church reads Scripture"? Each appears to compete with the other for normative priority. Positing the story as basic implies a self-identifying given and all the philosophical liabilities that follow such a foundationalist claim. To emphasize the tradition situatedness of the process, by contrast, appears to slide down the slope of communal use (either as a conscious decision made by the community or as community's habits happened to emerge). This is the apparent dilemma, and we want Frei to answer it.[63]

I am suggesting that the *sensus literalis* in Frei's account is not simply a feature inherent in a certain kind of literary narrative of which the gospel accounts present an instance. Neither is it simply a function of what the Christian community takes the text to mean. And yet, if it is both social-practical and yet theologically unique, how are we to characterize the *sensus literalis*? In other words, if it is not a simple *property* of the text nor merely a *function* of consensus, how best to articulate these claims? Here, again, I think we might find it illuminating to turn to recent pragmatist philosophical insights that have expanded upon similar claims in ways that help clarify this move and illuminate its potential significance. I aim to theorize only in passing, however—just enough to make sense of how Frei might cogently hold together the various strands of his account. To that end, in the remaining pages of this chapter, I attempt a philosophical redescription of the apparently contradictory set of claims set forth above. In the final chapter, I apply this redescription more explicitly to Frei's account of the literal sense as plain and fully trace out its theological implications.

V. "I Sing of Words and the World": Pragmatic Inferentialism as a Redescriptive Lens

Robert Brandom explicates Wittgenstein's conception of "meaning as use" at the level of concept application— that "the use of concepts determines their content, that is, that concepts can have no content apart from that conferred on them by their use."[64] But just as he forwards this thesis, Brandom cautiously sidesteps reducing content to use by drawing a distinction between conceptual *force* and conceptual *content*. He points out that, in using a concept, one commits one's self to be bound by a rule—namely, the normative constraint of the concept at hand (applying the concept "East" precludes the simultaneous application of the concept "West," just as it implicates other concepts—say, "cardinal direction"). What makes this rule authoritative is one's *taking it* to be authoritative and thus binding oneself by it. "The authority of the self-binder governs the *force* that attaches to a certain rule," Brandom writes. "[I]t is endorsement by the individual that makes the rule a rule for or binding on that individual." But this *force* is analytically distinct from its *content*:

> [T]hat authority [the concept's binding authority that ensues from a user committing herself to be bound by it] must not be taken to extend also to the *content* of the rule; to what is and is not correct according to the rule one has endorsed. For if it does, then one has not by one's endorsement really bound oneself by a rule or norm at all. What is chosen—the rule or law I bind myself to by applying a concept—must have a certain independence of the choosing of it.[65]

Brandom's contention is that, while social practices disclose the world, the world they disclose exerts a material counterthrust upon those practices. The world disclosed by our practices simultaneously shapes and forms, limits and enables, those social practices. The world's material and empirical counterthrust partially constitutes our practices. In other words, there is more to discursive practices than the normative leverage created by the inferential proprieties internal to those practices. Part of Brandom's innovation lies in bringing to light a *noninferential* normative dimension of our practices without forsaking the fundamentally social-practical character of the explanation, and doing so without smuggling back into the account a notion of "the thing in itself."

On Brandom's account, the meaning of assertions is contingent upon how one ought to use them in a given time and place in light of the socially instituted norms of concept use that constitute language use. As I read Frei above, analogously, participants in the practice of reading and consulting Christian

Scripture hold one another accountable to the norms constitutive of that practice and not merely community consensus about what the text means. This insight generates a conception of objectivity—that the norms constitutive of practices exert constraints upon what can count as a legitimate, acceptable, or appropriate performance of that practice. We have seen, however, that Frei encountered difficulty in clearly holding two sets of normative criteria for assessment together—traditional consensus with object-directed and practical constraints. This difficulty might account for the ambiguity in his description of the *sensus literalis* "not only as use-in-context but as unity of grammatical/syntactical sense and signified subject" and elsewhere his acknowledgement of the constraining features of the scriptural text while asserting that the concept "scripture" has no meaning apart from its use in church contexts.[66]

Brandom's account of the empirical and practical dimensions of discursive practices might help to relieve this ambiguity. It may help further illuminate Lovibond's point above, namely, that recognition of social practices as basic does not render the community's consensus the final court of appeal. Brandom proposes that we think of "the way things are" and "social practices" as seamless. The idea is basically this: discursive practices "disclose" or "make sense of" the world by conferring conceptual content upon that world. The practices in which we make sense of our world confer the cognitive content in and with which practitioners hold each other accountable. The contents of our assertions about that world are accountable to the norms implicit in these practices. But, says Brandom, our inferential practices are not only accountable to the recognition of our fellow concept users nor only the norms constitutive of the practice in question. We are also accountable to the ways things are in the world that those practices disclose. In other words, the material dimension of those practices practically and empirically constrains them. And this must factor into our assessments of our own (and our fellows') commitments and entitlements in giving and asking one another for reasons.

The key move here is to avoid thinking of practices and world as separate things. This move sidesteps the presupposition of "the thing in itself" as basic—the claim that our commitments are accountable to how things are in some sense apart from, or regardless of, our practical comprehension of them. In the case of the plain sense of Scripture, for instance, norms implicit in scriptural practices hold even obvious reading of the text—readings that have become second nature—accountable to the object around which the practices are oriented. This form of normative appraisal assesses appropriateness by asking questions like "Was all available evidence taken into account? Were the inferences made good ones, as far as the practitioners know? In general, did the speaker follow the rules of the game, so as not to be blameworthy for producing the assertion?"[67]

To say that the world is part and parcel of conceptual (paradigmatically, linguistic) practices is to assert that "discursive practices incorporate actual things":

> They are solid—as one might say, corporeal: they involve actual bodies, including both our own and others (animate and inanimate) we have practical and empirical dealings with. They must not be thought of as hollow, waiting to be filled up by things; they are not thin and abstract, but as concrete as the practice of driving nails with a hammer. (They are our means of access to what is abstract—among other things—not its product.) According to such a construal of practices, it is wrong to contrast discursive practices with a world of facts and things outside it, modeled on the contrast between words and the things they refer to. It is wrong to think of facts and the objects they involve as constraining linguistic practice from the outside—not because they do not constrain it but because of the mistaken picture of facts and objects as outside it. What determinate practices a community has depends on what the facts are and on what objects they are actually practically involved with, to begin with, through perception and action. The way the world is, constrains proprieties of inferential, doxastic, and practical commitment in a straightforward way from *within* those practices.[68]

The central point I am borrowing from Brandom here is fairly straightforward. It is that the material features in, through, and with which discursive practices confer conceptual content exert a counterthrust upon those sense-making practices. These practices are "solid (even lumpy)" because they are partially constituted by "the world," and the particular details of that "solidity" or "lumpiness" inform the normativity of those practices. "[O]ur discursive practices could not be what they are if the nonlinguistic facts were different," writes Brandom. "For those practices are not things, like words conceived as marks and noises, that are specifiable independently of the objects they deal with and the facts they make it possible to express. Discursive practices essentially involve to-ing and fro-ing with environing objects in perception and action."[69]

Brandom clarifies how this structural feature of discursive practices is due, in part, to their solidity. Conceptual contents "outrun the community's capacity to apply them correctly and to appreciate the correct consequences of their application."[70] In other words, the community can be wrong about what it takes to be the case, or even in how it takes things to be the case. As Brandom puts it:

[O]ur practice puts us in touch with facts and the concepts that
articulate them—we grasp them. But what we grasp by our practices
extends beyond the part we have immediate contact with (its handles,
as it were); that is why what we grasp is not transparent to us, why we
can be wrong even about its individuation. How the world really is
determines what we have gotten a hold of. . . . In this way the
proprieties governing the application of a community's concepts
are in part determined (according to the interpreter) by the actual
properties of and facts concerning the things the linguistic
practitioners are perceiving, acting on, and so talking about—which
are just features of their practice.[71]

With these claims Brandom confirms Lovibond's derivation of objectivity from
normative constraints implicit in (and constitutive of) practices in her reading
of Wittgenstein. Yet Brandom's account accentuates the empirical and practical
constraints exerted by causal features of discursive practices. He highlights
how appraisal "swings free of the attitudes of the practitioners [dispositional
factors which are, themselves, products of acculturation into social practices]
and looks, instead, to the subject matter about which claims are made for the
applicable norms," Brandom writes. "Here the central question is: Is the claim
correct in the sense that things really are as it says they are?"[72]

How might these insights help Frei forward a coherent account of the plain
sense that is at once contextually specific and yet reflects the textually articulated centrality of Christ? To say that the plain sense is a "discursive object" in
Brandom's sense clarifies at once its irreducibly social-practical character, and
that this text presents a state of affairs (the ink on the page; the grammar and
syntax of the sentence; the patterns arising from the interaction of the characters, circumstances, and themes of its narrative shape). With reference to Frei's
account we can say that our discursive practices are as solid as opening a book,
turning its pages, making sense of the syntax and grammar of the sentences
printed thereupon, grasping the subject signified thereby, asking if we agree on
what we find there, and discovering the patterns there to one another. These
are all part and parcel of the socially situated, discursive practices of reading
and consulting texts.[73]

From this vantage point, recognizing the plain sense of Scripture is neither
positing a *property* essential to the text nor solely a *product* of the discursive
practices of the community. Recognizing the plain sense is, rather, a *propriety*
in a set of communally situated uses of that text—one of the proprieties constitutive of the practice of consulting Scripture which uniquely orients Christian
communities. Such proprieties are simultaneously instituted linguistically and

nonlinguistically. And yet, the world and objects can be thought to "stand apart" from the discursive practices that disclose them only in a derivative sense. They are instituted "nonlinguistically" in the sense that the "world" and "objects" empirically and practically constrain the discursive activities of practitioners that institute those proprieties.[74] "The world" and "objects" are "conceptually articulated states of affairs" of which we discursive practitioners have a "conceptually articulated grasp."[75]

Borrowing from these terms, we might begin to clarify how the literal sense comes to be taken as plain and how, as such, it unifies text and context in precisely the way Frei sought to articulate, though with limited success.[76] The witness of the scriptural text to Christ's death and resurrection continues to take full and center stage. It, at once, precipitates from "object-directed," propriety-constituted social practice and provides the primary normative orientation for that practice. "The text is not inert but exerts a pressure of its own on the inquiring reader," as Frei put it.[77] And yet the reader, Frei would want to add, "is bound to bring his or her own pre-understanding and interests to the reading."[78] This relation is "asymptotic":

> In the self-description of the Christian community, the function of
> "Scripture" as a concept—it does not contain a "meaning" apart from
> interpretation or use in the Church—is to shape and constrain the
> reader, so that he or she discovers the very capacity to subordinate
> himself to it. In other words, the least that we can say is something
> that must be taken very seriously within the community, no matter
> how philosophers may view it: there can be no nonresidual reading,
> no complete "interpretation" of a text, not so much because
> interpreters' intellectual, moral, and cultural locations vary, but
> because a "good enough" text, to use an expression of Frank Kermode,
> has the power to resist; it has a richness and complexity that act on
> the reader. When we disagree in our interpretations of a text, it is well
> to check on what each of us is doing, but it would be silly to do that
> and not pay attention to the features of the text or act as though it had
> none or as though they varied simply as our reading of them varied.[79]

On one hand, here Frei asserts that the very concept of "Scripture" has meaning insofar as it finds use within the social practices of the church. And yet, he is clear in this passage that Scripture's "meaning"— the content of Scripture— does not reduce to use. Rather, here we see the interwovenness of normative constraints in Frei's account of scriptural practice. The conceptual independence of Scripture's content entails the accountability of readers to "the features of the text" as well as to each other vis-à-vis the features of the text and the normative constraints of the practice. Because of this "the text resists"; its "richness and complexity" (insofar as it has these) "act upon the reader." But this relation of reader presupposition and textual constraints is "asymptotic"—the reader comes to learn how to subordinate his preunderstandings and interests (which he cannot altogether forgo) to Scripture. This is a feature of the *sensus literalis*—"it bends to its own ends whatever general categories it shares—as indeed it has to share—with other kind of reading (e.g., "meaning," "truth," as well as their relation)."[80]

From the developmental perspective of Frei's work that I have been stressing throughout this book, the above passage from *Types* demonstrates an expansion to include an increasingly articulate and self-reflective awareness of several claims that Frei first set out in his "Remarks in Connections with a Theological Proposal" of 1967. There he claimed that "the constancy of the meaning of the text is the text and not the similarity of its *effect* on the life-perspectives of succeeding generations."[81] Frei's earlier formulation reflects a basic intuition that bears mature philosophical and theological fruit in the above passage from *Types*. That the gospel narratives portray the story of Jesus is a feature of this text that is, on the whole, perspicuous enough to conduct agreement—to have become a central trait of and orienting constraint upon—the various forms that the "plain sense" has taken.

Historically, plain reading was oriented by, and ought now to be oriented by, according to Frei, "the literal, ascriptive sense which serves simply to answer the question Who is Jesus in this text?" This is a claim in *Types* with which Frei brings his readers—now far more critically and self-reflectively—back to one of the primary concerns that animated *The Identity of Jesus Christ*.[82] In this later articulation the literal sense replaces the category of "realistic narrative" as the mode of its witness to Christ's identity.[83] Frei claims that the plain sense "manifests no underlying essence." But he adds, nonetheless, that this text depicts a theme "through the interaction of character and circumstances" as well as its unity with the grammar and syntax. As his later articulation would have it, the literal sense "comprehends together under 'literal' both the grammatical/syntactical sense and the storied sense, 'literal' thus meaning both syntactical and *literary*-literal (in contrast to allegorical) use."[84]

Recognizing the plain sense as a "discursive object" does not mean that it is a wholly indeterminate construct that awaits its meaning to be inscribed by being "taken as" something by someone or some community of readers. Nor is it simply a property of the structures of the text in abstraction from contexts of use. Rather, it is an object-oriented *propriety* that is partly constitutive of the very practices of "taking as" and "treating as." The plain sense is constrained by normative agreements in practitioners acting at the level of their practices of reading and consulting texts that have come, for example, to be codified in the forms of grammar and syntax. These norms internal to practices constrain practitioners' "taking as."[85] People do things with texts, and what a text is like (part and parcel to textual practices) empirically and practically constrains what people do with it.[86] Conversely, that people do things with texts places constraints upon what texts can be, and in fact are. From this vantage point, the literal sense is an object-oriented propriety of use that outruns—and thereby constrains—the dispositions of community members to recognize it as "plain." The gospel accounts exert a counterthrust upon practices of taking and treating those stories.

As Frei conceived them, these stories are where participants in these practices begin. How do they come to be central in this way? The plain sense of Scripture for both Frei and Tanner accrues, at least in part, from communal conventions of appealing to, and customary uses of, the scriptural text—"what a participant in the community automatically or naturally takes a text to be saying on its face insofar as he or she has been socialized in a community's conventions for reading the text as Scripture."[87] Socialization into these conventions engender community members' dispositions to take as obvious "what the text is about" and "the story it tells," against which further deliberate interpretations of the text will thrust.[88] As the plain sense is constrained by the norms implicit in the communal practices that are already up and running (permitting objectivity in the sense that Lovibond and Brandom share), so the plain sense constrains which inferential moves from it can be valid and which cannot. As such, these textual practices are "object directed." In other words, "they involve attentiveness to something being investigated as well as disciplined avoidance of wishful thinking, rationalization, and related intrusions of 'merely subjective' factors."[89] This conception of "object-directedness" helps to account for Frei's account of the traditional recognition of the literal sense as the plain sense.

Disposition-producing practices constitutive of this particular community (or range of communities) come to disclose the plain sense of the text as simply a matter of common sense—'immediately' or 'noninferentially.' So construed, recognition of the plain sense of the text comes to be "inferentially articulated but noninferentially elicited."[90] That is, recognizing the plain sense is a "noninferential" move into a practice that is basically inferential. In other words, as the "fount and origin" of that world of discourse that Frei saw as the social-practical conception of the church, the literal sense manifests the person of Christ to believers simply by narrating the events of Jesus' life, death, and resurrection.

Of course, Frei found himself drawn toward Barth's radical claim that it is, in fact, the biblical instances that portray the true and proper sense of the terms and practices that occur there. They all properly and originally belong to God in the first place. And Frei suggests as much when he claims that Scripture "must in principle embrace the experience of any present age and reader" in virtue of orienting the believer's "disposition, his actions and passions, the shape of his own life as well as that of his era's events as figures in that storied world."[91] To be caught up through faith into this world of discourse oriented by Scripture is to be grasped by certain storytellings and utterances as proclamation, instances of the otherwise ordinary practices of eating and drinking sacramental acts of communion, and discursive occasions of promising and commanding God's unique self-manifestation and claim upon the world and lives of God's creatures. We have here, in effect, the uniquely Christian set of social institutions and practices that constitute Christian community as a social organism.

Conclusion

Frei sought to articulate the literal and plain senses of Scripture in a way that unified text and context—Word and Spirit. The reading above accounts for the christological emphasis characteristic of his work in *Identity* and for the expansion of his focus to include the impact of context and readers' preunderstandings upon the practice of scriptural exegesis. I made the case above that Frei's account of the literal sense neither renders it simply a product of communal consensus nor posits a textual essentialism. I have attempted to demonstrate, nonetheless, that Frei's treatment of the literal sense is consistent with its development as a practice and formal articulation in the rule of faith in the context of the ancient church. Frei had keen insights into this approach to Scripture and spent much of his career searching and testing means by which he might bring those insights to full articulation. The challenge was how to think seamlessly of Scripture and tradition, Word and Spirit, without either simply conflating these or collapsing them into one another. I have drawn upon Brandom and Lovibond as fairly recent developments bearing a Wittgensteinian trajectory that might clarify some of Frei's efforts. My aim is to show that, from a philosophical perspective, it is possible that the various threads of normative constraint that stand in tension in Frei's description can be conceived as the whole cloth of scriptural practices.

Several questions still need to be addressed. The most pressing of these concerns is the historicizing effect that appears to result from an account of scriptural revelation that is articulated in contextually situated, social, and practical terms. If I have succeeded demonstrating how we might conceive of text and context as seamless in social-practical redescription, are we still in a position to accommodate the radical ingression of God's revelation in and through the scriptural witness? Is the scriptural witness understood in social-practical terms sufficient to account for God's revelation in history?

My reading of Frei as holding in tandem the basic insights of Barth's theology and the pragmatist themes in Wittgenstein's work stands or falls with this question. If the social-practical account cannot accommodate the otherness and priority of God's revelatory act, then the purely anthropological component of the account will exert normative control. In the following chapter I demonstrate why I think Frei's social-practical account does, in fact, account for the radical otherness and ingression of God's revelation in history. Moreover, I show how it is precisely the turns in his account that accommodate God's revelation and that can assuage lingering suspicions of "scriptural foundationalism" leveled at Frei's project.

8

"Christ Called Himself Truth, Not Custom"

—Tertullian, De virginibus velandis I, I, *CChr* 2:208.

John Webster has expressed deep suspicions about the kind of social-practical account of scriptural practices that I attributed to Frei in the preceding chapters. He writes:

> If recent essays in ecclesial hermeneutics have done much to draw discussion of scripture and its interpretation away from the generic and a-social and steer it towards the Christianly specific, they have nevertheless customarily lacked an eschatology of sufficient strength to resist the naturalizing tendencies of the notions of virtue and social practice.[1]

In the last chapter I argued that Frei's attention to contexts of use and tradition does not hinder its theological uniqueness or the christological irreducibility of his account of the literal sense. The broader concerns raised by Webster's foregoing remark remain to be addressed. Does Frei's increased explicitness about the social and practical account of Christian scriptural practices risk "naturalizing" God's revelation? Does an account of God's revelation as historically immanent, social, and practical render it so dependent upon human concepts and concept use as to anthropocentrize it? Is it possible to acknowledge the inescapability of culture and language, and the social-practical dimension of scriptural uses in church contexts in particular, and yet still maintain the prevenience of God's revelation? In this chapter I will propose an answer to these questions by way of redescribing Frei's claim that the biblical narratives *embrace* the "experience of any present age and reader."[2]

I. Treasure in Earthen Vessels

Frei used the phrase "scriptural world of discourse" to refer to all the embodied and historically situated social practices that constitute the life of the church. One of his basic claims was that, within the practices of consulting, meditating upon, interpreting, disputing, and applying the discursive inferences and implications extending from Scripture's accounts, the concrete set of characters and events that the narrative depictively renders is, in an important sense, observable.[3] Frei cast this claim against the backdrop of the three-phase engagement of Scripture as it was commonly understood prior to the Enlightenment—*explicatio, meditatio,* and *applicatio.* In the preceding chapters we saw how this multidimensional conception of engaging Scripture formally articulates what Frei described as "ruled reading" in the Christian tradition. We saw, further, that this approach models the process by which the rule of faith and eventually the creeds were derived and then further constrained and enabled scriptural interpretation and contestation. In the pages that follow I draw upon my philosophical redescription of the literal reading in the previous chapter in order to explicate how this three-level process might account for the distinctively christological character Scripture's "embrace" of the present age and reader.

Frei described *explicatio* as the level of reading and listening to the basic *sensus* of the text—"the sheer retelling of the story or other texts, together with philosophical and other aids that go into that activity for the more technically trained."[4] *Explicatio* presents the moment of engagement with the biblical narrative by observing what is going on in the story. Events and claims that confront readers in the biblical narratives can be described as "embracing" them by eliciting normative attitudes and commitments that orient perception and understanding as well as serving as reasons for acting. Thus the entry level of "following the story" shades into (while remaining logically distinct from) the process of *meditatio,* the level at which those attitudes and commitments come to be formally articulate and refined. Barth described this moment as "the transition of what is said into the thinking of the reader or hearer."[5] The initial encounter is explicated and reflected upon by way of commentary, criticism, and deliberation.[6] The normative attitudes and commitments elicited in *explicatio* and explicated in *meditatio* exert certain logical and material implications that issue in *applicatio*—practical application.

What appears to be the "humdrum" following of the surface description and plot as the entryway into interpretation and practice exerts considerable normative sway in the Christian tradition. It both orients and circumscribes that tradition. "We are governed first by the story and, in the second place, by the way it functions in the Christian religion," Frei wrote, indicating that *meditatio* and *applicatio* are oriented by *explicatio*. This occurs in recognition of what Frei described as the "urging of the *sensus literalis* that between the Christian narrative and the interpreter there is the nexus of the common linguistic world, which is rendered by the diachronic, agential, i.e., narrative web of that world."[7] Those who believe and follow the scriptural witness to Christ find themselves grasped by and grafted onto the grace-initiated inferences and implications that extend from what these stories portray. Being so caught up shapes and constrains their practical attitudes, dispositions, and thus their actions. The stories elicit peculiarly constraining and enabling normative attitudes and thereby shape a new life—thus "embracing the experience of any present age and reader."[8]

Of course, engaging the *sensus* of the story does not occur in a vacuum. Charles Wood described the dimensions of this engagement in terms particularly influential upon Frei. "[T]he accurate explication of the verbal sense of a text depends upon our own mastery of the concepts it involves," Wood wrote. At the same time, he added, "our mastery of those concepts is guided by the sense of the text which explication discloses." Wood continued:

> *Meditatio* is not an introspective venture carried out at a remove from the text. If it is to be the reader's "realization" of the text, which enables the reader not only to understand the text (i.e., fulfill the aim of *explicatio*) but also to understand through the text (i.e., to consider and embark upon *applicatio*), it must be controlled closely and constantly by the text.[9]

Consider, for example, how the scriptural stories express and portray God's commands and promises—at times in the forms of specific illocutionary acts of commanding and promising, and sometimes in virtue of their narrative shape of the stories. Both are discursive "motivating expressions" in that they elicit actions and activities from their readers. These presuppose that the practitioners in question have been acculturated into certain general inferential and linguistic practices, that is, that they have become sufficiently competent users of the "intralinguistic moves or 'logical grammar' of these expressions."[10] In other words, promises and commands exert the practical constraints that they do because the social practices in which they participate are already in place.

Discursive moves such as commanding and promising are not *sui generis* within Christian communities. They occur in the normative relations that obtain between mutually recognizing fellow language and concept users.[11] They must inform the reader's "preunderstanding" in order for recognition of these scriptural instances to occur in the first place. This insight would appear to vindicate Kelsey's claim that such discursive instances portrayed in the biblical writings—that *God* commands and promises—are not unique as such. They acquire uniqueness because they occur in the context of Christian *praxis*. As Kelsey put it, they "come to bear authoritatively on theology . . . only in the context of the intentional activities of individual persons and communities who understand themselves to be having their identities shaped in distinctively Christian ways."[12] This point brings us to the crux of Webster's concern with which I opened this chapter. Does the efficacy of God's narrated promises and commands depend upon the particular *praxis* of the Christian community that presupposes a general, nontheological account of social practices? More broadly, does the social-practical conception of the church, Scripture and theology that Frei offers "naturalize" God's revelation by making it contingent upon generic, human social practices? To answer this question it will help to look once again at the influence of Barth's work upon Frei.

Barth identified an uninvertible asymmetry between human promise- and command-making practices and the commands and promises of God. But this neither eliminated nor negated the sense-making efficacy of those human social practices in making sense of—rendering intelligible—God's promises and commands. In Barth's terms, these stories exhibit "coherent continuity that is expressed logically and grammatically" through hearing the words preached or narrated in Scripture.[13] Faith shares this basic awareness in common with unbelief of the basic perspicuity of the *sensus literalis*.

On this basis, for instance, Frei thought someone like Erich Auerbach could recognize and articulate with remarkable accuracy and elegance the peculiar, self-involving character of the claims made by these narratives without himself assenting to their force.[14] Barth's distinction between the "outer" and "inner" texts of Scripture, in effect, distinguishes between the social-practical givenness of writing, reading, and consulting the scriptural text on one hand and its mediation of the person of Christ to the recipient mode of faith effected by God's act of self-revelation on the other. The response of faith is distinguished by the Spirit-solicited assent to the truth of this *vox significans rem* in addition to the basic comprehension shared by readers of this text, believer and unbeliever alike.[15]

Discursive moves such as commanding and promising constitute, in part, the sense-making social practices in and through which fellow practitioners recognize God's commands and promises in Scripture. That these moves precipitate out of communal *praxis*, and thus make sense of instances of commanding and promising in Scripture, accounts for the intelligibility of that content. However, the *force* of those claims—the world-orienting uniqueness of the scriptural occurrences and claims that show up in virtue of communal *praxis*—is due to the fact that these narrated promises and commands are God's. It is God's act of revelation that accounts for the uniqueness that discursive moves such as God's promising and commanding acquire within the world of discourse, of which Scripture is the primary cause. In and through the scriptural accounts God takes up discursive moves such as promising and commanding and breaks and transforms them in order to manifest God's particularity through them. This occurs, as Frei put it, in "the coincidence of letter and spirit."[16] As such, common concepts and practices are "conscripted, broken and reformed" so as to become "serviceable for the depiction of God's unique particularity."[17] On this view, God's choice and use of human, sense-making social practices "allow our concepts to be interpreted by the particularity of God, not God by the particularity of our concepts."[18] As Barth put it, "God's true revelation comes from out of itself to meet what we can say with our human words and makes a selection from among them to which we have to attach ourselves in obedience."[19] Thus does the scriptural witness embrace the present and work-a-day world of the contemporary believer within history without reducing itself to a simply historical—or conventional—phenomenon.

In the case of scripturally conveyed promises and commands, God's use of these transforms the meaning of those institutions for believers by orienting their actions and understandings in ways that are unique in kind. God's commands impel and oblige believers to take action in the world in certain ways, hope for certain things, pray for certain kinds of intercession. God's promises in Scripture lead believers to understand themselves as participants in a certain kind of world, a world in which, for instance, the arc of the universe bends toward justice, or in which one's always partial acts of love can only be the responses to a Love that loved one first.[20]

In and through the Gospels' narrative rendering of the person and work of Christ, the otherwise ordinary speech acts of promising become "the unconditional offer of salvation which comes through God's grace."[21] And yet, this occurs not merely on the basis of a sequence of discrete, promissory speech acts strung together in a way that secondarily constitutes the story. These features of the story do not rely upon general theories about the nature of textual interpretation, speech acts, or promise-making *as such*. Rather, the story itself takes the shape of a promise. The form of the stories is a central way that God has used (and uses) Scripture to convey God's promises, both in the patterns these stories portray as well as specific assertions attributed to the characters and assertions made by authors. A central point behind Frei's use of "identifying descriptions" in *The Identity of Jesus Christ* was that, in the gospel accounts, God's promises come irreducibly in the form and content of the life, death, and resurrection of Jesus. Similarly, God's promises are conveyed throughout the Bible by portraying who God is, what God has done, as well as specific assertions attributable to God. To reduce these accounts to allegedly more basic components is to render them something other than what they are. As a result, any application of speech-act theory categories must remain delicate and piecemeal. It would need to be used for redescriptive purposes—to illuminate these more basic patterns rather than as a prefabricated theoretical framework that sets the terms of the engagement independently of, or antecedently to, engaging the stories.[22]

This approach refuses to confine God's role to that of "speaker." God's promising is portrayed in the "complex narrative structure" and often made explicit in doctrinal reflection and liturgical practice (*meditatio* and *applicatio*). On this basis, "Whenever words of pardon and absolution are spoken in Christ's name, believers recall the narrative scope of God's promises in Christ and become participants in the world that narrative depicts."[23] God's promise in the life, death, and resurrection of Christ "evokes the remembrance of God's promises to Israel, the fulfillment of those promises in Messiah's coming, the bestowing of the promised blessing and the renewal of the promise in forgiveness and justification, and the further promise of a final consummation in eternal life."[24] The world-orienting force of God's promise exerts itself through the practices that make up the life of the church and embrace the world of believers, reorienting all human acts of promising as figurations of God's promise.[25]

In this way, the scripturally oriented discursive practice of promising sheds some light on what Frei means in claiming that "we are embodied agents and understand what we do, suffer, and are in the contexts in which we are placed as the world is shaped upon and by us. In that way the gospel story and we ourselves inhabit the same kind of world."[26] While social practices permit scriptural analogies to God's internal being to show up as such, it is not simply this community's "taking as true" those representations narrated in Scripture that they reveal God. This account does not, in other words, "turn 'thus saith the Lord' into 'thus heareth the Man.'"[27] Rather, scriptural accounts analogically reveal God because God chooses these accounts, these claims and concepts. The promises and commands through which God manifests God's self in Scripture break in upon the historically situated social practices within which such things as commands and promises show up. We have this truth in earthen vessels. Insofar as these earthen vessels contain this truth, it is God's free and graceful election of these particular vessels—these practices, these concepts, these words.

II. On Scripture's "Speaking for Itself"

The account above is predicated upon the claim that in the literal sense the name and narrative of Christ allegedly "speaks for itself." This claim recalls the description of these stories as operating "noninferentially" in virtue of their uses in context and again raises the specter of "scriptural foundationalism."[28] As we saw in chapter 6, in epistemological circles the term "noninferential" is synonymous with "self-evidence," "immediacy," or "incorrigibility"—all descriptors used to characterize foundationalist epistemology. Claims for the scriptural text as the revelatory *fons et origo* of the Christian world of discourse— and as "speaking for itself"—might appear as assertions of self-evidence in a classically epistemological sense.[29] Drawing upon my earlier discussion of these points, we are now in a position to ask "Is it adequate to construe 'beginning with the plain sense' as a 'noninferential' transition into the practice of giving and asking for reasons about this text?" Clearly, reading a text appears to present a far more complicated activity than observing the happenings in one's immediate environment or acting in response to some chain of inferences. Moreover, if we do construe consulting the *sensus literalis* as a noninferential entry into discursive practices, do we not invite further charges of "scriptural foundationalism"?[30] Does Frei's appeal to the irreducibility of the biblical narratives simply replace "clear and distinct ideas" or "unmediated experience" with the scriptural text's self-presentation or, as Barth phrased it, "letting Scripture speak for itself"?

Jeffrey Stout provides an instructive example for answering these questions when he addresses the role of noninferential, normative attitudes in moral deliberation.[31] Taking up the debate between Thomas Paine and Edmund Burke about the relative merits and moral character of the French Revolution, Stout explains how prose and narrative accounts noninferentially elicit certain normative attitudes in their readers. Both Paine and Burke employed "observational criticism" at important points in their writings. Each was differently disposed to perceive and experience—and deliberate about—the events of the French Revolution. Each adopted opposing normative attitudes about what he saw and experienced. Each conveyed his moral experience in writing, often in the forms of eyewitness accounts, and intended these descriptions to arouse in their readers similar moral responses—at first as noninferential, dispositional responses. However, in so doing, Burke and Paine invited their readers to discursively examine, justify, act upon, and amend as need be their own normative, noninferential observations.[32]

Stout explains that Paine and Burke were both gripped by moral visions. Their commitments and respective moral dispositions caused them to view and respond to the events before them in particular ways, and they sought to persuade their readers to see and respond to those events similarly. Each of these authors invited his readers to reflect and deliberate in ways that would, hopefully, lead them to embrace a similar moral vision. "Their writings are designed in part to cause others to see what they see," Stout explains. "Here is a word-picture of someone—a queen or pauper—being maltreated. Do you not intuitively take this to be horrible, the violation of something precious? If not, there is no hope for you as an observer of moral affairs. Either you see it, or you don't. Coming to see it is the process of conversion that each side is trying to initiate in its opponents."[33]

In a comparable way, many of the realistic biblical narratives of Jesus' life, death, and resurrection present observational accounts. The gospel writers have been grasped by faith in Christ and seek to witness to the life events and encounters with this Person who gave rise to their faith. "Now Jesus did many other signs in the presence of his disciples, which are not written in this book," reads the Gospel of John's summation of its account. "But these are written so that you may come to believe that Jesus is the Messiah, the Son of God, and that through believing you may have life in his name."[34] Much like the events reported by Burke and Paine, this gospel writer's descriptive accounts mean to elicit noninferential responses and initiate (and perhaps cultivate) normative attitudes in their readers. Those who follow—those grasped by these accounts—find their lives and world involved in and oriented by the world of discourse initiated by these stories. "Either you see it or you don't," as Stout puts it. "Coming to see is the process of conversion."[35] Such an altered way of seeing, which recognizes one's participation in "the narrative web of that world," is certainly an appropriate characterization of what the gospel authors hope for their readers.

I mention this example in order to demonstrate that speaking of a "noninferential" grasp of the biblical accounts need not implicate them in an epistemologically foundationalist claim. As I argued in chapter 6, "noninferential" observation (or perception) requires skills that are just as much the product of acculturation into certain inferential social practices as are explicitly inferential skills such as, say, assessing and exploring the truth or moral value of a commitment that proceeds from such an observation. Noninferential skills are acquired and can be honed to better or worse degrees of proficiency and reliability.

Attending to the *sensus literalis* of Scripture—far from being an appeal to narrative foundationalism (Scripture's incorrigible self-interpreting presentation)—appeals instead to an acquired skill, namely, sufficient adeptness in (and perhaps on the way to relative mastery of) the skills of concept application in virtue of which these noninferential moves are possible. Concept users come to be immediately (though not *incorrigibly*) beholden to these proprieties for judgment and experience—grasped by them, and thus disposed to reliably respond in certain ways. Through the acquisition of such skills of concept application, readers come to discern letters and words on a page. With practice come the skills of discerning the propositional regularities of grammar and syntax that make elementary reading possible. Gradually, one so trained and acculturated acquires and develops the capacity for reading comprehension, out of which arises sustained understanding of and eventual expansion upon what one encounters there. With such acculturation into the practice of reading, discerning the sensory presentation of character and circumstance that make up some story, such as the story of Jesus of Nazareth, becomes a noninferential affair. To recognize what the words say—the "way the words go"—is to recognize what they portray.[36] "We start from the text," Frei wrote, "that is the language pattern, the meaning-and-reference pattern to which we are bound, and which is sufficient for us."[37]

Construed in this way, Frei's retrieval and reconfiguration of the literal sense as plain overcomes what had been one of the most detrimental features of Christian scriptural practices by emphasizing the priority of what the stories portray (depictively render) over what the text "means." Auerbach argued that the witness of the text's literal presentation in all its *sensory* immediacy was lost when a concern for the text's "meaning" became the basic level of engagement. This loss, he argued, was exacerbated by the figural interpretation of Scripture. According to Auerbach:

> The total content of the sacred writings was placed in an exegetic
> context which often removed the thing told very far away from its
> sensory base, in that the reader or listener was forced to turn his
> attention away from the sensory occurrence and toward its meaning.
> This implied the danger that the visual element of the occurrences
> might succumb under the dense texture of meanings. Let one
> example stand for many: It is a visually dramatic occurrence that God
> made Eve, the first woman, from Adam's rib while Adam lay asleep;
> so too is it that a soldier pierced Jesus' side, as he hung dead on the
> cross, so that blood and water flowed out. But when these two
> occurrences are exegetically interrelated in the doctrine that Adam's

sleep is a figure of Christ's death-sleep; that, as from the wound in
Adam's side mankind's primordial mother after the flesh, Eve, was
born, so from the wound in Christ's side was born the mother of all
men after the spirit, the Church (blood and water are sacramental
symbols)—then the sensory occurrence pales before the power of
figural meaning. What is perceived by the hearer or reader . . . is
weak as a sensory perception, and all one's interest is directed toward
the context of meanings.[38]

On Frei's account, the biblical narratives say what they say first by portraying it,
by showing rather than saying. Or, perhaps more aptly put, saying in virtue of
showing. As Placher restated this insight, "Such narratives help us know a person in the way a great novelist or narrative historian can, and they provide
insights we lose if we try to summarize the narrative in nonnarrative form."[39]
Thus, the life events of Jesus confront us in our comprehension of the words
and sentences on the page in narrative form.

Frei thought that Scripture's depictive renderings of these events cannot be
reduced to something more basic—either a collection of discrete assertions or
doctrines—without becoming something other than the depictive rendering,
something other than the story. "[W]hat one knows about the story's central agent
[Christ] is not known by 'inference' from the story," David Kelsey helps to sharpen
this point. "On the contrary, he is known quite directly in and with the story, and
recedes from cognitive grasp the more he is abstracted from the story."[40] The
depiction rendered by the story presents the entry level into the practice of interpretation, commentary, and application. "The first plainly distinguishable aspect
of the process [of scriptural interpretation] is the act of observation. In this phase,
exegesis is entirely concerned with the *sensus* of the words of Scripture as such,"
Barth explains. "If we ourselves or others are to be in a position to follow the
sense of the words of Scripture, they must first be put before us clearly, that is, as
in themselves intelligible, in contrast to mere noises."[41]

I am proposing that this is what it means to describe recognition of the
sensus literalis as a *propriety* of the practices oriented by this text, a propriety that
uniquely situates the life of Christian communities and followers. As a propriety, it gives rise to certain practical implications for readers who, on the basis
of engaging these stories, acquire commitments to the claim that "Jesus loves
me" or the command "Give to everyone who begs from you, and do not refuse
anyone who wants to borrow from you" (Matt 6:41) or the promise, "I am with
you always, to the close of the age" (Matt 28:20).

The normative attitudes elicited by the claims of Scripture, when Christian, will be oriented by the witness of Christ. They will impel believers to act

in certain ways by initiating dispositions and shaping sensibilities about the way the world is. Viewed in this way, the *sensus literalis* is the noninferential entryway into the practice constitutive of discerning and assessing and following the practical implications of these stories. It is the entry into the inferential discursive practices and actions of learning "to interpret the Bible in order to apply it in the church, in the secular society, in prayer, praise and personal relation."[42] The dispositional responses and moves into the practice of consulting Scripture exert that first grasp by which the strange new world within the Bible embraces the believer and the world.

Redescribing recognition of the *sensus literalis* in terms of a noninferential move into an essentially inferential set of practices allows the charges of revelational positivism or scriptural foundationalism to fall away. With this insight in view, one can appeal to the *sensus literalis* as a noninferential propriety without invoking it as "given," much like Wilfrid Sellars invoked his noninferential move of observation without reverting the "given" of classical foundationalist epistemology. Frei's account of the *sensus literalis* need not tie him to an epistemic foundation. But do we dare assert that what is the *sensus literalis* is uniquely christological as Frei would have us? Well, yes. And this answer sheds light on the limits of the ad hoc insights I have employed in explicating and redescribing the social-practical character of Scripture's *witness* to the person of Christ in the story it tells.

III. "No Matter How Philosophers May View It"

Asserting the christological character of the scriptural witness means that the gospel narratives' accounts of the identity of Christ flies free of the dispositions of the community members. It resides rather at the level of the congruity of our practices (including those object-oriented states of affairs we call texts, pages, sentences, and grammar as well as intelligent actions such as reading and giving and asking for reasons in our consulting this text). As such, Jesus is the literal, ascriptive subject not simply because the community ascribes that status to him, but also because of how the narratives portray him. Claiming that the plain sense is christological in this way does not jeopardize the theoretical frugality of the Wittgensteinian rule of thumb that Frei found helpful—"don't ask about meaning; look for the use." Rather, it highlights the fact that the statement "meaning is use" is itself multivalent. On one hand, texts are things that are used. Scripture is the object part and parcel of the object-directed textual practices and stories of the One that gathers the church together and makes it a church. At the same time, this Wittgensteinian quip conveys the sense that texts are used in particular times and places, with particular interests and purposes at hand, and in relation to previous and future uses and traditions of use. Employed in this way, this phrase serves as a proviso that we do not have "Scripture" in abstraction from the life of the church.

But here we must continue to press further, for our attempt to recognize text and context as a seamless (yet differentiated) whole in virtue of a philosophically redescribed account is only partially complete at this point. The conceptual character by which Scripture *witnesses* to the identity of Christ is simultaneously the means by which the Spirit *mediates* Christ's presence. Again, as Frei put it, "the reality of God is given in, with, and under the concept and not separably, and that is adequate for us."[43] And here, at last, we have the final warrant for ascription of predicates to the person of Jesus as rendered by the *sensus literalis*.

While "what the text says" makes possible and warrants predicate ascription to the person of Jesus, it does not ultimately *govern* that predicate ascription. The final warrant for seeing Jesus as the unsubstitutable ascriptive subject of the gospel narratives is the person of Christ himself. This is not merely Christ as a narratively deposited character in the story. It is Christ as the living person present even now. It is the person whose conscription of these concepts—as well as the practices that make predication, storytelling, writing, reading, and meaning possible in the first place—breaks and transforms them in order to thereby objectively, though analogically, mediate his person to believers.[44] This is the sense in which engaging Scripture is irreducibly social-practical but theologically unique in kind. That is, while it is the text in and through which the literal sense is possible, it is, according to Frei, the living and present person of Christ who governs—and thus warrants—the predicates ascribed to him in the literal sense of Scripture, not the consensus of the Christian community (even consensus understood as congruity at the level of their practices).

"Jesus Christ is known to the Christian believer in a manner that incorporates ordinary personal knowledge, but also surpasses it mysteriously," Frei had claimed as far back as *Identity*. This story makes certain radical claims upon its readers in virtue of the identity of the person it portrays. Making sense of this text implicates one in recognizing an event. This event is constituted by any number of mutually interrelated events (or "life acts") that comprise the story of Jesus of Nazareth.[45] Readers may, of course, dismiss this account as absurd, mistaken, or untrue. The identity of Jesus Christ is given with the story of his life and work, and in this story Christ comes as the one who lived and died and lived again.[46] "Either we believe with the New Testament in the risen Jesus Christ, or we do not believe in Him at all. This is the statement which believers and nonbelievers alike can surely accept as a fair assessment of the sources."[47]

Ultimately, the *sensus literalis* authentically, if indirectly, ascribes predicates to the person of Christ *neither* because, as some instance of the category of text, it is imbued with a special status or property nor simply because the tradition takes it as such. The scriptural text can so ascribe these predicates to the person of Christ because God acts in these stories to mediate the person of Christ to believers, indirectly but nevertheless authentically, by manifesting Christ in person and act through them, always under the proviso that "the subject matter governs concepts as well as method, not vice versa."[48] The Word, conceptually articulated and conceptually grasped, cannot be conceptually bound.[49] God's self-revelation is predicated on God's sovereignty, freedom, and grace.[50]

This seems to me to be the substance of—and final warrant for—Frei's claim that identification of the 'literal sense' as plain was not a "logically necessary development" in the ancient church. "[T]here was no a priori reason why the 'plain' reading could not have been 'spiritual' in contrast to 'literal,'" he wrote. As we saw, the emergence of the creed, "rule of faith," or "rule of truth" asserted "the primacy of their literal sense."[51] The absence of "logical necessity" is not a claim on behalf of believers' autonomy to simply *opt to make* the literal sense plain, even if in the form of purely accidental, gradual accumulation of traditional consensus. In my judgment, Frei's claim must finally be on behalf of *God's freedom*. God, not bound by logical necessity, could have done things otherwise.

This point presupposes, again, the interwovenness of apostolic tradition and constraints exerted by scriptural texts and practices. I think that a normative strand implicit in Frei's view is that the absence of "logical necessity" is treated as an implication of God's agency in this complex process.[52] Brevard Childs helps to clarify on this point in his discussion of the process of canonization of Scripture:

> [C]rucial to the concept of the Christian canon is that the apostolic church never claimed to have created its canon of scripture, but understood its formation as a response to the divine coercion of the living Word of God. Thus the concept of canon was a corollary of inspiration. It set the boundaries within which God's voice was heard. Only in this sense is the formation of the canon the work of the church. Nevertheless, scripture did not fall from heaven, but arose within the bosom of the community of faith, shaped by its usage in worship, preaching, and catechesis. Even though the exact

range of books designated canonical was never fully settled within
the Christian church—tension between a larger and a shorter canon
remained—there was full agreement in all the branches of the
church that sacred scripture consisted of two testaments, the
Old and the New, both of which bore witness to Jesus Christ in
different ways.[53]

This point holds analogously for the scriptural practices of the tradition, namely, the emergence of the primacy of the literal sense. In the emergence of the *sensus literalis* as plain reading, the "fact of faith" found itself formally articulated in the form of a "rule" (the "rule of faith" or "rule of truth" invoked by Frei) and thereby "asserted the primacy of the literal sense," as Frei recounts the story. But even the rule of faith has its origins in the gospel accounts of Christ's death and resurrection. It comes from the "objective encounters" to which the biblical narrative witnesses, in and through which Christ comes "again and again."

Faith was, and is, fashioned in encounter with the history-like accounts rendered in the literary-literal accounts of the event. Barth writes:

> God Himself, the object and ground of their faith, was present as the
> man Jesus was present in this way. That this really took place is the
> specific content of the apostolic recollection of these days. The fact of
> faith was created in this history. This faith did not consist in a
> reassessment and reinterpretation *in meliorem partem* ["in a better
> sense"] of the picture of the Crucified, but in an objective encounter
> with the Crucified and Risen, who Himself not only made Himself
> credible to them, but manifested Himself as the ["captain of their
> salvation"] (Heb. 2:10) and therefore the ["author and finisher"] (Heb.
> 12:2). The concrete demonstration of this God, His appearance, is the
> meaning of the appearance and appearances of this man Jesus, alive
> again after His death, in the forty days.[54]

Barth is not concerned with reinterpretations of this material that might unlock their hidden meaning, attempts to translate them into motifs and maxims usable for modern readers or which might simply be beneficial for Christian communities. Their "meaning" is their concrete demonstration of apostolic witness to the objective encounters with the Crucified and Risen.[55] For Barth, these cannot be independent from—and in fact, presupposes—their truth. Frei agreed with Barth that the possibility is predicated upon the actuality. As Frei characterized Barth's position, "the possibility and even the necessity for God's assuming man unto himself by incarnating himself may be affirmed and explored *because he did so* and only for that reason."[56] Frei endorsed this view, writing, "I agree with Karl Barth . . . that it is not the business of Christian theology to argue the possibility of Christian truth any more than the instantiation or actuality of that truth. The possibility follows logically as well as existentially from its actuality."[57] As we saw, such a view is consistent with Frei's construal of the rule of faith and its interpretive use in the Christian tradition, namely that "the singular agent enacting the unity of human finitude and divine infinity, Jesus of Nazareth, is taken to be itself the ground, guarantee, and conveyance of the truth of the depicted enactment."[58] With this set of claims Barth stands jeek by jowl with Frei—"[F]or the Christian tradition truth is what is written, not something separable and translinguistic that is written 'about.'"[59]

Barth's appeals to authorial intention, compulsion, and "what the text says," with which I expound Frei's more tersely articulated project, appear to raise again precisely some of the conceptual knots that I spent the foregoing chapters attempting to distinguish and untangle. While I have argued that Frei's claims for the literal sense do not implicate him in a form of textual essentialism or scriptural foundationalism, questions about the role played by *perspective* in the *sensus literalis* continue to press in upon my account. Surely the counterthrust exerted by the text does not negate the impact that some readers' or reading communities' perspectives—the contextually particular interests and purposes they bring to the reading of the text—bear upon the implications of their reading. The roles played by perspective and significance of context are, in my judgment, two of the points on which Frei's ideas most matured over the course of his career from his "Remarks" of 1967.[60] As a few final words to the present set of reflections on Frei's theology, I will consider these concerns about perspective and disagreement within the framework of Frei's effort to fashion a "generous orthodoxy."

Conclusion

The "literal sense" was traditionally the "plain sense" for the Christian tradition because it served the interests and purposes of faithfulness to the freedom and sovereignty of the Word of God. Chief among such scriptural texts are those that relate the story of Jesus of Nazareth. But faith comes—mysteriously, miraculously—in response to the command of the person manifest in this story, whether attested to in narrative form or preached in the Ministry of the Word. The story of Jesus affords "a kind of loose organizing center for the whole."[61] This "looseness" suggests that the constraints it exerts upon Christian exegesis are flexible. They provide interpretive leeway. The literal sense "bends." It can accommodate an array of emphases and immediate implications depending upon the context in which these stories grasp those who read or hear them. Nevertheless, the literal sense of the story of Jesus is where faithful reading begins.

Frei was not concerned simply to document the historical development of the literal sense and then account for its eventual decline. Nor did he mean to conduct an act of retrieval of a premodern or precritical approach to Scripture in any simple sense, as if the developments he documented in *Eclipse* had never occurred or could somehow be undone. Rather, Frei traced out historically and worked out the *sensus literalis* in order to revive and reconceptualize this approach to Scripture for contemporary Christian communities in full awareness of all that transpired in the preceding centuries. He thought that the story of Jesus, as such, ought to have priority in the reading of Scripture. And of course, he thought that Barth's theological exegesis pointed concretely in the directions that this kind of reading could lead.[62]

Far from overdetermining "meaning," the literal sense of the text exerted constraints flexible enough to accommodate uses that differed by degree from context to context, extending over time. We have now seen at length that Frei pinpointed a normatively christological sense to the surface of the biblical accounts even as he softened his use of literary categories to redescribe them. In other words, his work of the 1980s reconciled his earlier claims for the normative priority of the plainly christological character of these history-like (formerly "realistic") narratives with his increasingly explicit articulation of the social-practical character of engaging Scripture. Most basically, the literal sense characterized what he called Scripture's "basic ascriptive Christological sense"—the sense in which "the subject matter of these stories is not something or someone else, and that the rest of the canon must in some way or ways, looser or tighter, be related to this subject matter or at least not in contradiction to it."[63] This enabled Frei to attend to the influence that interpretive context bears upon the practices of engaging Scripture with increasing explicitness. In particular, he pinpointed the ascriptive christological sense as a basic point of normative orientation—often practically embodied and informally articulated yet in some variation or other basically nonnegotiable—by which Christian reading of the Christian Scriptures had been identified as Christian.[64]

The guidelines for reading into which the story's priority translates do not, however, come with a "method" for application.[65] Rather, they present the formal caution that whatever interests, purposes, and preunderstandings faithful readers bring to their reading of the Bible—and they inevitably bring them—they must have a fundamental awareness that the content they come up against therein, an encounter with the name and narrative of Jesus Christ, inescapably stands in grace-inscribed judgment over precisely those interests and purposes.[66] There can be no systematic or general theory of how to read, aside, that is, from subordinating our human interests and purposes to the reading of Scripture. This subordination of the recognition that the subject matter of these stories is bound to overcome them, and us with them, in unexpected ways. And this insight of Barth's establishes a fundamental normative edge. Christian commentary upon the Bible, then, ought to serve the interests and purposes of faithfulness to the freedom and sovereignty of God. But this means holding loosely even the best intentions of faithfulness and ardent efforts to do justice to the scriptural text. The results of such reading will have to be largely open ended, as they will be impossible to predict prior to actually taking up the task of exegesis and commentary.

Viewed in this way, faithful reading of Scripture, exegesis, and commentary may entail genuine—even radical—variation. Christians ought to come to expect such variation insofar as "the object mirrored in the text"—the Word of God—is "master of our thinking."[67] In fact, it was on precisely this basis that Barth claimed that "it is possible to regard scriptural exposition as the best and perhaps the only school of truly free human thinking—freed, that is, from all the conflicts and tyranny of systems in favour of this object. But, however that may be, the task of scriptural exposition demands both caution and also openness with regard to all the possibilities of human thought because no limits may be set to the freedom and sovereign power of its object."[68]

Frei expanded upon the implications of this insight. He pointed out that Christians take the risk incumbent upon subordinating themselves to the text "in the confidence that in, with, and under our identical or very different, indispensable auxiliary philosophical tools we may be able to reach agreement or at least mutually understanding disagreement in the reading of crucial biblical texts."[69] The possibility of radical variation presumes a great deal of agreement about the object of investigation as well as the practice of investigation and consultation itself. These tasks presume that "the text is not inert but exerts a pressure of its own back upon the inquiring reader." They presume that the embodied and contextually situated activity of reading and consulting Scripture is an object-directed practice for which there are certain loose rules of the game and better or worse performances of the practice. "Sound exposition," on this reading, will recognize that the story of Jesus asserts itself as the place that inquiry ought to begin and end, just as its radical possibilities norm the entire enterprise.[70]

But textual practices of explication and application are riven with disagreement and contestation about how the *sensus literalis* itself ought to be construed as plain—*which* themes ought to be emphasized, *which* passages normative. And thus, the practice of consulting Scripture is necessarily critical. The discursive practice into which the *sensus literalis* is an entryway is so central to the identities of Christian communities, and thus Frei's overall project, because not every use of Scripture, not every conceptual redescription of the story, is equally sound, or true for that matter. Again, insofar as "the object mirrored in the text"—the Word of God—is "master of our thinking," the very tasks of reading, exposition, and commentary of Scripture will entail a critical edge aimed at the Christian community itself.[71]

David Dawson points out that "for Frei, Christian theological reflection demands critical self-assessment regarding the community's identity, even to the point of concluding that the community has in fact betrayed its identity" and that "[t]he activity of Christian self-criticism is carried out by means of debates about the faithfulness of competing conceptual redescriptions of its identifying narratives."[72] The "modest second-order discipline called systematic or dogmatic theology" takes up the tradition-constitutive arguments embodied in claims, such as:

> "This is a better way to express it than that; this is normative and that
> is peripheral," and, above all, to decide what is more than attitudinal
> within the communal self-description and how, what could be taken
> to be appropriate conceptual redescriptions of specific beliefs in our
> day, and how they are authorized within community and tradition.[73]

Such claims are practices of reason exchange, deliberation, and debate. As such, they are tradition-constitutive arguments in which endorsements of noninferential encounters with these stories implicate believers. This is a biblically inspired and oriented "tradition" in the sense of "an historically extended, socially embodied argument, and an argument precisely in part about the goods which constitute that tradition."[74] However, we cannot emphasize the note of variability and radical unpredictability without noting, at the same time, that God has miraculously enacted God's revelation through these stories and words and continues to do so. This never occurs without remainder and provision. Nonetheless, it occurs authentically. And this fact renders all the more crucial our sorting through, contesting, and redescribing all the conceptual inner and outer workings of the practices of engaging Scripture. So conceiving scriptural practices situates the tradition they constitute as altogether different from a "windowless monad." It is a multifaceted, historically extended set of arguments that are neither immune from criticism nor lodged in a "theological ghetto."

Frei thought that this account of Scripture and tradition would move in the direction of a "generous orthodoxy." Such a stance entailed elements of both liberalism and evangelicalism. And yet, it could in no way be reduced to a simple sum of their best insights. Frei's theological program encourages us to move beyond this dichotomy. It pushes any would-be theologian beyond any easy dichotomies between church and academy or between church and world. At the same time, it refuses to compromise its confessional commitments. This interdisciplinary posture and conversational form—modeled best by Frei's own temperament and generous sensibility—holds out possibilities for the future of theology in an age in which its role continues to be contested.

Notes

INTRODUCTION

1. Hans Frei, *The Eclipse of Biblical Narrative* (New Haven: Yale University Press, 1974), hereafter cited as *Eclipse*.

2. Van A. Harvey reflects upon this tenuous transition in the life of academic theology in his essay "The Intellectual Marginality of American Theology," in *Religion and Twentieth-Century American Intellectual Life*, ed. Michael J. Lacey (Cambridge: Cambridge University Press, 1989), pp. 172–92. Harvey provides more personal (though no less trenchant) observations about this transition in his introduction to the 1996 edition of *The Historian and the Believer* (Urbana and Chicago: University of Illinois Press: [1966] 1996), p. x. For other treatments of this pivotal period in theology, see also "The Voice of Academic Theology" in Jeffrey Stout, *Ethics After Babel* (Princeton: Princeton University Press, [1988] 2001), pp. 163–88, and chapter 7 of Stout, *The Flight from Authority* (Notre Dame: University of Notre Dame Press, 1981), pp. 128–48. Alasdair MacIntyre offered withering diagnoses of theology's emaciated condition during this period in his essays "God and the Theologians" and "The Fate of Theism," reprinted in *Against the Self-images of the Age* (Notre Dame: University of Notre Dame Press, 1978) and *The Religious Significance of Atheism* (New York: Columbia University Press, 1969); see also Peter Berger, "A Sociological View of the Secularization of Theology," *Journal of the Scientific Study of Religion* 6 (Spring 1967): 3–16.

3. Stout, *The Flight from Authority*, p. 147.

4. John Woolverton provides a detailed discussion of Frei's context at midcareer in "Hans W. Frei in Context: A Theological and Historical Memoir," *Anglican Theological Review* 79 (Summer 1997): 369–93. For an extended account of the contextual specifics and historical developments

contributing to the rise of "postliberal" theology, see Paul J. DeHart, *The Trial of the Witnesses: The Rise and Decline of Postliberal Theology* (Oxford: Blackwell, 2006), chapter 1; Mike Higton provides important background to this period in his article, "An American Theologian of History: Hans W. Frei in 1956," *Anglican and Episcopal History* 71, no. 1 (2002): 61–84.

5. Alasdair MacIntyre, "Interpretation of the Bible, Review of Hans Frei's *The Eclipse of Biblical Narrative*," *Yale Review* 65 (1976): 251–55 (here 255); George Steiner's review of *Eclipse* echoed MacIntyre's assessment, though toward a less favorable verdict. See Steiner's review of *The Eclipse of Biblical Narrative* in *Philosophy and Literature* 1, no. 1 (1977): 238–43.

6. Brevard S. Childs, "The *Sensus Literalis* of Scripture: An Ancient and Modern Problem," in *Beitrage zur alttestamentlichen Theologie: Festschrift fur Walther Zimmerli zum 70 Geburtstag*, ed. Herbert Donner, Robert Hanhart, and Rudolph Smend (Gottingen: Vandenhoek & Ruprecht, 1977), pp. 80–95; Raphael Loewe, "The 'Plain' Meaning of Scripture in Early Jewish Exegesis," in *Papers of the Institute of Jewish Studies, London*, ed. J. G. Weiss (Jerusalem: Magnes, 1964), 1:181.

7. Peter Ochs, *The Return to Scripture in Judaism and Christianity: Essays in Postcritical Scriptural Interpretation* (New York: Paulist, 1993) presents a similarly framed project of critical recovery.

8. James Gustafson, "The Sectarian Temptation: Reflection on Theology, the Church, and the University," *Proceedings of the Catholic Theological Society* 40 (1985): 83–94; David Tracy, "Lindbeck's New Program for Theology: A Reflection," *The Thomist* 49 (1985): 460–72. Some of Frei's friendliest readers characterize his work as "church theology" due to what they take to be the limits of its focus. See, for instance, Nicholas Wolterstorff, "What New Haven and Grand Rapids Have to Say to Each Other," in *Seeking Understanding: The Stob Lectures, 1986–1998* (Grand Rapids, MI: Eerdmans, 2001), pp. 251–94.

9. Cornel West, "On Hans Frei's *The Eclipse of Biblical Narrative*," in *Prophetic Fragments* (Grand Rapids, MI: Eerdmans, 1988), pp. 236–39.

10. Paul Ricoeur sounded this cautionary note to any would-be "narrative theologian" in his exchange with Frei at the Symposium on Narrative Theology at Haverford College in 1982. Ricoeur's paper was published much later as "Toward a Narrative Theology: Its Necessity, Its Resources, Its Difficulties," in *Figuring the Sacred: Religion, Narrative, and Imagination*, ed. Mark I. Wallace, trans. David Pellauer (Minneapolis: Fortress, 1995), pp. 236–37.

11. Frank Kermode, "What Precisely are the Facts?" in *The Genesis of Secrecy: On the Interpretation of Narrative* (Cambridge, MA: Harvard University Press, 1979), chapter 5 (esp. 116–23); Mark Wallace, *The Second Naiveté: Barth, Ricoeur and the New Yale Theology* (Macon, GA: Mercer University Press, 1995), pp. 104, 109, 112.

12. Dan Stiver, *Theology After Ricoeur* (Louisville, KY: Westminster / John Knox, 2001), pp. 46–56 (esp. p. 51); see also Stiver's "Theological Method," in *The Cambridge Companion to Postmodern Theology*, ed. Kevin Vanhoozer (Cambridge: Cambridge University Press, 2003), p. 181.

13. Carl F. H. Henry, "Narrative Theology: An Evangelical Appraisal," and Frei's response in *Trinity Journal* 8 (1987): 3–24.

14. N.T. Wright, *The Resurrection of the Son of God* (Minneapolis: Fortress, 2003), p. 21; cf. Henry, "Narrative Theology: An Evangelical Appraisal," p. 12.

15. Nancey Murphy, *Theology in the Age of Scientific Reasoning* (Ithaca: Cornell University Press, 1990), p. 22. Murphy aims this point specifically at Barth.

16. An example of such "family resemblance" analysis would be a pair of articles by Gary Dorrien: "The Origins of Postliberalism: A Third Way in Theology?" *Christian Century*, July 4–11, 2001, pp. 16–21, and "The Future of Postliberal Theology: Truth Claims," *Christian Century*, July 18–25, 2001, pp. 22–29.

17. Ralph Waldo Emerson, "Self-Reliance," *Self-Reliance and Other Essays*, (Mineola, NY: Dover Publications, 1993), p. 23.

18. Karl Barth, *Church Dogmatics*, trans. G. T. Thomson (Edinburgh: T&T Clark, 1936), 1/1, p. 1 (hereafter *CD*), as quoted by Frei in *Types of Christian Theology* (New Haven: Yale University Press, 1992), p. 78 (hereafter cited as *Types*).

19. John Howard Yoder captures Barth's use of the term *Gemeinde* to explicate the church as a multiform and ever-reforming "gathering-under-the-Word" as opposed to reducing it to the structural dimensions of polity or hierarchy (*Kirche*). For Yoder's illuminating discussion, see his *Karl Barth and the Problem of War and Other Essays on Barth*, ed. Mark Thiessen Nation (Eugene, OR: Cascade Books, 2003), pp. 96–97, 173.

20. The position I am sketching here I explicate and develop in detail in chapter 4. For meticulous exposition of this point see George Hunsinger, *How to Read Karl Barth: The Shape of his Theology* (Oxford: Oxford University Press, 1991), p. 73.

21. Frei, *Types*, p. 79.

22. Karl Barth, "The Authority and Significance of the Bible," in *God Here and Now*, trans. Paul M. van Buren (New York: Routledge, 2004), pp. 64–65.

23. Friedrich Schleiermacher, *The Christian Faith* (Philadelphia: Fortress Press, 1976), p. 26. Frei came to challenge this reading of Schleiermacher in certain of the writings posthumously collected in *Types*. DeHart provides important analysis of these developments in *The Trial of the Witnesses*.

24. George Hunsinger, "Beyond Literalism and Expressivism," *Disruptive Grace* (Grand Rapids: Eerdmans, 2000), p. 216.

25. Frei, *The Identity of Jesus Christ* (Eugene, OR: Wipf & Stock, 1997), p. 59, hereafter cited as *Identity*.

26. Barth, *CD* 1/1, p. 1.

27. Frei, *Types*, p. 78.

28. Ibid., p. 112, referring to Elizabeth Anscombe and Gilbert Ryle, among others. For a seminal articulation of the point, see Ludwig Wittgenstein, *Philosophical Investigations* (Oxford: Blackwell, 2001), Sec. 208.

29. Frei, *Identity*, p. 59. Frei avoids the claim that "the self-involving quality of religious statements is the indispensable logical condition or interpretive setting for the intelligibility of the doctrine that Jesus is the crucified and risen Savior."

30. Frei, *Types*, p. 112.

31. Ibid., pp. 78–79.

32. Stanley Hauerwas, for instance, has identified Frei as his first teacher in Barth's theology as well as among the earliest to recognize the value of Wittgenstein's later thought for theological purposes. See Hauerwas's "The Narrative Turn: Thirty

Years Later," in *Performing the Faith* (Grand Rapids, MI: Brazos, 2004), pp. 137–38. George Hunsinger acknowledges having learned how to read Barth from Mr. Frei, and under Frei's supervision he wrote the dissertation which later became a standard primer in Barth's theology, *How to Read Karl Barth*.

33. Karl Barth, *Evangelical Theology: An Introduction* (Grand Rapids, MI: Eerdmans, 1963), p. 35.

34. Gilbert Ryle, *The Concept of Mind* (Chicago: University of Chicago Press, 1949).

35. Fergus Kerr points out that Wittgensteinian insights motivated even Frei's earliest uses of Ryle, though Kerr remains silent about the fact that Frei's work presents one of the earliest examples of "theology after Wittgenstein." See his "Frei's Types," *New Blackfriars* 5 (April 1994): 184–93.

36. Frei, "Letter to Gary Comstock," November 5, 1984 (YDS 12-184), as quoted by Mike Higton in *Christ, Providence and History: Hans W. Frei's Public Theology* (New York: T&T Clark, 2004), p. 199 (hereafter cited as *CPH*); italics added.

37. Frei, *Types*, pp. 78–91.

38. Ibid., pp. 40–41.

39. Barth, *CD* 1/1, pp. 53–56. Barth offers an example of this in detailing the significant lessons that conceptions of *eros* in ancient Greek religion, mysticism, and philosophy have to teach Christian conceptions of *agape*. See *CD* 3/2, pp. 279–85.

40. Barth, "Theological and Philosophical Ethics," a lecture delivered at Marburg in 1930, in *Briefwechsel Karl Barth-Eduard Thurneysen, 1913–1921, 1973*, p. 526; cf. Eberhard Busch, *Karl Barth: His Life and Letters and Autobiographical Texts* (Philadelphia: Fortress, 1975), pp. 194–95.

41. Sheila Greeve Davaney, "Mapping Theologies," in Dwight N. Hopkins & Sheila Greeve Davaney, eds., *Changing Conversations: Religious Reflection and Cultural Analysis* (New York: Routledge, 1996), pp. 29–32.

42. Frei, "Theology and the Interpretation of Narrative," in George Hunsinger and William Placher, eds., *Theology and Narrative* (Oxford: Oxford University Press, 1993), p. 108 (hereafter cited as *T&N*).

43. Barth, "Humanism," *God Here and Now* (New York: Routledge, 2003), p. 132.

44. Barth, "The Proclamation of God's Grace," *God Here and Now*, pp. 43–44.

45. Ibid.

46. Barth, *CD* 2/1, pp. 257–321.

47. Eugene Rogers, "Supplementing Barth on Jews and Gender: Identifying God by Anagogy and the Spirit," *Modern Theology* 14 (January 1998), p. 50.

48. Frei appealed to the notion of a "generous orthodoxy" in response to Carl Henry. See Frei's "Response to 'Narrative Theology: An Evangelical Appraisal,'" *T&N*, pp. 207–12.

49. Dan Stiver, *The Philosophy of Religious Language* (Oxford: Blackwell, 1996), pp. 143–45.

50. See, for instance, Frei's contributions to a Festschrift for Lindbeck, in *Theology and Dialogue*, ed. Bruce Marshall (Notre Dame: University of Notre Dame Press, 1990), pp. 149–64 & 275–82.

51. Bruce McCormack, *Orthodox and Modern: Studies in the Theology of Karl Barth* (Grand Rapids, MI: Baker Academic, 2008), pp. 109–66.

52. These shared worries include positivist theories of meaning, correspondence theories of historical factuality and truth, metaphysical conceptions of "inner intention," "mind" and "consciousness" as the seat of personal identity and intention, and the idea that experience is "given," and thus an immediate form of knowing.

53. Frei, " Theology and the Interpretation of Narrative," pp. 111–12; "The 'Literal Reading' of Biblical Narrative," *T&N*, pp. 122–23.

54. Barth, *CD* 1/2, pp. 729–30 (italics added).

55. Wittgenstein, *Philosophical Investigations*, Sec. 133.

56. See, for instance, *Types*, pp. 84–87; "Theology and the Interpretation of Narrative," (1982), *T&N*, pp. 110–14.

57. Nicholas Wolterstorff shared with me the story of a student visiting Frei in the hospital during the last weeks of his life. The student asked Frei why he never turned his attention to writing a dogmatics. Frei responded by referring to Barth and saying "That's already been done."

CHAPTER 1

1. Barth, *Church Dogmatics* (Edinburgh: T&T Clark, 1956), 1/2, pp. 727–28 (hereafter cited as *CD*).

2. Ibid., pp. 729–30 (italics added). Frei dealt with this complex dimension of scriptural exegesis with explicit reference to Barth's work in the work collected in *Types of Christian Theology* (New Haven: Yale University Press, 1992) pp. 84–87 (hereafter cited as *Types*), and in the earlier essay, "Theology and the Interpretation of Narrative," (1982) *T&N*, pp. 110–14.

3. *Identity* originally appeared as a series of articles entitled "The Mystery and Presence of Jesus Christ" in *Crossroads,* a Presbyterian journal of Christian education. Frei published these articles in 1975 as *The Identity of Jesus Christ*, unaltered with the exception of a new preface and an epilogue entitled "A Meditation for the Week of Good Friday and Easter," both written in 1974.

4. Frei walks his readers through detailed assessments of such figures as Anthony Collins, S. J. Baumgarten, Christian Wolff, J. P. Gabler, G. T. Zacharia, Johannes Cocceius, along with such standards as Spinoza, Kant, Locke, Herder, Strauss, and Schleiermacher.

5. Frei, "On Interpreting the Christian Story," The 10th Annual Greenhoe Lectureship (Louisville, KY: Louisville Presbyterian Theological Seminary; Cass: Greenhoe, 1976), transcript in *Hans W. Frei: Unpublished Pieces, Transcripts from the Yale Divinity School Archive,* ed. Mike Higton, p. 55, http://www.library.yale.edu/div/ Freitranscripts/Freicomplete.pdf.

6. Barth, *CD* 1/2, p. 727.

7. Ibid., p. 734.

8. Frei, *The Identity of Jesus Christ* (Philadelphia: Fortress, 1975), hereafter *Identity* (Eugene, OR: Wipf & Stock, 1997), p. 101.

9. Ibid., p. 102.

10. Frei, *Identity*, p. 53.

11. Some key texts that account for the application of evidential conceptions of "reasonableness" applied to Scripture and religious belief include, for instance, Baruch Spinoza's *Theologico-Political Treatise*, John Locke's *The Reasonableness of Christianity*, David Hume's "Of Miracles" and his *Dialogues Concerning Natural Religion*.

12. The following paragraphs provide a brief sketch of Frei's account. See specifically *Eclipse*, pp. 255–66.

13. Ibid., p. 11.

14. S. J. Baumgarten (1706–57) is the particular case Frei examines. Ibid., pp. 88–91.

15. Ibid.

16. Ibid., p. 89.

17. Ibid.

18. See Frei's "David Friedrich Strauss," in *Nineteenth Century Religious Thought in the West*, ed. Ninian Smart, John Clayton, Patrick Sherry, and Steven T. Katz (Cambridge: Cambridge University Press, 1985), 1:215–57. For the interpretation of Jesus' resurrection from the dead as "the rise of faith in the risen Lord, since it was this faith which led to the apostolic preaching," see Rudolf Bultmann, *Kerygma and Myth: A Theological Debate, Vol. 2* (New York: Harper and Row, 1961), p. 42 (cf. Karl Barth, *CD* 3/2, p. 443).

19. Frei, *Eclipse*, pp. 113–14.

20. Frei, *Identity*, p. 54.

21. Frei, "On Interpreting the Christian Story," pp. 45–46.

22. Ibid., p. 55.

23. Frei, *Eclipse*, p. 313.

24. Frei, "On Interpreting the Christian Story," p. 51.

25. Frei, *Identity*, p. 59.

26. Ibid.

27. Frei, "On Interpreting the Christian Story," p. 51.

28. Frei, *Eclipse*, p. 312.

29. Ibid., pp. 13–14. "[T]he narrative depiction is of that peculiar sort in which characters or individual persons, in their internal depth or subjectivity as well as in their capacity as doers and sufferers of actions or events, are firmly and significantly set in the context of the external environment, natural but more particularly social."

30. Frei, *Identity*, p. 134.

31. Ibid., p. 102.

32. Ibid.

33. Ibid., p. 136.

34. Ibid., p. 140.

35. Ibid., p. 141.

36. "Things happen to a person that enter into the very identification of him; they are enacted or occur upon or through him. Do such external acts or occurrences become embodied in him? Do they become part of his identity since they are woven into his story? Undoubtedly, yes, and in part by his own response to or incorporation

of these happenings. What is to be stressed here is that our categories for identity description break down at this very point. They cannot describe how external events become ingredient in a person's identity directly, i.e. other than by his own response to them. All that one can do to describe a person in that situation of direct impact by circumstances upon him (and not as refracted through his own response) and how he becomes himself in and through these circumstances is simply to tell the story of the events." Ibid., pp. 137–38.

37. Ibid., p. 139; "Remarks in Connection with a Theological Proposal," *T&N*, p. 35. "I want to say that intentional action description *categories* finally break down, though the description itself does not," wrote Frei ("Remarks," p. 37).

38. Frei, "Remarks," p. 37.

39. Frei, *Identity*, p. 61.

40. Ibid.

41. Ibid.

42. Ibid., 63.

43. Ibid., 61.

44. Frei, "Remarks," p. 41.

45. Ibid., pp. 32–33.

46. Ibid.

47. *Identity*, p. 60.

48. Frei, "Theological Reflections on the Accounts of Jesus' Death and Resurrection," *T&N*, p. 46.

49. Frei, *Identity*, p. 61; cf. *Types*, pp. 85–86.

50. Frei, "Theological Reflections on the Accounts of Jesus' Death and Resurrection," *T&N*, p. 58.

51. Ibid., p. 46.

52. Frei, *Types*, pp. 85–87.

53. Ibid., p. 86, Frei quoting Barth, *CD* 1/1.

54. Frei, "On Interpreting the Christian Story," p. 61.

55. Frei, "Remarks," (1967) *T&N*, pp. 32–33, 41; cf. Frei, "On Interpreting the Christian Story," pp. 60–61.

56. Kevin Vanhoozer helpfully articulates this temptation in Frei's case. See his *Biblical Narrative in the Philosophy of Paul Ricoeur* (Cambridge: Cambridge University Press, 1990), p. 164.

CHAPTER 2

1. Dan Stiver, *The Philosophy of Religious Language* (Oxford: Blackwell, 1996), p. 143 (Stiver's emphasis); cf. Hans Frei, *The Eclipse of Biblical Narrative* (New Haven: Yale University Press, 1974), pp. 34–35.

2. Stiver, *The Philosophy of Religious Language*, p. 143.

3. Ibid.

4. Ibid., p. 144.

5. For such accounts of the shift in Frei's thinking, see, for instance, Kevin Vanhoozer, *The Drama of Doctrine: A Canonical-Linguistic Approach to Christian*

Theology (Louisville, KY: Westminster John Knox, 2005), pp. 10–11; cf. George Hunsinger, afterword in *Theology and Narrative*, ed. George Hunsinger and William Placher (Oxford: Oxford University Press, 1993), p. 259 (hereafter cited as *T&N*). Charles Campbell locates Frei's "turn" to cultural-linguistic theory squarely in his essay "Theology and the Interpretation of Narrative" (1982). While this would predate Lindbeck's *The Nature of Doctrine*, Campbell reads Frei's account as more or less consistent with the general theory that Lindbeck articulates. See Campbell's *Preaching Jesus: New Directions for Homiletics in Hans Frei's Postliberal Theology* (Grand Rapids: Eerdmans, 1997), chapter 3 (esp. p. 64 n. 5).

6. George Lindbeck, *The Nature of Doctrine* (Philadelphia: Westminster, 1984), pp. 32–41.

7. Ibid., pp. 32–33.

8. Mike Higton, *Christ, Providence & History: Hans W. Frei's Public Theology* (New York: T&T Clark, 2004) (hereafter *CPH*).

9. Higton's account also appears in his article, "Frei's Christology and Lindbeck's Cultural-Linguistic Theory," *Scottish Journal of Theology* 50, no. 1 (1997): 92–95.

10. Higton, *CPH*, p. 178.

11. Ibid.

12. Ibid.

13. Ibid.; cf. p. 19.

14. Higton proposes that Frei's cultural-linguistic shift reflected his worries in the late 1970s that the historical developments recounted in *Eclipse* needed further supplementation by social and cultural history. Ibid., pp. 178–79.

15. Paul DeHart suggests that some mixture of David Kelsey's text of 1975, *The Uses of Scripture*, and Charles Wood's *The Formation of Christian Understanding* of 1981 introduced the pivotal ideas that catalyzed the shift in Frei's thinking. See DeHart, *The Trial of the Witnesses* (Oxford: Blackwell, 2006), pp. 26–27. In fact, much earlier in *Eclipse* Frei acknowledged the influence of many of those ideas in Wood's 1972 Yale dissertation—a Wittgensteinian assessment of the strand of hermeneutics stretching from Schleiermacher to Gadamer. See *Eclipse*, pp. 341–42 n. 1.

16. Much of Frei's work still in progress at the time of his death was edited by his former students, George Hunsinger and William Placher, and published as *Types of Christian Theology* (New Haven: Yale University Press, 1994). Frei's occasional essays were collected and published in *T&N*. In 2004 Mike Higton edited and circulated lecture manuscripts, notes, and other occasional writings remaining in Frei's archive under the title *Hans W. Frei: Unpublished Pieces, Transcripts from the Yale Divinity School Archive*, http://www.library.yale.edu/div/Freitranscripts/Freicomplete.pdf.

17. Higton, *CPH*, p. 178.

18. Ibid., p. 21. Higton takes up Frei's "later work" in chapter 8 of his book.

19. Vanhoozer, *The Drama of Doctrine*, pp. 10–11, 172–73.

20. Frei, "Remarks in Connection with a Theological Proposal," (1967), *T&N*, pp. 32–33.

21. Frei identified this date in an interview with John Woolverton in 1975. See Woolverton's "Hans W. Frei in Context: A Theological and Historical Memoir," *Anglican Theological Review* 79, no. 3 (Summer 1997): 385.

22. Ibid.

23. Frei, *Eclipse,* pp. vii–ix.

24. Robert H. King's dissertation was later published as *The Meaning of God* (Philadelphia: Fortress, 1973). Frei cites the dissertation in "Theological Reflections on the Accounts of Jesus' Death and Resurrection" of 1966; see *T&N,* p. 91 n. 6; King relies upon Frei's account of Barth in the Niebuhr Festschrift and in the published version cites Frei's "Theological Reflections" essay as an example of the kind of philosophical analysis he describes (*The Meaning of God,* p. 111 n. 9).

25. All of these thinkers, as well as Wittgenstein, were key resources for Robert King's dissertation. Frei, "Remarks in Connection with a Theological Proposal" (1967), *T&N,* p. 35; cf. "Theological Reflections on the Accounts of Jesus' Death and Resurrection" (1966), *T&N,* pp. 45–93 (here 64–68).

26. Frei, "Remarks," pp. 36–37.

27. Frei, *The Identity of Jesus Christ* (Philadelphia: Fortress, 1975), p. 42.

28. Frei, *Identity* (Wipf and Stock), p. 137.

29. Frei wrote that "Intention and action logically involve each other in verbal usage. 'To perform intelligently,' says Gilbert Ryle quite correctly, 'is to do one thing and not two things.' Hence, each has to be described by reference to the other. An intention is nothing other than an implicit action; but to say this is not to make intention and action one and the same. The necessary use of the qualifying adjective 'explicit' and 'implicit' in defining each by the other makes that point clear" (*Identity,* p. 137, quoting *The Concept of Mind* (New York: Barnes and Noble, 1949) p. 40.). This passage from Ryle turns out to be pivotal to Clifford Geertz's enterprise as well.).

30. Frei, *Eclipse,* p. 281. This passage follows Frei's citation of Ryle's *The Concept of Mind,* p. 40.

31. Even A. J. Ayer acknowledged that the claim that "all our talk about the mind is translatable into talk about behaviour" is one that Ryle "probably does not hold," in spite of the fact that "his programmatic statements often imply that he does." See Ayer's "An Honest Ghost?" in *Ryle: A Collection of Critical Essays* (New York: Doubleday, 1970), p. 67.

32. Frei, *Identity,* p. 43.

33. Frei, "Remarks," p. 35.

34. Frei, *Identity,* pp. 186–95.

35. Frei, *Eclipse,* p. 281 (quoting *The Concept of Mind,* p. 40,).

36. Ibid.

37. Frei, *Identity,* pp. 186–95.

38. Ibid., p. 190.

39. Woolverton, "Hans W. Frei in Context," p. 385.

40. Part 1 of *Philosophical Investigations*—by far the largest part of that text— was complete by 1945. Wittgenstein wrote part 2 from 1947–49, though the entirety of the text was not published until 1953. See editor's note by G. E. M. Anscombe and Rush Rhees in Anscombe translation of *Philosophical Investigations* (Oxford: Blackwell, 2001). The similarities between several of Wittgenstein's anecdotes and Ryle's claims in *The Concept of Mind* are considerable. In section 194, for instance, Wittgenstein employs the image of a shadow animating a machine in order to illustrate agent

volition and intentionality. For other important instances of Ryle's engagement of Wittgenstein, see his "Ludwig Wittgenstein," *Analysis* 12 (1951): 1-9, and "Review of Ludwig Wittgenstein: Remarks on the Foundations of Mathematics," *Scientific American* 117 (1957): 251-59, both reprinted in Ryle's *Collected Papers*.

41. In perhaps the definitive biography of Wittgenstein's life and thought to date, Ray Monk reports an encounter in which Wittgenstein identified Gilbert Ryle as the person who best understood his thinking at that time. Monk goes on to characterize this remark as an overstatement on Wittgenstein's part.

42. By the late 1930s, *The Blue Book*—dictations taken by his students of his 1933–34 lectures entitled "Philosophy" and "Philosophy for Mathematicians" and considered "an early prototype for subsequent presentation of Wittgenstein's later philosophy"—circulated among the Oxford philosophy faculty with whom Ryle spent his formative philosophical years and joined in 1945. For comments on his relationship with Wittgenstein, see Ryle's "Autobiographical" in *Ryle: A Collection of Critical Essays*, ed. Oscar P. Wood and George Pitcher (Garden City: Anchor, 1970), pp. 5, 11; see also Ray Monk's commentary on their time together in *Wittgenstein: The Duty of Genius* (New York: Penguin, 1990), pp. 275, 336–37, 436.

43. Frei, *Types*, p. 13. I explicate in detail the relevant family resemblances between Wittgenstein, Ryle, and Geertz in part 1 of chapter 3.

44. Frei, "Theology and the Interpretation of Narrative," *T&N*, pp. 96–97. Frei cites Geertz's *Islam Observed* (Chicago: University of chicgao Press, 1968) as an example of the analysis he here describes (96 n. 4).

45. Geertz borrowed this term from Gilbert Ryle's essay, "The Thinking of Thoughts: What Is *Le Penseur* Doing?" in *Collected Papers* (London: Hutchinson, 1971), 2:480–84. Frei also cites this essay at various points.

46. Frei, "The 'Literal Reading' of Biblical Narrative," *T&N*, pp. 145–49; *Types*, pp.13–14.

47. Clifford Geertz, preface to his *Available Light: Anthropological Reflection on Philosophical Topics* (Princeton, NJ: Princeton University Press, 2000), pp. xi–xii. For a more extensive treatment of Wittgenstein's influence upon Geertz, see my essay, "What Cultural Theorists of Religion Have to Learn from Wittgenstein, Or, How to Read Geertz as a Practice Theorist," *Journal of the American Academy of Religion*, 76 (December 2008): 934–69.

48. Frei, *Types*, p. 13.

49. Geertz explicitly invokes Ryle and Auerbach at various points in his account, and his entire approach to ethnography is predicated upon this complementarity. Again, the central passages where this is played out occur in "Thick Description" and "The Growth of Culture and the Evolution of Mind," *The Interpretation of Cultures* (New York: Basic Books, 1973) (hereafter *IC*), pp. 55–83 (esp. 55–61). For his identification of Auerbach (along with Ryle and Wittgenstein, among others) as central to his project, see "Ideology as a Cultural System," *IC*, p. 208. Stephen Greenblatt helpfully explicates the role of Auerbach's work in Geertz's idea of thick description in "The Touch of the Real," *The Fate of Culture: Geertz and Beyond*, ed. Sherry Ortner (Berkeley: University of California Press, 1999).

50. Frei, "The 'Literal Reading' of Biblical Narrative," pp. 140–41.

51. Ibid.

52. Ibid. "This will obviously mean a humbler hermeneutics for rather low-level guidance in interpretation than we have become accustomed to." Cf. Frei, preface to *Identity*, pp. 60–63.

53. Frei, "Remarks," *T&N*, p. 33.

54. Frei borrows the term from Geertz, "Thick Description," *IC*, p. 10.

55. Frei, "Theology and the Interpretation of Narrative," *T&N*, pp. 111–14.

56. Frei, *Identity*, p. 190.

57. Frei, "Scripture as Realistic Narrative: Karl Barth as Critic of Historical Criticism," Lecture for the Karl Barth Society of North America, Toronto, Spring 1974, in *Hans W. Frei: Unpublished Pieces*, p. 31.

58. See Higton, *CPH*, 227–30; Campbell, *Preaching Jesus*, chapter 4.

59. Stanley Hauerwas, "The Church as God's New Language," in *Scriptural Authority and Narrative Interpretation*, ed. Garrett Green (Eugene, OR: Wipf and Stock, 2000), p. 188.

60. Ibid., p. 196.

61. Frei, "Remarks," p. 43.

62. Ibid., p. 42.

63. Barth, *CD* 3/2, p. 443.

64. Ibid., p. 442.

65. Frei, "Scripture as Realistic Narrative: Karl Barth as Critic of Historical Criticism," in *Hans W. Frei: Unpublished Pieces*, p. 35. Frei spends much of this piece working through Barth's thoughts about the difference between *Geschichte* and *Historie* ("empirical history, history to which our fact questions are relevant").

66. As such, Frei explains, the gospel accounts of Jesus' death and resurrection are the hinge on which the depictions of him earlier in the gospel accounts, and teachings and sayings attributed to him, must revolve. "If the depicted Jesus' (not even to mention the 'historical' Jesus') sayings are to function Christologically, they will have to do so as expressions of the person who comes to be portrayed in the last stage of the story," Frei wrote. "One cannot with any confidence proceed in the reverse direction" (*Identity*, p. 176). On these points there are striking parallels between Chapter 13 of *Identity*, and Paragraph 47 of Vol. 3, Part 2 of Barth's *Church Dogmatics*.

67. Joseph F. Mitros, SJ, has meticulously excavated the intricate strands of this complex development during the period of the Apostolic Fathers (early part of the second century). "As to the written record of apostolic teaching, the main body of the apostolic writings was completed by the end of the first century. Although it was elevated to the status of the Word of God only by the middle of the second century, it enjoyed an extraordinary respect among the Fathers as the 'memoirs' and 'letters' of the apostles, the eyewitnesses of Christ, commissioned by Him. . . . Thus the whole body of doctrines and beliefs comprising the Christocentrically interpreted Old Testament and the writings of the apostles, the kerygmatic, catechetical, and liturgical doctrinal elements of the Christian message, constituted the apostolic deposit or gospel" (Mitros, "The Norm of Faith in the Patristic Age," *Theological Studies*, 29, no. 3

(Sept. 1968): 444–71 (here p. 449); cf. Rowan Greer, "The Rise of the Christian Bible," in James Kugel and Rowan Greer, *Early Biblical Interpretation* (Louisville, KY: Westminster John Knox, 1986), pp. 109–25). According to Mitros, the term "tradition" was not applied to this "apostolic deposit" until the latter part of the second century. In chapter 7 I address these developments in much greater detail. Mitros provides important background for my exposition of the "rule of faith" and "rule of truth" in Frei's account of the history and character of the plain sense of Scripture.

As will become apparent in chapter 7, I am also following accounts of the church-Scripture-tradition relation set forth by Brevard Childs' *Biblical Theology of the Old and New Testaments* (Minneapolis: Fortress, 1993). K. E. Greene-McCreight sifts the broader literature on these points in the opening chapter of her important book *Ad Litteram: How Augustine, Calvin, and Barth Read the 'Plain Sense' of Genesis 1–3* (New York: Peter Lang, 1999).

68. Barth, *CD* 3/2, p. 438.

69. Ibid., p. 455; cf. pp. 473–74.

70. As Paul explained to the Christians in Corinth about "liturgical order" (1 Cor. 11:1–16), Barth writes, "Without Christ's commission and Spirit, there was no apostolic word, but without the apostolic word there was no Christian hearing, no hearing of the Word of Christ, no life in the Holy Spirit" (Ibid., p. 309).

71. Mitros describes it thus: "[F]or all practical purposes, Christ was the source and norm of faith for the Fathers. . . . Christ committed His gospel to the apostles as His eyewitnesses, and the apostles in their turn handed it down to the churches they had founded, orally and in writing, that is in Scripture and tradition. Scripture and tradition became in their turn the norm of faith for the Church, but in unequal measure. Scripture was to the Fathers the supreme and ultimate norm, but to be interpreted in the light of tradition by the Church, which is the home of the Holy Spirit" (Mitros, "The Norm of Faith in the Patristic Age," 448). In investigating how St. Irenaeus derived the *regula fidei*, Mitros claims that it was not natural to think about text and tradition separately. He writes: "If we ask what served for Irenaeus as the norm of the Church's teaching and the basis of her faith, the answer would be: both Scripture and tradition. Scripture is 'the basis and support of our faith,' and the tradition is substantially identical with the canon of the (apostolic) truth. Which of them is the superior or the ultimate norm? He never asked this question (as a matter of fact, no Father ever asked it); understandably, then, he never gave a direct and explicit answer to it. Indirectly, however, he seems to have used the Scriptures as the last court of appeal. As we have seen, he calls Scripture the *foundation* of Christian faith, defends orthodoxy by appealing to Holy Writ, and views even the canon of the truth as a condensation of Scripture." (455)

72. Frei, *Identity*, pp. 178-79, 192; cf. Barth, *CD III/2*, pp. 452-56.

73. In fact, this claim issues in a kind of functionalism—in which case Scripture is such in virtue of its *function* of the liturgical practices of the community. As I argue extensively in chapters 7 and 8, Frei manages to avoid this kind of functionalism. In fact, both Scripture and liturgical practices occur at all because of the *Geschichte* of Christ.

74. Frei, *Identity*, p. 194.

75. This is especially the case for chapter 14.

76. Frei, *Identity*, p. 198. In claiming that scriptural narration and liturgical reenactment "render present" the original, Frei does not suggest that they *repeat* the original. That would permit a proliferation of certain unrepeatable events—events that are unique in kind, and which happened "once for all." The events remembered and reenacted by the scriptural accounts and sacraments "make present" these events—as the One portrayed in and through those events draws near—"again and again."

77. Ibid., pp. 199–200. Such claims contrast with Campbell's claims that Frei sets forth a "mentalistic" conception of meaning that pays no attention to the embodied character of reading (*Preaching Jesus*, pp. 102–3).

78. *Identity*, p. 199. These claims in Frei's "Meditation" point back to his claims in the final installment of the original essays (pp. 187–88).

79. Ibid.

80. The fact that Frei's project culminates in these claims renders odd David Demson's attempt to sever Frei's approach to Scripture from Barth's on the grounds that Frei does not explicitly deal with the narrative details of Jesus' appointment, calling, and commissioning of his disciples. "Frei, having left out of account Jesus as Gatherer and Upholder of the disciples (in the earlier stages) and Sender of the disciples (in this third stage), cannot specify the definite shape of Jesus' sharing himself with the apostles." This means that, allegedly, Frei omitted the means by which the presence of Christ mediated through the stories incorporates the present-day believer into the apostolate. And yet, as the above passage demonstrates, Frei provided an intricate account of believers' incorporation into the community of the faithful through Word and Sacrament and the real presence of Christ in the activity of the Spirit. The fact that he does this by way of his meditation on Paul's claims in Romans rather than the accounts that Demson identifies is no indication that Frei could not highlight the centrality of those narratives (or would not in a more expansive project), nor that Paul's charge does not itself presuppose Christ's appointing, calling, and commissioning his disciples. Scripture is rich enough to afford several possibilities for explicating this central point, even if the accounts of Jesus as gatherer and upholder of the disciples provide the "definite shape." In my judgment, the lacuna Demson ascribes to Frei's account is neither a terminal omission nor one that identifies a qualitative distinction between Frei and Barth. So far as I can tell, Demson gives no reason that Frei's use of Paul in Romans to explicate Christ's call to "follow him" and believers' ever-halting incorporation into Christ's body through a "gathering under the Word" (*Gemeinde*) is either incompatible with, precludes, or does not presuppose the narrative accounts of Christ's calling, commissioning, and sending of his apostles. For Demson's criticisms of Frei on this point, see *Hans Frei and Karl Barth: Different Ways of Reading Scripture* (here pp. 106–7).

81. Frei addresses the role of the Spirit in relation to the identity and presence of Christ in chapter 14 of *Identity*.

82. Christomonism is the claim that Christ alone is real—in abstraction from humanity and the other persons of the Trinity. Paul DeHart identifies this concern in Frei's treatment of Barth in *The Trial of the Witnesses*, chapter 6.

83. Barth, *CD* 3/2, p. 467.

84. Ibid., pp. 476–77.

85. Frei, "Remarks," pp. 42–43.

86. Frei, *Identity*, pp. 188–89.

87. Ibid., p. 189.

88. Ibid., p. 194.

89. Ibid., pp. 190–91.

90. Ibid., p. 55.

91. Ibid., p. 54.

92. Ibid., pp. 54, 56.

93. Note that Frei does not rule out using presence as a "technical category" altogether in his later reflections. Rather, he states that if he found that he needed to use the category, he would confine himself to the claim that "*if* one thinks about him under this rubric one cannot conceive of him as *not* being present." He adds, "Further than that I would not go" (ibid., p. 55).

94. Vanhoozer clarifies that Frei continued to speak of "the presence of Christ" informally, much like he would later treat the term "narrative." Vanhoozer, *Biblical Narrative in the Philosophy of Paul Ricoeur* (Cambridge: Cambridge University Press, 1990), p. 164.

95. *Identity*, p. 56. Frei writes, "[M]ost important is the fact that I am of the same mind now about the essay's central affirmation as I was when I wrote it."

96. Ibid.

97. Lindbeck, *The Nature of Doctrine*, pp. 113–18. Hunsinger provides a helpful account of the most important differences between Frei and Lindbeck in his essay "Postliberal Theology," in *The Cambridge Companion to Postmodern Theology*, ed. Kevin Vanhoozer (Cambridge: Cambridge University Press, 2003), pp. 42–57. In my judgment, William Placher's discussion of the complex interrelation of "the narrated world of the Gospels and 'our world'" suggests what a reliable expansion upon Frei's basic ideas on the matter might look like. See Placher, *Narratives of a Vulnerable God* (Louisville, KY: Westminster John Knox, 1994), chapter 4 (esp. pp. 101–4). Placher points out that a crucial text for comparison is Barth's *CD* 2/2, pp. 136ff.

98. Frei, "On Interpreting the Christian Story," The 10th Annual Greenhoe Lectureship (Louisville, KY: Louisville Presbyterian Theological Seminary; Cass: Greenhoe, 1976), transcript in *Hans W. Frei: Unpublished Pieces, Transcripts from the Yale Divinity School Archive*, ed. Mike Higton, p. 52, http://www.library.yale.edu/div/Freitranscripts/Freicomplete.pdf.

99. Frei, "The 'Literal Reading' of Biblical Narrative," pp. 147–49.

CHAPTER 3

1. Frei, "Theology in the University," *Types of Christian Theology* (New Haven: Yale University Press, 1992), pp. 95–132 (hereafter cited as *Types*); see also his "Barth and Schleiermacher: Divergence and Convergence," in George Hunsinger and William Placher, eds., *Theology and Narrative* (Oxford: Oxford University Press, 1993), pp. 177–99 (hereafter cited as *T&N*).

2. Frei continued, "The language is religion-specific, and theology is the constant testing of the way it is used in a given era, against a norm that consists not only of some ordering of the paradigmatic instances of the language (such as the sacred text), but also the cumulative tradition and the most supple and sensitive minds and consciences in the community past and present." See "Theology and the Interpretation of Narrative," *T&N*, p. 100.

3. Frei, "Eberhard Busch's Biography of Karl Barth," *Types*, pp. 158–59.

4. Ibid., p. 161.

5. Ibid.; cf. Frei, "Theology and the Interpretation of Narrative," pp. 111–14.

6. Frei employed this phrase in reference to Lindbeck's conception of "intratextuality," which he then endorsed as the general form of which "the literal sense" is the paradigmatic example ("The 'Literal Reading' of Biblical Narrative," *T&N*, p. 147).

7. Frei, "The 'Literal Reading' of Biblical Narrative," p. 113 (quoting Lindbeck's *The Nature of Doctrine*).

8. Lindbeck, *The Nature of Doctrine* (Philadelphia: Westminster, 1984), p. 118 (hereafter *ND*).

9. "What would it mean to let the biblical world absorb the modern world? Would it mean that we eat their food and wear their clothes and speak their language? And at which time would we emulate their life?" Dan Stiver writes, pressing the point in an unfortunate direction. Elsewhere, he takes Lindbeck's claim to imply that "we emulate cultural details of the ancient world, such as giving up cars and TVs in favor of donkeys and scrolls." Clearly, these are helpfully concrete examples of what Lindbeck has in mind when he speaks in terms of "absorption." Dan Stiver, *Theology After Ricoeur* (Louisville, KY: Westminster John Knox, 2001), esp. pp. 50–53, and his "Theological Method," in *The Cambridge Companion to Postmodern Theology*, ed. Kevin Vanhoozer (Cambridge: Cambridge University Press, 2003), p. 181.

10. Lindbeck, "Scripture, Consensus, and Community," in *The Church in a Postliberal Age*, ed. James J. Buckley (Grand Rapids, MI: Eerdmans, 2003), p. 219.

11. Ibid.

12. "In religious belief and practice a group's ethos is rendered intellectually reasonable by being shown to represent a way of life ideally adapted to the actual state of affairs the world view describes, while the world view is rendered emotionally convincing by being presented as an image of an actual state of affairs peculiarly well-arranged to accommodate such a way of life." Geertz, "Religion as a Cultural System," *The Interpretation of Cultures* (New York: Basic Books, 1973), pp. 89–90 (hereafter *IC*). For a thorough explication and vindication of Geertz's work in this essay, see Kevin Shilbrack's article ""Religion, Models of, and Reality: Are We Through with Geertz?" *Journal of the American Academy of Religion*. Vol 73, No 2 (2005): 429-452.

13. Geertz, "Religion as a Cultural System," pp. 111–12.

14. Geertz, *Islam Observed*, p. 99.

15. Ibid. This practice-oriented dimension of Geertz's work derives from the influences of Max Weber and Ludwig Wittgenstein. Cf. Springs, "What Cultural Theorists of Religion Have to Learn from Wittgenstein; Or, How to Read Geertz as

a Practice Theorist," *Journal of the American Academy of Religion*, Vol. 76, No. 4 (Dec 2008), pp. 934-969.

16. Lindbeck, *ND*, p. 33.

17. Ibid., pp. 32–42.

18. Lindbeck, "Scripture, Consensus and Community," p. 211.

19. Frei, "The 'Literal Reading' of Biblical Narrative," *T&N*, pp. 147–48.

20. Lindbeck, "The Gospel's Uniqueness: Election and Untranslatability," in *The Church in a Postliberal Age*, ed. James Buckley, pp. 225–36. Lindbeck's discussion of uniqueness in this essay expands upon the themes of Lindbeck's "Many Religions and the One True Faith" chapter in *The Nature of Doctrine*.

21. Ibid., p. 230.

22. Ibid., pp. 225–33.

23. Lindbeck cites John Hick as an example of the "pluralist" position (ibid., p. 228).

24. Lindbeck cites Karl Rahner's account of "anonymous Christianity" as an example of one such "inclusivist" position (ibid.); cf. *ND*, pp. 56–57.

25. ibid., pp. 226–30.

26. These debates played out in such articles as John Hick, "On Grading Religions," *Religious Studies*, 17 (1982): 451-67; Paul Griffiths and Delmas Lewis, "On Grading Religions, Seeking Truth, and Being Nice to People," *Religious Studies* 19 (1983): 75–80, and Hick's reply following in the same volume (No. 4, 1983), "On Conflicting Religious Truth Claims," Pp. 485-91.

27. Lindbeck, *ND*, pp. 63–69.

28. Ibid., pp. 130–31.

29. The role of "truth" in Lindbeck's project is threefold and has been the source of much debate. Two of the key claims that are helpful to keep at hand for the present discussion run as follows: "A religion thought of as comparable to a cultural system, as a set of language games correlated with a form of life, may as a whole correspond or not correspond to what a theist calls God's being and will. As actually lived, a religion may be pictured as a single gigantic proposition" (*ND*, p. 51). This system, moreover, works like a map that situates a landscape, becoming true both insofar as it is properly used and rightly guides the traveler. "To the extent that a map is misread and misused, it is a part of a false proposition no matter how accurate it may be in itself. Conversely, even if it is in many ways in error in its distances, proportions, and topographic markings, it becomes constitutive of a true proposition when it guides the traveler rightly. . . . To draw the moral of the metaphor, the categorically and unsurpassably true religion is capable of being rightly utilized, of guiding thought, passions, and actions in a way that corresponds to ultimate reality, and of thus being ontologically (and 'propositionally') true, but is not always and perhaps not even usually so employed" (*ND*, pp. 51-2). The most helpful overview of Lindbeck's position can be found in C. C. Pecknold's *Transforming Postliberal Theology* (New York: T&T Clark, 2005).

30. Lindbeck, "The Gospel's Uniqueness," p. 229.

31. Ibid., p. 232. "[T]he Bible as interpreted within the Christian mainstream purports to provide a totally comprehensive framework, a universal perspective, within

which everything can be properly construed and outside of which nothing can be equally well understood."

32. Erich Auerbach, *Mimesis* (Princeton, NJ: Princeton University Press, 1953), p. 15.

33. Bruce Marshall entertains this concern in what remains perhaps the most illuminating expansion upon Lindbeck's account, entitled "Absorbing the World: Christianity and the Universe of Truths," in *Theology and Dialogue*, ed. Bruce Marshall (Notre Dame: Notre Dame University Press, 1990), pp. 69–102. Marshall demonstrates what it would look like to account for and move beyond the risks of "imperialism" to which Lindbeck's account of "assimilative success" is prone.

34. Frei intimates this concern in his essay "Epilogue: George Lindbeck and the Nature of Doctrine," *Theology and Dialogue*, pp. 279–80. As was often the case for Frei, his concern could not be expressed more subtly. Initially, in fact, Frei characterizes the theory of religion forwarded in *The Nature of Doctrine* as "solely for the service it can render to the ongoing description or self-description of the Christian community." Frei's second subpoint to this point, however, prodded Lindbeck to "Go on, [and] show people how to use Christian language properly" as opposed to sorting out questions about truth as a special question that needs to be answered prior to turning to the explicitly theological task (other concerns of prolegomena would pertain here as well). This point prompted Frei's third subpoint, namely, that Lindbeck's work on a theory of religion prior to Christian self-description positioned him close to Schleiermacher and distanced him from Barth. Ronald Theimann provided detailed clarification of the differences between Barth and Lindbeck in his response to Lindbeck's article, "Barth and Textuality," *Theology Today* 43, no. 3 (1986): 361–76. Other work on their important differences includes Hunsinger, "Truth as Self-involving," *Journal of the American Academy of Religion* 61 (Spring 1993), pp. 41–56.

35. Lindbeck, "The Gospel's Uniqueness," pp. 235.

36. Ibid.

37. Ibid.

38. Ibid.

39. Ibid.

40. Wolterstorff, "Inhabiting the World of the Text" in *Ten Year Commemoration to the Life of Hans Frei*, ed. Giorgy Ogilovich (New York: Semenenko Foundation, 1999.) p. 79. Paul DeHart also raises important criticisms of Lindbeck on this point in *The Trial of the Witnesses* (Oxford: Blackwell, 2006).

41. Frei, *Types*, p. 161.

42. Frei, *Eclipse*, p. 3.

43. Frei, "Theology and the Interpretation of Narrative," *T&N*, p. 111. The same type of asymmetry must be noted of Frei's use of Geertz. He finds it helpful to speak of the Christian tradition's use of the *sensus literalis* as a central feature of its semiotic system. But to apply the Geertzian category in abstraction from this concrete instance of such uses is to make it a misplaced metaphor ("The 'Literal Reading," p. 146). For a meticulous account of Frei's appropriations of Auerbach's work, and their important differences, see David Dawson's *Christian Figural Reading and the Fashioning of Identity* (Berkeley: University of California Press, 2002), pp. 145–60.

44. Wolterstorff, "Inhabiting the World of the Text," p. 80.

45. Karl Barth, *Anselm: Fides Quarens Intellectum* (London: SCM Press, 1960), p. 23.

46. Ibid., pp. 23–24.

47. Wolterstorff, "Inhabiting the World of the Text," p. 79.

48. Barth, *Anselm*, p. 23.

49. Frei, *Eclipse*, p. 3.

50. Frei, *Types*, p. 160. This refusal of a "biblical point of view" was the one of the bases upon which Frei refused the characterization of his thinking (and Barth's) as simply a form of *Heilsgeschichte*. The charge was leveled by Paul Ricoeur in "Toward a Narrative Theology," (1982) in *Figuring the Sacred: Religion, Narrative and Imagination*, ed. Mark Wallace (Minneapolis: Fortress, 1995), pp. 236–48; See also Ricoeur's "Thinking Creation" in André LaCocque and Paul Ricoeur, *Thinking Biblically: Exegetical and Hermeneutical Considerations*, trans. David Pellauer (Chicago: Chicago University Press, 1998), p. 31.

51. Frei, *Types*, p. 159.

52. Hans Frei, "The Doctrine of Revelation in the Thought of Karl Barth, 1909–1922: The Nature of Barth's Break with Liberalism" (PhD diss., Yale University, 1956), p. ii (hereafter cited as *Barth's Break with Liberalism*).

53. Frei, *Types*, p. 160.

54. Barth, *CD* 2/2, p. 73

55. Hunsinger, *How To Read Karl Barth* (Oxford: Oxford University Press, 1991), p. 53. Frei recognized the centrality of this point in his exploration of Barth's use of analogy. See "Analogy and the Spirit in the Thought of Karl Barth," in *Hans W. Frei: Unpublished Pieces: Transcripts from the Yale Divinity School Archive*, ed. Mike Higton, p. 18.

56. Hunsinger, *How To Read Karl Barth*, p. 53.

57. Barth, *CD* III/2, p. 447.

58. See Stephen Fowl, "Could Horace Talk with the Hebrews? Translatability and Moral Disagreement in MacIntyre and Stout," *Journal of Religious Ethics* 19 (Spring 1991): 4–6, for a helpfully concrete example.

59. The point is also developed by William Werpehowski in his seminal article "Ad Hoc Apologetics," *Journal of Religion* 66 (July 1986): 301.

60. Frei, *Types*, pp. 161–62.

61. Ibid., pp. 45–46.

62. Barth, *CD* 3/2, p. 442.

63. Ibid., p. 447.

64. In *The Identity of Jesus Christ* Frei provided opening reflection on the differing types of relevance that study had for believer and nonbeliever: "For the believer, we have agreed, it is a purely formal procedure, useful in praising God with the mind," and added, "What it can mean for the nonbeliever is only a clarification of the procedural order of reflection of those who think about the content of belief" (pp. 70–71).

65. Frei, "Theology and the Interpretation of Narrative," *T&N*, p. 111.

66. Again, see Donald Davidson, "On the Very Idea of a Conceptual Scheme," in *Inquiries into Truth and Interpretation* (Oxford: Oxford University Press, 2001) pp. 183–98; Jeffrey Stout, *Ethics After Babel* (Princeton: Princeton University Press, 2001), chapters 1–2, 5 and the postscript to the second edition; Stout, *Democracy and Tradition* (Princeton: Princeton University Press, 2004); Fowl, "Could Horace Talk to the Hebrews?" pp. 1–20 (esp. 5–7).

67. Lindbeck, "The Gospel's Uniqueness," p. 231.

68. Ibid.

69. MacIntyre, "Relativism, Power, and Philosophy," in *After Philosophy*, ed. Kenneth Baynes, James Bohman, and Thomas McCarthy (Cambridge, MA: MIT Press, 1987), pp. 385–411 (here p. 390).

70. MacIntyre, *Whose Justice? Which Rationality?* (Notre Dame: University of Notre Dame Press, 1988), pp. 370–71.

71. MacIntyre, "Relativism, Power, and Philosophy," p. 391.

72. Ibid., p. 393.

73. MacIntyre, *Whose Justice? Which Rationality?* p. 380.

74. Fowl, "Could Horace Talk to the Hebrews? pp. 1–20 (here 5–6).

75. This point finds much fuller articulation in Stout, *Ethics After Babel*, esp. pp. 216–18. Stout meticulously unpacks MacIntyre's claims about incommensurability throughout this book. See also Fergus Kerr, *Theology After Wittgenstein* (Oxford: Basil Blackwell, 1986), pp. 105-09.

76. For a brief example of what such a position might look like, see Alvin Plantinga, "Pluralism: A Defense of Religious Exclusivism," in *A Defense of Religious Exclusivism*, ed. Philip Quinn (New York: Oxford, 2000), pp. 172–92. For a helpful example of the application of Davidson to Lindbeck's project—one which highlights how Frei differs on precisely this point—see Adonis Vidu, "Lindbeck's Scheme-Content Distinction: A Critique of the Dualism between Orders of Language," *Journal for the Study of Religions and Ideologies* 9 (Winter 2004): 110–22.

77. For a lucid account of how "worldview" talk actually fuels the realism/antirealism debate, see John Bowlin and Peter Stromberg, "Representation and Reality in the Study of Culture," *American Anthropologist* 99 (March 1997): 123–34.

78. Kathryn Tanner, *Theories of Culture* (Minneapolis: Fortress, 1997), p. 150.

79. Frei, *Types*, p. 81.

80. Frei, "Theology and the Interpretive of Narrative," *T&N*, p. 108.

81. Barth, "Humanism," *God Here and Now*, trans. Paul M. van Buren (New York: Routledge, 2004), pp. 131–32.

82. Ibid.

83. Frei, "The 'Literal Reading'," *T&N*, pp. 147–48.

84. Frei, *Eclipse*, p. 3.

85. William Placher, "On Being Postliberal: A Response to James Gustafson," *Christian Century*, April 7, 1999, p. 391.

86. Wolterstorff, "Inhabiting the World of the Text," p. 79. See also Wolterstorff, "What New Haven and Grand Rapids Have to Say to Each Other," in *Seeking Understanding: The Stob Lectures, 1986–1998* (Grand Rapids, MI: Eerdmans, 2001), pp. 251–94.

87. See the point as I explicate at the end of the introduction, citing Eugene Rogers, "Supplementing Barth on Jews and Gender: Identifying God by Anagogy and the Spirit," *Modern Theology* 14 (January 1998): 50.

88. In chapters 7 and 8 I work through the multiple strands of normative constraint that render a tradition-situated account of scriptural practices an entirely objective affair.

89. Frei, "Theology and the Interpretation of Narrative," *T&N*, pp. 113–14.

CHAPTER 4

1. Carl F. H. Henry, "Narrative Theology: An Evangelical Appraisal," and Frei's response in *Trinity Journal* 8 (1987): 3–24. This particular debate has been mediated by George Hunsinger in an essay entitled, "What Can Evangelicals and Postliberals Learn from Each Other? The Carl Henry–Hans Frei Exchange Reconsidered," in *The Nature of Confession: Evangelicals and Postliberals in Conversation*, ed. Timothy R. Phillips and Dennis R. Okholm (Downers Grove, IL: InterVarsity, 1996).

2. Frei, "Theology and the Interpretation of Narrative," in George Hunsinger and William Placher, eds., *Theology and Narrative* (Oxford: Oxford University Press, 1993), p. 108 (hereafter cited as *T&N*).

3. Ibid.

4. Jacques Derrida, *Of Grammatology*, trans. Gayatri Chakravorty Spivak (Baltimore: Johns Hopkins, 1976), p. 156.

5. For a helpfully succinct account of this feature of Barth's theology, see Bruce McCormack, "Beyond Non-foundational and Postmodern Readings of Karl Barth: Critically Realistic Dialectical Theology," *Orthodox and Modern: Studies in the Theology of Karl Barth* (Grand Rapids, MI: Baker Academic, 2008), pp. 109-13.

6. Hunsinger, "What Can Evangelicals and Postliberals Learn from Each Other?" p. 137.

7. Henry, "Narrative Theology," p. 11.

8. Frei, "Response to 'Narrative Theology: An Evangelical Appraisal,'" *T&N*, p. 211.

9. Ibid., pp. 211 & 212.

10. Ibid., p. 209.

11. Hunsinger, "What Can Evangelicals and Postliberals Learn from Each Other?" p. 143, citing pp. 151 and 51 of the 1975 Fortress edition of Hans Frei, *The Identity of Jesus Christ* (Eugene, OR: Wipf and Stock, 1997).

12. Frei, *The Identity of Jesus Christ*, p. 183.

13. Frei, "Historical Reference and the Gospels: A Response to a Critique of *The Identity of Jesus Christ*," in *Hans W. Frei: Unpublished Pieces*, ed. Mike Higton, p. 67. Frei's comment here refers to claims that appear on pp. 175–77 of *Identity*. The operative paragraph reads: "I have argued that Jesus' individual identity comes to focus directly in the passion-resurrection narrative rather than in the account of his person and teaching in his earlier ministry. It is in this final and climactic sequence that the storied Jesus is most of all himself, and there—unlike those earlier points at which we can get to his individual identity only ambiguously—we are confronted with him

directly as the unsubstitutable individual who is what he does and undergoes and is manifested directly as who he is. Whether or not we know much or anything about the 'historical' Jesus is probably a well nigh insoluble question; but once again, *if* the accounts rendering the storied Jesus are to be joined to fact claims about the "historical" Jesus in such a way as to make the depicted Jesus genuinely accessible and thus give the historical person significant history-like religious content, the union will have to be in the sequence where the crucified Jesus is raised from the dead as the Christ" (177). Frei advocates roughly this same position in his 1986 lecture, "Conflicts in Interpretation," *T&N*, pp. 164–65. Hunsinger's treatment of Frei on this point is illuminating, see his "The Daybreak of the New Creation: Christ's Resurrection in Recent Theology," *The Scottish Journal of Theology* 7, no. 2 (2004): 14–16.

14. Frei, "Response to 'Narrative Theology: An Evangelical Appraisal,'" p. 208.

15. Frei, *Identity*, p. 59.

16. Frei, "Response to 'Narrative Theology: An Evangelical Appraisal,'" p. 209.

17. Ibid.

18. For an expansion upon this point, see William Placher, "Scripture as Realistic Narrative: Some Preliminary Questions," *Perspectives in Religious Studies* 5 (Spring 1987), pp. 32–41; cf. Placher further developed these claims in his *Narratives of a Vulnerable God* (Louisville, KY: Westminster John Knox, 1994), chapters 1 & 4 (esp. pp. 92–95). Placher's explanation of this point is helpful enough to quote at length: He writes: "Reading these stories, one learns who Jesus is—that is, one learns both the characteristics of his human life and the fact that that human life was somehow the self-revelation of God. Many of the individual episodes serve as biographical anecdotes, 'true' if they illustrate his character authentically even though the particular incident they narrate never happened, and the overall shape of the narrative portrays something of Jesus' identity. While such an identity description need not be correct in all its particulars in order to get someone's identity right, its general themes do have to capture a person's essential features, and *some* of its particulars may be crucial. . . . [I]f Jesus never taught about love, or if the disciples, as Reimarus argued two hundred years ago, conspired to invent the story of the resurrection so that they would not have to go back to fishing, then the Gospels are wrong about Jesus" (92).

19. Frei, *Identity*, p. 182.

20. Ibid.

21. Frei, "Of the Resurrection of Christ," (1987), *T&N*, p. 203.

22. While Frei stands in concert with Barth against abstraction and speculation, Frei's account of historical reference differs from Barth's in a crucial way. Hunsinger has identified the character and significance of this difference, writing: "In his treatment of the question of knowledge, Barth did not keep the same balance between historicity and transcendence. He focused almost entirely on the transcendent aspect while denying any significance to modern historical inquiry (IV/2, pp. 149–50). The possibility of disconfirmation, as explored by Frei, apparently did not interest him; consequently; Frei's thoughtful emendation of Barth's position was arguably more nuanced and satisfying. Nevertheless, Barth richly developed the transcendent aspect in a way that remains unsurpassed. He was untiring in his stress that if Christ was risen from the dead, so as to be present as the risen Lord, then his own self-witness as

the One who lives was always necessarily decisive. Faith depended not on historical investigation but on an encounter with the living Christ" ("The Daybreak of the New Creation," p. 17).

23. Frei, "Of the Resurrection of Christ," p. 203.

24. Frei, "Response to Narrative Theology," pp. 211 & 212.

25. Frei, *Identity*, p. 194. For all of the reasons above, I think that Wolterstorff is mistaken when he claims that "the traditional view that proper reading of the scriptures is a mode of revelation in the present (and was a mode of revelation in the past) is as absent from Frei's line of thought as it was from Locke's; that this is 'the Word of God' does not function in his argument." Wolterstorff, "Is Narrativity the Linchpin? Reflections on the Hermeneutic of Hans Frei" in *Relativism and Religion*, ed. Charles M. Lewis (London: Palgrave Macmillan, 1995), p. 101.

26. Henry wrote, "Narrative hermeneutics removes from the interpretative process any text-transcendent referent and clouds the narrative's relationship to a divine reality not exhausted by literary presence" ("Narrative Theology," p. 13).

27. Frei, *Types of Christian Theology* (New Haven: Yale University Press, 1992), p. 79 (hereafter cited as *Types*).

28. Hunsinger, "What can Evangelicals and Postliberals Learn from each Other?" pp. 145–46.

29. Frei, "Theology and the Interpretive of Narrative," (1982), *T&N*, p. 108.

30. McCormack, *Orthodox and Modern*, p. 123.

31. John Franke, "Karl Barth, the Postmodern Turn, and Evangelical Theology," in *Karl Barth and Evangelical Theology: Convergences and Divergences*, ed. Sung Wook Chung (Grand Rapids, MI: Baker Academic, 2006), p. 273.

32. Ibid., pp. 272–73. Hans Urs von Balthasar, *The Theology of Karl Barth: Exposition and Interpretation,* trans. Edward T. Oakes, SJ (San Francisco: Ignatius, 1992); Karl Barth, *Anselm: Fides Quaerens Intellectum: Anselm's Proof of the Existence of God in the Context of His Theological Scheme* (London: SCM, [1960] 1985) (hereafter *Anselm*).

33. McCormack, *Orthodox and Modern*, p. 124 n. 45.

34. Ibid., pp. 113, 158.

35. Ibid., p. 123.

36. Hans Frei, "The Doctrine of Revelation in the Thought of Karl Barth, 1909–1922: The Nature of Barth's Break with Liberalism" (PhD diss., Yale University, 1956), p. 194 (hereafter cited as "Barth's Break with Liberalism"). He further developed this suggestion in a dense discussion of Barth's work for an article adapted from his dissertation and included in a 1957 Festschrift for H. Richard Niebuhr. Cf. Frei, "Niebuhr's Theological Background," in *Faith and Ethics*, ed. Paul Ramsey (New York: Harper and Row, 1957), pp. 49–53 (this essay includes pages 174–202 of Frei's dissertation). In both this essay and in his dissertation Frei bases this characterization of the shift primarily upon Barth's own retrospective admission that the Anselm book "characterize[s] the change in his thinking in the decade following 1928." Barth's remarks appear in "How My Mind Has Changed," *Christian Century*, Sept. 13 & 20, 1939. For an overview of von Balthasar's thesis, its problems, and the ensuing developments, see Bruce McCormack, *Karl Barth's Critically Realistic Dialectical*

Theology (Oxford: Clarendon Press, 1995), pp. 1–28. To date, the literature has addressed Frei's dissertation only to a limited extent. Mike Higton addresses Frei's treatment of 'relationalism' and the challenges of 'epistemological monophysitism' in *Christ, Providence & History* (New York: T&T Clark International, 2004); John Allan Knight explicates with exceptional clarity how Frei's dissertation thematically oriented his engagement with Barth throughout his career in "The Barthian Heritage of Hans W. Frei," *Scottish Journal of Theology* 61/3 (2008): 307-326.

37. "Where von Balthasar was at least tempted to see the *Christliche Dogmatik* as initiating Barth's turn to analogy, for Hans Frei that volume belonged without question to the dialectical period and the shift which was thought to take place with the Anselm book was seen to be dramatic in character—in Frei's word, it represented a 'revolution' in Barth's thought" (McCormack, *Karl Barth's Critically Realistic Dialectical Theology*, p. 4); "Frei believed that the Anselm book constituted a methodological revolution in Barth's thought" (McCormack, *Orthodox and Modern*, p. 124 n. 45); "On the one hand, Frei could speak of the Anselm book in 1931 as having wrought a 'revolution' in Barth's thought and could find evidence for this in an alleged retreat from actualism in the doctrine of God (though what he meant by the latter point is not especially clear). . . . And yet, Frei is also well aware that the mature Barth of the *Dogmatics* continued to insist that God is revealed in hiddenness, in the givenness of an object with which God is not identical" (McCormack, *Orthodox and Modern*, p. 160 n. 159);. Cf. John Franke, "Karl Barth, the Postmodern Turn, and Evangelical Theology," pp. 272–73.

38. Frei, "Barth's Break with Liberalism", p. 198.

39. Ibid., p. 197.

40. Ibid., p. 199.

41. Ibid., p. 200.

42. Ibid., p. 198.

43. Ibid., p. 196.

44. Ibid., p. 198.

45. Ibid., pp. 197–200. Frei identifies the *analogia fidei* in *CD* 1/1, pp. 250 ff.; 2/1, pp. 63–93, 252–67. In the following sentence he identifies the *analogia relationis* between God and man in *CD* 3/2, pp. 262ff.

46. Frei, "Barth's Break with Liberalism", pp. 520 ff., 557 & 568; Frei explicates long passages from the 1922 edition of Barth's *The Epistle to the Romans*, trans. Edwyn Hoskyns (London: Oxford University Press, 1933), pp. 39ff. & 78ff. Note that the word "or" in this passage is an error. Frei intends to write "of." Nearly forty pages later he provides a correct restatement of this point, writing, "The more [Barth] turns to *a doctrine of analogy* (which was, as we have seen, not quite absent even at the height of the dialectical period, in his understanding of faith), the more we see through revelation a freedom that is in God himself" (557, italics added). At the end of the parenthetical remark in the preceding sentence Frei refers his reader by way of a footnote to his previous demonstration of this point, citing the passage from page 520 quoted above, the one containing the (mis-worded) phrase "doctrine or analogy."

47. Barth, *Die Christliche Welt* (1923), cols. 249f. (Frei also cites pp. 193ff.); quoted by Frei in "Barth's Break with Liberalism", p. 522.

48. Ibid., pp. 520ff., 557 & 568.

49. Ibid., pp. 522–23.

50. Frei, "Niebuhr's Theological Background," p. 52.

51. This, Frei explains, occurs in virtue of what Barth identified as the *analogia fidei*. Frei locates Barth's account of this in *CD* 1/1, p. 250ff., and 2/1, pp. 68–93 and 252–67 (ibid.)

52. Frei, "Niebuhr's Theological Background," p. 52.

53. Ibid., p. 53.

54. Ibid.

55. Ibid., p. 52. It should come as no surprise if Frei's description of the analogical form reflects a Chalcedonian pattern (without separation and division; without confusion or change; the parts then uniquely ordered in relation to the person of Christ). Hunsinger credits Frei with having first taught him to see the Chalcedonian affirmation of Christ's incarnation as a heuristic pattern. On these points, see Hunsinger's "Karl Barth's Christology: Its Basic Chalcedonian Character," *Disruptive Grace* (Grand Rapids: Eerdmans, 2000), pp. 131–47. For an overview of the history and character of Barth's use of analogy, see McCormack, *Karl Barth's Critically Realistic Dialectical Theology*, pp. 16–26, 312–14 & 367.

56. Busch cites Barth's comment to his friend Eduard Thurneysen of January 9, 1931 (Busch, p. 214). Busch also cites *CD* 1/1, p. 162.

57. Barth, "How My Mind Has Changed."

58. Frei, "Barth's Break with Liberalism", p. 522. These subtleties of Frei's account contrast with McCormack's characterization of Frei's treatment of this issue. McCormack construes Frei as (1) locating the *Christliche Dogmatik* of 1927 within the so-called "dialectical period" without qualification, (2) characterizing Barth's "turn" to analogy as dramatic ("revolutionary"), and (3) positioning that turn squarely within the *Anselm* text. See McCormack's *Karl Barth's Critically Realistic Dialectical Theology*, p. 4.

59. Frei, "Barth's Break with Liberalism", pp. 562, 568 & 576–77. Frei acknowledges that his comments extending beyond that period present a far too cursory examination of what he takes to be "the later, analogical period of Barth's thought."

60. I am not suggesting that this retrieval and repositioning of Frei's account finally gets the full development of Barth's thought correct. There remain other points of disagreement between McCormack's account and other of Frei's claims about Barth's development. Examples would be Frei's locating Barth's shift to dialectical method as occurring between Romans 1 and 2, and his claim that Barth did not finally break with "relationalism" until some time between the two editions of *Romans*. Cf. McCormack, *Karl Barth's Critically Realistic Dialectical Theology*, pp. 202, 147.

61. See, for instance, Frei, "Theology and the Interpretive of Narrative," (1982), *T&N*, p. 108; Frei, "Analogy and the Spirit in the Theology of Karl Barth," pp. 9–10 & 21–23; "Response to 'Narrative Theology: An Evangelical Appraisal,'" (1985), *T&N*, p. 209.

62. Frei, "Analogy and the Spirit in the Theology of Karl Barth," pp. 9–10 (italics added). In this passage, Frei is explicating Barth's claim in *CD* 2/1, p. 190 (Frei's translation). Frei reads this passage as descriptive of the "positive, special presence of God who is invisible and unpronounceable because he is not there in the manner in which the corporeal and spiritual world which he has created is there. Rather, in this . . .

world he is there in his revelation, in Jesus Christ, in the proclamation of his name, in his witnesses and sacraments and thus visible only for faith. . . . This means that he is to be seen only as the Invisible one, pronounced as he who cannot be pronounced—and both not as the inclusive concept of limit or as origin of our vision and speech but as the one who orders and permits . . . and in free, gracious decision enables this our hearing and speaking."

63. John Franke, "Karl Barth, the Postmodern Turn, and Evangelical Theology," p. 273.

64. Frei, "Karl Barth: Theologian," (1969), *T&N*, p. 170.

65. Frei, "Eberhard Busch's Biography of Karl Barth," (1978), *Types*, pp. 158–59.

66. Frei, "Response to Narrative Theology," p. 212.

67. Frei, "Conflicts in Interpretation," (1986), *T&N*, pp. 163–64.

68. Frei, "Of the Resurrection of Christ," (1987), *T&N*, p. 205.

69. Ibid.

70. Kevin Vanhoozer, for instance, characterizes Frei's later work as a "cultural-linguistic correction" to his earlier work. On this account, Frei's later thinking comes off as textual functionalism that epitomizes what is most erroneous about "cultural-linguistic" approaches. Vanhoozer alleges that Frei confines the theological task to describing the logic implicit in the practices that constitute the church, and thus a task incapable of criticizing and correcting "Christian malpractice." Vanhoozer, *The Drama of Doctrine* (Louisville, KY: Westminster John Knox, 2005), esp. pp. 10–11, 172–73.

71. McCormack acknowledges some of the realist claims in Frei's account (*Types*, 39), only to set them aside as ambivalent and underdeveloped by Frei. He conjectures that Frei was reluctant to be sufficiently forthcoming about Barth's theological realism because Frei worked as a theologian in a secular, university context, where such claims were unfashionable, and theological inquiry in general was difficult to justify. In my judgment, such an explanation is inadequate to the content and motivating concerns of Frei's work from early to late and is inaccurate when viewed in light of all the examples set forth in the preceding pages, and in the chapter that follows. McCormack, *Orthodox and Modern*, p. 123.

72. McCormack, *Orthodox and Modern*, p. 160.

73. Frei, "Response to 'Narrative Theology: An Evangelical Appraisal,'" *T&N*, p. 212.

CHAPTER 5

1. Bruce McCormack, *Orthodox and Modern: Studies in the Theology of Karl Barth* (Grand Rapids, MI: Baker Academic, 2008), pp. 123–24.

2. George Hunsinger, *How to Read Karl Barth: The Shape of His Theology* (Oxford: Oxford University Press, 1991), p. 55.

3. Ibid., pp. 59–60.

4. Ronald Thiemann, *Religion in Public Life: A Dilemma for Democracy* (Washington, D.C.: Georgetown University Press, 1996), p. 133.

5. Consider Thiemann's explication of the matter: "While these background beliefs are not immune to revision, they must remain relatively fixed for the framework to remain stable. Revision or suspension of a background belief or basic conviction requires a rearrangement of all dependent beliefs and the possible rejection

of some. These defining convictions are resistant to change, because they provide the community's essential identity. . . . [W]hile these fundamental beliefs resist revision, they are not in a logically strong sense incorrigible. The history of religion is replete with examples of fundamental restructuring of communal identity that have occurred when basic convictions have been revised or jettisoned (e.g., the Gentile mission of early Christianity, the Protestant reformations, the rise of historical criticism of the Bible)." (*Religion in Public Life*, p. 134).

6. Hunsinger, *How to Read Karl Barth*, p. 57.

7. For an example see Thiemann, *Revelation and Theology: The Gospel as Narrated Promise* (Notre Dame: University of Notre Dame Press, 1985), see chapter 4 (esp. pp. 77 & 78).

8. Hunsinger, *How to Read Karl Barth*, p. 56.

9. Frei, "Types of Academic Theology," in *Types of Christian Theology* (New Haven, CT: Yale University Press, 1992), p. 126.

10. "Through a kind of doctrinal-hermeneutical feedback loop, the results of doctrinal construction, having arisen (however complexly) from scripture, can then be brought to bear on the interpretation of scripture," explains Hunsinger, *How to Read Karl Barth*, pp. 56–57. For a succinct restatement of how this played out in Frei's theology, see William Placher's *Narratives of a Vulnerable God* (Louisville, KY: Westminster/John Knox, 1994), pp. 15–16.

11. Hans Frei, *The Identity of Jesus Christ* (Eugene, OR: Wipf and Stock, 1997), pp. 164–65.

12. Ibid., n. 16. See Karl Barth, *Church Dogmatics* 4/1: *The Doctrine of Reconciliation* (Edinburgh: T&T Clark, 1956), pp. 224 ff.

13. Kathryn Tanner, *Theories of Culture* (Minneapolis, MN: Augsburg Fortress, 1997), p. 73 (hereafter *TC*).

14. Ibid., p. 74.

15. She cites Frei in *Types*, pp. 2, 20–21, 124, stating that "the ideas in this book of his represent in many ways the founding ideas of postliberalism" (*TC*, p. 184 n. 22).

16. Frei quoting Barth, *CD* 1/1, trans. G.T. Thomson (Edingburgh: T&T Clark, 1936), p. 1, in *Types*, p. 78.

17. Frei, "Remarks in Connection with a Theological Proposal," (1967) *Theology and Narrative* (Oxford: Oxford University Press, 1993), p. 33.

18. Frei, *Types*, p. 5. "'[L]iteral' is not referentially univocal but embraces several possibilities. All other senses of the quite diverse and changing notion 'literal' are secondary to this (to my mind, basic ascriptive Christological) sense of 'literal.' . . . That is the minimal agreement of how 'literal' reading has generally been understood in the Western Christian tradition."

19. Ibid., p. 79.

20. Ibid. (italics added).

21. Ibid., p. 40.

22. Frei, "On Interpreting the Christian Story," The 10th Annual Greenhoe Lectureship (Louisville, KY: Louisville Presbyterian Theological Seminary; Cass: Greenhoe, 1976); transcript in *Hans W. Frei: Unpublished Pieces, Transcripts from the*

Yale Divinity School Archive, ed. Mike Higton, p. 58, captured from http://www.library.yale.edu/div/Freitranscripts/ Freicomplete.pdf.

23. Ludwig Wittgenstein, *Philosophical Investigations* (Oxford: Blackwell, 2001), Sec. 43; Cf. Wittgenstein, *Philosophical Grammar* (Oxford: Basil Blackwell, 1974), pp. 58–62.

24. Frei, "On Interpreting the Christian Story," pp. 58–59.

25. Ibid., p. 57.

26. Ibid., pp. 57–58.

27. Frei, "Theology and the Interpretation of Narrative," *T&N*, pp. 96–97.

28. Frei, *Types*, p. 39 (emphasis added).

29. Frei, "Epilogue: George Lindbeck and the Nature of Doctrine," in Bruce Marshall (ed) *Theology and Dialogue* (Notre Dame: University of Notre Dame Press, 1990), pp. 278–79.

30. Frei, *Types*, p. 42.

31. Ibid.

32. Frei, "Types of Academic Theology," *Types*, pp. 124–25.

33. Ibid., p. 125.

34. Ibid., p. 126 (italics added).

35. Frei, "Theology and the Interpretation of Narrative," in *T&N*, pp. 96–97. Cf. Geertz, *Islam Observed* (New Haven: Yale Universtiy Press, 1968), p. 96 n. 4.

36. Geertz, "Thick Description," *The Interpretation of Cultures* (New York: Basic Books, 1973), p. 9.

37. Ibid.

38. Ibid., p. 10.

39. Ibid.

40. Frei, *Types*, pp. 12–13.

41. Frei, "Literal Reading," *T&N*, p. 148.

42. Geertz, *After the Fact* (Cambridge, MA: Harvard University Press, 1996), pp. 18–19.

43. Ibid.

44. Frei, *Types*, p. 39.

45. Frei makes this point starkly in a letter to Gary Comstock of 1984 quoted by Higton, *Christ, Providence and History* (London: T&T Clark, 2004), p. 218 n. 93.

46. Tanner, *TC*, p. 76. Charles Campbell makes a similar charge that Frei presents a notion of culture in "monolithic"— and thus insufficiently "dynamic" and "nuanced"—terms. Such a criticism similarly misses its mark (in Frei's case, at least) for all the reasons rehearsed in the above section. Further, Campbell's criticism is based upon a comparison of Raymond Williams and Geertz that suggests an inadequate account of the latter. I have addressed criticisms that misread Geertz's approach as insufficiently historical and proposing an overly-integrated account of culture in my article "What Cultural Theorists of Religion have to Learn from Wittgenstein, or, How to Read Geertz as a Practice Theorist," *Journal of the American Academy of Religion* Vol. 76, No. 4 (Dec 2008), pp. 934–969; see Campbell, *Preaching Jesus* (Grand Rapids, MI: Eerdmans, 1997), pp. 80–82.

47. Tanner, *TC*, p. 76.

48. Ibid., pp. 138–39.

49. Ibid. Beyond her own articulation of it, Tanner ascribes some version of this criticism to David Bryant, "Christian Identity and Historical Change: Postliberals and Historicity," *The Journal of Religion* 73 (January 1993): 31–41; see also Mary McClintock-Fulkerson, *Changing the Subject* (Minneapolis, MN: Fortress Press, 1994), pp. 158–64; James Buckley, "Doctrine in Diaspora," *The Thomist* 49 (July 1985): 443–59.

CHAPTER 6

1. Ronald Thiemann, *Revelation and Theology: The Gospel as Narrated Promise* (Notre Dame: University of Notre Dame Press, 1985), p. 45.

2. For a helpful historical contextualization of the emergence and debate over foundationalism, see Jeffrey Stout, *The Flight from Authority* (Notre Dame: University of Notre Dame Press, 1981); see also William Placher, *Unapologetic Theology* (Louisville, KY: Westminster/John Knox, 1989).

3. Wittgenstein offers a helpful illustration of the point in *Philosophical Grammar*, (Oxford: Basil Blackwell, 1974), pp. 55–65; perhaps the most influential treatment of this point of criticism of classical foundationalism is Wilfrid Sellars *Empiricism and the Philosophy of Mind* (Cambridge, MA: Harvard University Press, 1997). Sellars' criticisms are not without their detractors. For historical and philosophical contextualization of his attack on 'the given' see Robert Brandom's *Tales of the Mighty Dead* (Cambridge, MA: Harvard University Press, 2002); for helpful entrée' into the ensuing debates see Michael P. Wolf and Mark Norris Lance, eds., *The Self-Correcting Enterprise* (Amsterdam: Rodopi, 2006).

4. John Dewey, *The Quest for Certainty* (Carbondale: Southern Illinois University Press, 1988), pp. 160–65; for an influential account of Dewey's contribution to these developments, see Richard Rorty, *Philosophy and the Mirror of Nature* (Princeton: Princeton University Press, 1979), and more broadly, Richard Bernstein, *Between Objectivism and Relativism* (Philadelphia: University of Pennsylvania Press, 1983).

5. Among numerous accounts, Nancey Murphy provides a systematic interrogation of foundationalism from a theologically concerned perspective in *Beyond Liberalism and Fundamentalism* (Harrisburg, PA: Trinity Press International, 1996); another helpful and particularly trenchant analysis can be found in Bruce D. Marshall's *Trinity and Truth* (Cambridge: Cambridge University Press, 2000), chapters 3 and 4.

6. W. V. O. Quine, *Word and Object* (Cambridge, MA: MIT, 1960), pp. 3–4.

7. John E. Thiel, *Nonfoundationalism* (Minneapolis: Augsburg Fortress, 2000), pp. 1–2; for a thorough treatment of the issue, see Stanley J. Grenz and John R. Franke, *Beyond Foundationalism* (Louisville, KY: Westminster John Knox, 2001).

8. Frei, "Letter to Gary Comstock," November 5, 1984 (YDS 12-184), as quoted by Mike Higton in *Christ, Providence and History* (London: T&T Clark, 2004), p. 199.

9. This character of Frei's work is evident from its beginning to its end content-wise. He reflects explicitly upon making such connections nowhere more clearly than in his response to Carl Henry. See *Theology and Narrative* (Oxford: Oxford

University Press, 1993), pp. 207–12. Hunsinger further refines this insight when he suggestively describes an account of revelation that seeks to be nonfoundationalist without falling prey to either subjectivism or fideism. He then identifies helpful texts for understanding and explicating this theological approach such as Wittgenstein's *On Certainty*, Alasdair MacIntyre's *Whose Justice? Which Rationality?* and Robert Brandom's *Making It Explicit*. "The Harnack/Barth Correspondence: A Paraphrase with Comments," in *Disruptive Grace* (Grand Rapids: Eerdmans, 2000), p. 333 n. 13.

10. Wilfrid Sellars, "Some Reflections on Language Games," in *Science, Perception and Reality* (London: Routledge and Kegan Paul, 1963), p. 170.

11. Hunsinger, *How to Read Karl Barth* (Oxford: Oxford University Press, 1991), p. 281 n. 1.

12. See Sellars's *Empiricism and the Philosophy of Mind*, introduction by Richard Rorty and study guide by Robert Brandom (Cambridge, MA: Harvard University Press, 1997), esp. 152–55.

13. I am awkwardly restating a description of Sellars' account that Jeffrey Stout sets forth in his essay "Davidson, Rorty, and Brandom on Truth," in *Radical Interpretation in Religion*, ed. Nancy Frankenberry (Cambridge: Cambridge University Press, 2002), esp. 36–37. At a pivotal turn in the explanation he writes, "Sellar's great breakthrough was precisely to notice that we are not faced with an exclusive choice between seeing perception as completely unshaped by inferential capacities— "the myth of the given"— and seeing it as a variety of inference. The Sellarsian alternative is to see perception, in the epistemically relevant sense of the term, as noninferential but also as something only a concept-using reason-exchanger can engage in. An analogous reinterpretation of intentional action is also required by Sellars's approach. Once these ideas are incorporated into inferentialism, perception and action can be factored into a broadly inferentialist account of conceptual content along with the contribution of strictly inferential relations. This is the revision in inferentialism that is required to avoid idealistic inferentialism's loss of contact with the world" (36 n. 14).

14. Wolterstorff draws on the basic insights of this idea as well. See "Can Belief in God be Rational if it has no Foundations?" in *Faith and Rationality*, ed. Plantinga and Wolterstorff (Notre Dame: University of Notre Dame Press, 1984), p. 176

15. Sellars, *Empiricism and the Philosophy of Mind*, pp. 68–79, and Brandom's explication, pp. 152–62.

16. Alvin Plantinga, "Is Belief in God Properly Basic?" in *Contemporary Classics in Philosophy of Religion*, ed. Ann Loades and Loyal D. Rue (La Salle, IL: Open Court, 1991), p. 101 (italics added).

17. Ibid., pp. 101–2.

18. Plantinga, "Justification and Theism," in *Christian Theism and the Problems of Philosophy*, ed. Michael Beaty (Notre Dame: University of Notre Dame Press, 1990), pp. 44–45.

19. Wittgenstein, *On Certainty* (Oxford: Blackwell, 1975), sections 520–49; cf. Stout, "Davidson, Rorty and Brandom on Truth," p. 36 n. 14.

20. Plantinga, "Is Belief in God Properly Basic?" p. 101.

21. Wittgenstein, *On Certainty*, sections 524–31; cf. *Philosophical Investigations*, section 381ff.

22. Though heavily influenced by this portion of Sellars' account, Robert Brandom departs from Sellars on this point. Sellars is committed to withholding the attribution of knowledge to a claimer who cannot, at some point, explicitly justify his or her claim. Brandom, by contrast, endorses the view that a claimer can be recognized by an observer as being justified in making a claim that he or she simply cannot justify. In such cases, it is recognition from a third-person perspective that confers justification upon the practitioner in question. See *Making It Explicit* (Cambridge, MA: Harvard University Press, 1994), pp. 219–21; cf. "Vocabularies of Pragmatism," in *Rorty and His Critics*, ed. Robert Brandom (Oxford: Blackwell, 2000), pp. 165–66.

23. Plantinga, "Is Belief in God Properly Basic?" p. 101.

24. Hunsinger, *How to Read Karl Barth*, p. 58. I take Hunsinger's use of the word "interpretation" here to be consistent with the approach to scriptural interpretation (hermeneutics) that I explicated in Frei and Barth's thinking in chapter 1 above. I make this case in detail throughout chapters 7 and 8. Plantinga agrees with the basically coherentist shape of the complex of beliefs. Some will be properly "immediate and basic," others will not. Plantinga, *Warranted Christian Belief* (Oxford: Oxford University Press, 2000), pp. 267–68.

25. Plantinga, "Justification and Theism," p. 66; "Is Belief in God Properly Basic?" pp. 45–46. In more recent work Plantinga has developed and defended his position on warrant and proper function at a length and level of detail that I cannot do justice to here without something along the lines of a book-length digression. For present purposes of contrast and illustration, however, I refer merely to the fact that in the article to which I presently allude, Plantinga concedes that his articulation of his position there amounts to something similar to epistemic reliabilism. Along with the two requirements mentioned in the previous sentence, he adds that a belief has warrant as knowledge when belief formation occurs "according to a design plan aimed at the production of true beliefs, when there is a high statistical probability of such beliefs being true." For a helpful critical engagement, see Richard Swinburne, "Plantinga on Warrant," *Religious Studies* 37 (2001): 203–14, and Plantinga's rejoinder, pp. 215–22.

26. The Brandomian pragmatist does as well. However, I should hold that concern in abeyance in order to avoid a digression. Cf. *MIE*, pp. 206–13.

27. As we saw in chapter 4, Frei has the passion and resurrection in mind in particular.

28. Barth, *CD* 4/2, p. 131. See my discussion at the end of chapter 2.

29. This is merely to construe "faith seeking understanding" as an embodied set of practices extended over time rather than isolated instances in abstraction from fellow believers, community, and tradition. It is also to add the possibility of attributing knowledge from third-person recognition of one's reliability in making noninferential reports about Scripture. Brandom offers the crucial explanation of how a related tradition of critical inquiry contributes to (what I am calling) the "justifying conditions" of noninferential reports in "Vocabularies of Pragmatism: Synthesizing Naturalism and Historicism," in *Rorty and His Critics*, pp. 165–67.

30. Cf. Alvin Plantinga, *Warranted Christian Belief*, chapter 8. Plantinga more explicitly emphasizes the sufficiency of the Spirit's testimony than does Frei's account

of the *sensus literalis*, though the activity of the Holy Spirit is logically implicit in Frei's account. However, this difference in emphasis aside, their accounts are compatible.

31. Wolterstorff, "Second Lecture," *What New Haven and Grand Rapids to Say to Each Other?* in *Seeking Understanding* (Grand Rapids, MI: Eerdmans, 2001), pp. 290–91. Neil B. MacDonald has used this compatibility about properly basic beliefs to clarify the confusion invited by Frei's appeal to "meaning as reference" in *Eclipse*. His redescriptive use of the similarity seems to be harmonious with my point here. See MacDonald's "Illocutionary Stance in Hans Frei's *The Eclipse of Biblical Narrative*: An Exercise in Conceptual Redescription and Normative Analysis," in *After Pentecost: Language and Biblical Interpretation*, ed. Craig Bartholomew, Colin Greene, and Karl Moller (Grand Rapids: Zondervan, 2001), pp. 312–28.

32. Wolterstorff, "Evidence, Entitled Belief, and the Gospels," *Faith and Philosophy* 6 (October 1989): 442–47; and Wolterstorff, "Will Narrativity Work as Linchpin? Reflections on the Hermeneutic of Hans Frei." In *Relativism and Religion*, edited by Charles Lewis, 111–53. London: MacMillan, 1995.pp. 98–99. Plantinga's emphasis upon the sufficiency of the Holy Spirit's testimony differs from Frei on precisely this point. It makes even minimal historical considerations irrelevant (see his *Warranted Christian Belief*, pp. 266–68). Cf. Hunsinger, "What Can Evangelicals and Postliberals Learn from Each Other? The Carl Henry–Hans Frei Exchange Reconsidered," in *The Nature of Confession: Evangelicals and Postliberals in Conversation*, ed. Timothy R. Phillips and Dennis R. Okholm (Downers Grove, IL: InterVarsity, 1996), p. 137; Cf. Bruce Marshall, *Trinity and Truth*, pp. 165–69.

33. How such noninferential beliefs are possible in virtue of inferential conceptual practices that have Christian Scripture as their object is the general topic I investigate in chapter 7. In chapter 8 I attempt to apply these inferentialist insights as tools with which to clarify and expand upon Frei's account of the *sensus literalis* as the plain sense. Plantinga draws a subtle distinction between the "proper basicality" that characterizes ordinary perceptual beliefs and the kind that characterize faith. The latter lack the "detailed phenomenological basis, the rich and highly articulated sensuous imagery that is involved in perception" (*Warranted Christian Belief*, p. 264). In the remaining chapters of this book I redescribe Frei's account of the *sensus literalis* in a way that illuminates its sensory and "observable" renderings of the narratives (*explicatio*) as affording the kind of "proper basicality" that Plantinga ascribes here to "perception."

34. Alvin Plantinga and Nicholas Wolterstorff, *Faith and Rationality* (Notre Dame: University of Notre Dame Press, 1983); Frei, *Types*, pp. 79–80.

35. Frei, "Karl Barth," *T&N*, pp. 170–71.

36. Hunsinger, *How to Read Karl Barth*, p. 50.

37. Ibid. Cf. Frei, *Identity*, pp. 187–88.

38. Ibid. (italics added). Plantinga treats this dimension of faith in a fashion compatible with the present account in *Warranted Christian Belief*, chapter 9 ("The Testimonial Model: Sealed Upon Our Hearts").

39. Ibid. Hunsinger cites Barth in *CD* 4/3 (p. 882): "Theological work is surely inconceivable and impossible at any time without prayer."

40. Frei, *Types*, 78.

41. Emmanuel Katangole levels the charge of "fideism" at Barth's theology in *Beyond Universal Reason* (Notre Dame: University of Notre Dame Press, 2000), pp. 183–85. Hauerwas raises the charge against "Barthians, reinforced by Wittgensteinian 'language game' analysis" in "The Church as God's New Language" in *Scriptural Authority and Narrative Interpretation*, ed. Garrett Green (Eugene, OR: Wipf and Stock, 2000), p. 190.

42. *Types*, p. 80. Frei identifies *Wissenschaft* as "inquiry into the universal, rational principles that allow us to organize any and all specific fields of inquiry into internally and mutually coherent, intelligible totalities; perhaps, if we just watch our language and do not try too hard for lucidity, it may be translated as 'an inquiry into the transcendental principles justifying all systematic method and explanation'" (*Types*, 98).

43. Sheila Davaney, *Pragmatic Historicism: A Theology for the Twenty-First Century* (New York: State University of New York Press, 2000), esp. pp. 29–41.

44. Sheila Davaney, "Mapping Theologies," in *Changing Conversations: Religious Reflection and Cultural Analysis*, ed. Dwight N. Hopkins & Sheila Greeve Davaney (New York: Routledge, 1996), pp. 30–31.

45. Davaney, "Mapping Theologies," p. 30.

46. Ibid., 31. She writes, "While postliberals insist that we do or should so reside within primary communities, in fact, many people today cannot easily find such a primary, encompassing perspective and are compelled to fashion, creatively and critically, the diverse traditions that impact them into some new, more adequate whole."

47. On this point Frei differs subtly from Lindbeck. In particular, Lindbeck's rule theory of doctrine permits "inexhaustible semantic novelty" against a background of "syntactic continuity." As he puts it, "grammatical features . . . remain unchanged even while the lexicon expands indefinitely" ("The Gospel's Uniqueness: Election and Untranslatability," *The Church in a Postliberal Age*, ed. James Buckley (Grand Rapids: Eerdmans, 2002), p. 235). Higton highlights this crucial distinction between Lindbeck and Frei when he writes that Frei's refusal of a general theory allows him to "accommodate the idea that instead of rule-governed behavior with a split between the unchanging second-order rules and the changing first-order enactments, we should think in terms of skilled improvisation on themes provided by a habitus, non-identical repetitions of past paradigms in ever new, really new situations" ("Frei's Christology and Lindbeck's Cultural-Linguistic Theory," *Scottish Journal of Theology* 50 (1997), p. 93).

48. See, for instance, Robert Brandom, "Freedom through Constraint by Norms," in *Hermeneutics and Praxis*, ed. Robert Hollinger (Notre Dame: University of Notre Dame Press, 1985), pp. 173–91; for further development of these ideas, see my article "'Dismantling the Master's House': Freedom as Ethical Practice in Robert Brandom and Michel Foucault," *Journal of Religious Ethics*, Vol. 37, No. 3 (Sept. 2009), pp. 419-448.

49. So, for instance, the difference between the refusal of the all-fields-encompassing or universal rules of discourse is that for D.Z. Philips this conclusion

is final, while for Barth it is provisional. For Barth (according to Frei), "There might be enough overlap among contexts to allow limited overlap between logics or criteria. That fact in turn would clue us in on the proviso, important for Barth, that this kind of overlap might mean that criteria—for example, of coherence and noncontradiction—are field-encompassing in God's eyes, though not in ours, and that the declaration *in principle* that they are not and cannot be is therefore too *prescriptive* a rule" (*Types*, p. 51).

50. Frei, *Types*, pp. 89–90.

51. Stout, *Democracy and Tradition* (Princeton: Princeton University Press, 2004), pp. 69–70, esp. 73.

52. As I mentioned in the introduction, again, this point presumes the test of exegesis and discernment of the Spirit. See Eugene Rogers, "Supplementing Barth on Jews and Gender: Identifying God by Anagogy and the Spirit," *Modern Theology* 14 (January 1998), p. 50.

53. Barth, *Anselm: Fides Quaerens Intellectum: Anslem's Proof of the Existence of God in the Context of his Theological Scheme* (London: SCM, [1960] 1985)., pp. 70–71.

54. Thiemann helpfully illustrates: "To inquire concerning the faith of an individual or community, it is necessary to explore the set of practices within which the convictions of faith are displayed. To understand Christian notions of 'love,' for example, it would be helpful to read biblical texts (e.g., the parable of the Good Samaritan, the teachings on love in the Gospel and Epistles of John), to study theological treatises on the topic, and to learn about the benevolent practices of Christian communities across the centuries. Such a process is no more unusual or difficult than that which is required to understand a notion like 'freedom' in the American constitutional tradition." (*Religion in Public Life* (Washington, D.C.: Georgetown University Press, 1996), p. 155). Richard Bernstein sketches an analogous controversy of alleged "fideism"—and an analogous resolution—that occurred among philosophers of science. See Paul Feyerabend's *Against Method* (New York: Verso, 1993), pp. 250–51, and Bernstein's account of the controversy in *Between Objectivism and Relativism*, pp. 84–88.

55. Barth, *CD* IV/2, p. 545.

56. Frei, *Types*, 44–46.

57. Barth, *CD* 1/2, pp. 732–33.

58. Ibid., p. 732.

59. Ibid., p. 730.

60. Ibid., p. 726.

61. Ibid., p. 718.

62. Ibid., p. 733.

63. Frei, *Types*, p. 46. It was Barth, Frei says, who came "as close as anybody in his generation and in his geographical area to discovering a specific mode of studying Scripture in which external and internal Christian description converge." Paul DeHart pursues the themes of the preceding paragraphs to a conclusion about Barth very different from mine. See DeHart, *The Trial of the Witnesses* (Oxford: Blackwell, 2006), esp. 222–25. For all the foregoing reasons, I agree with William Placher and Keith L. Johnson that DeHart's book—while excellent in many ways—remains insufficiently

attuned to the nuances of Barth's position. See Placher, *Conversations in Religion and Theology* 5, no. 2 (2007): 136–40, followed by DeHart's rejoinder, and Keith L. Johnson, "Review of *The Trial of the Witnesses*," *Scottish Journal of Theology*, forthcoming.

CHAPTER 7

1. Ludwig Wittgenstein, *On Certainty* (Oxford: Blackwell, 1969), sections 61–65.

2. Frei, "'Narrative' in Christian and Modern Reading," in *Theology and Dialogue*, ed. Bruce Marshall (Notre Dame: Notre Dame University Press, 1990), pp. 159–60.

3. After assigning general theory ("hermeneutical or antihermeneutical" and including New Criticism) as secondary and dependent relevance, Frei writes, "Equally clearly it is once more a case of putting the cart before the horse—but this time the wagon is theological rather than literary—if one constructs a general and inalienable human quality called 'narrative' or 'narrativity,' within which to interpret the Gospels and provide foundational warrant for the possibility of their existential and ontological meaningfulness. The notion that Christian theology is a member of a general class of 'narrative theology' is no more than a minor will-o'-the-wisp." Frei, "The 'Literal Reading' of Biblical Narrative," (1983), ed. George Hunsinger and William C. Placher *Theology and Narrative* (Oxford: Oxford University Press, 1993), p. 148, (hereafter T&N).

4. Frei, "The 'Literal Reading' of Biblical Narrative," pp. 142–43. Frei put the point emphatically here. "There may or may not be a class called 'realistic narrative,' but to take it as a general category of which the synoptic Gospel narratives and their partial second-order redescription are a dependent instance is first to put the cart before the horse and then cut the lines and claim that the vehicle is self-propelled."

5. Frei, "The 'Literal Reading' of Biblical Narrative," pp. 142–43.

6. Tanner, "Theology and the Plain Sense," in *Scriptural Authority and Narrative Interpretation*, ed. Garrett Green (Eugene, OR: Wipf and Stock, 2000), pp. 59–78.

7. Ibid., p. 62.

8. Ibid., p. 63.

9. Wood, *The Formation of Christian Understanding* (Philadelphia: Westminster, 1981), p. 43, quoted by Frei in "Theology and the Interpretation of Narrative," T&N, p. 104.

10. Tanner, "Theology and the Plain Sense,", p. 65.

11. Ibid., p. 62; David Kelsey, *Proving Doctrine: The Uses of Scripture in Recent Theology* (Philadelphia: Fortress, 1975).

12. Tanner, "Theology and the Plain Sense," p. 64.

13. Brevard Childs levels this criticism, suggesting that Tanner "move[s] into the liberal hermeneutical orbit of David Kelsey and [is] again trapped by communal 'construal.'" See Childs, "Toward Recovering Theological Exegesis," *Pro Ecclesia* 6, no. 1 (1997): 20 n. 8.

14. Ronald Thiemann, *Revelation and Theology: The Gospel as Narrated Promise* (Notre Dame: University of Notre Dame Press, 1985), pp. 56–70.

15. Ibid., pp. 62–63.

16. Tanner, "Theology and the Plain Sense," p. 63. Tanner here cites Charles Wood's *The Formation of Christian Understanding* (Philadelphia: Westminster, 1981), pp. 40ff., 116ff.

17. For a helpfully succinct account of this point, see Brandom, "Remembering Wilfrid Sellars," in *In Memoriam*, ed. Susanna Downie (1990): http://www.ditext.com/brandom/brandom.html.

18. Brandom, *Tales of the Mighty Dead* (Cambridge, MA: Harvard University Press, 2002), p. 48.

19. Sellars, "Some Reflections on Language Games," *Science, Perception and Reality* (Atascadero, CA: Ridgeview Publishing, 1991), p. 350. See also Brandom, *Making It Explicit* (Cambridge, MA: Harvard University Press, 1994),p. 235 (hereafter *MIE*).

20. Tanner, "Theology and the Plain Sense," p. 66.

21. "'Does human agreement *decide* what is red? Is it decided by appeal to the majority? Were we taught to determine colour in *that* way?'" Wittgenstein, *Zettel* (Los Angeles, CA: University of California Press, 1970), section 431. Cf. Lovibond, *Realism and Imagination in Ethics* (Minneapolis: University of Minnesota Press, 1983), p. 148 (hereafter *RIE*), cited in Tanner's "Theology and the Plain Sense," pp. 63–66. Tanner follows closely Lovibond's explication of Wittgenstein's conception of "rationality," citing *RIE*, sections 35, 37 & 48. Jeffrey Stout employs many of these insights from Lovibond in *Democracy and Tradition* (Princeton: Princeton University Press, 2004), pp. 270–78 to identify the objectivity at the heart of Wittgenstein's account of practices. For a compatible account of the social-practical basis of objectivity in Wittgenstein's work, see Fergus Kerr's *Theology After Wittgenstein* (Oxford: Blackwell, 1986), pp. 109–12.

22. For an extended exposition of this feature of social practices, please see my article "'Dismantling the Master's House': Freedom as Ethical Practice in Brandom and Foucault," *Journal of Religious Ethics* 37 (September 2009): 419–448.

23. The enrichment of the practice here need be no more the enrichment of textual meaning and practice effected through the "hermeneutical feedback loop" (*explicatio, meditatio, applicatio*).

24. This may be an objection that Tanner has little interest in addressing. See Tanner's account of her project in Gary Dorrien's article "Truth Claims," *Christian Century*, July 18–25, 2001, pp. 22–30.

25. Frei, *Types of Christian Theology* (New Haven, CT: Yale University Press, 1992), pp. 15–16; "Theology and the Interpretation of Narrative," pp. 112–13.

26. This way of characterizing Frei's development was first suggested to me by George Hunsinger.

27. Frei, "Theology and the Interpretation of Narrative," p. 110.

28. Frei, *Types*, p. 5.

29. Frei, "Theology and the Interpretation of Narrative," p. 114.

30. Hunsinger, afterword in *T&N*, p. 259. "What is clear is that a "cultural-linguistic" turn, under the influence of George Lindbeck, has been effected in Frei's

thought," Hunsinger continues. While this claim stands as an example of seeing a significant break and turn in Frei's work, taken in abstraction I do not think it accurately reflects Hunsinger's views on the matter. As he has articulated his position in conversation and group discussion, he seems inclined to describe the movement internal to Frei's work in terms of a broadening of scope (cf. n. 26 above).

31. Frei, "The 'Literal Reading' of Biblical Narrative," pp. 122–23.

32. This characterization of Frei's project orients Wolterstorff's treatment of him in *Divine Discourse* (Cambridge: Cambridge University Press, 1995), pp. 235–36.

33. This dense passage is set within an equally dense section in the "Literal Reading" essay (which is itself notoriously complex). There Frei explicitly addresses "The Primacy of the Literal Sense in Christian Interpretation," *T&N*, pp. 120–24. The following discussion is informed by K. E. Greene-McCreight's programmatic overview of the plain sense in Christian scriptural interpretation and meticulous exposition of its role in the work of Augustine, Calvin, and Barth. See her *Ad Litteram: How Augustine, Calvin, and Barth Read the 'Plain Sense' of Genesis 1–3* (New York: Peter Lang, 1999).

34. Here and in the ensuing pages I follow the account provided by Rowan Greer, "The Rise of the Christian Bible," in *Early Biblical Interpretation*, ed. Wayne Meeks (Louisville, KY: Westminster John Knox, 1986), here pp. 109, 115; Greene-McCreight also provides a illuminates its earliest origins (particularly in the writings of Tertullian), and catalogues much of the pivotal literature addressing its influence, in the opening chapter of *Ad Litteram*.

35. Greer, "The Rise of the Christian Bible," pp. 109, 111–12.

36. Jospeh F. Mitros, "The Norm of Faith in the Patristic Age," *Theological Studies* 29:3 (Sept. 1968), p. 455; Brevard Childs perhaps encapsulates the complex of considerations and processes that went into the devising of the *Regula Fidei*. He writes: "[T]he rule is a summary of the truth which comprises the faith of the church. It refers to the totality of the faith as the criterion of correct interpretation. It is the content of scripture, but not identical with the Bible; rather, it is that to which scripture points. It is contained in the proclamation of church tradition, but it is not as if the written Bible required an additional oral formulation. Its content is decisive for faith and is reflected in a unified teaching in both its oral and written form" (*Biblical Theology of the Old and New Testaments* (Minneapolis, MN: Augsburg Fortress, 1993)p. 31).

37. My account here expands upon my treatment of Frei's ecclesial interests in the final segment of chapter 2. Nils Dahl points out that corroboration by Old Testament Scriptures was another normative constraint in the formation of "apostolicity" in the ancient church. See Dahl, "The Crucified Messiah and the Endangered Promises," *Word and World*, 3, no. 3 (1983): 251–62.

38. Greer, "The Rise of the Christian Bible," p. 112.

39. Ibid., p. 110. Greer reports that Irenaeus is the first to use the expression "New Testament" (*Against Heresies* 4.9.1). He adds, "This development should not be regarded as a radical break with earlier attitudes. It is simply a question of taking seriously the authority of the Christian writings that constituted the apostolic witness to Christ and of the inevitable eclipse of the oral tradition, the content of which differed in no way from what could be found in the New Testament writings" (115).

40. Ibid., p. 111. "Apostolicity" meant that: "[T]he decision as to which Christian writing could be considered the apostolic witness to Christ was really a decision that these books interpreted Christ correctly from a theological point of view. For Christians, the dialogue between God and his people found its fullest expression in Christ, and so Christ became the key to the whole of Scripture. The theological and even Christological convictions that determined how a Christian Bible was to be constituted then became central in shaping the interpretation of that Bible" (111).

41. Mitros, "The Norm of Faith in the Patristic Age," p. 455 (see the relevant quotation in chapter 2, n. 71). Though a detailed exposition and comparison of the two would take me too far afield for present purposes, there appear to be important similarities that remain to be worked out between the foregoing account of the background of the rule of faith and the description offered by Wolterstorff in his "Sketch of a Historical Answer" segment of *Divine Discourse*, pp. 288–96.

42. Mitros, "The Norm of Faith in the Patristic Age," p. 447. So, for instance, as a matter of historical fact, there were two contending schools of thought that arose in Alexandria and Antioch. The former, heavily influenced by the neo-Platonism of Philo, maintained that insofar as the unseen and finally incomprehensible Word of God entered human language, that language could serve as a shadow of the divine reality, necessitating spiritual, allegorical interpretation. For this school of thought, initiated members of the church would recognize plainly that the sense which presented itself in literal form was, in fact, an allegory for a higher, divine truth and would need to have that truth derived. Those associated with Antioch, by contrast, were more influenced by Aristotelian epistemology and the biblical practices of Palestinian Judaism. As Mitros put it, "Antiochene Christology always showed a tendency to stress the humanity of Christ at the expense of its union with the divinity, to underscore the importance of our Lord as the model to be imitated by man in his pursuit of Christian perfection. In the interpretation of Scripture, its human aspect, i.e., the literal sense, was brought out." Both schools engaged in typological reading of scripture. While both schools were influenced by the elements of Greek philosophical traditions, Mitros makes clear that their approaches to Scripture were motivated and oriented by their respective christologies. Frei explicitly mentions Origen in the regard, as well the Antiochene school. His account is informed by James Preus's *From Shadow to Promise* ("The 'Literal Reading,'" pp. 121–22).

43. Greer, "The Rise of the Christian Bible," p. 116.

44. Brevard Childs, "Speech-act Theory and Biblical Interpretation," *Scottish Journal of Theology* 58, no. 4 (2005): 381.

45. Childs, "Speech-act Theory and Biblical Interpretation," p. 383.

46. Greer writes that "[T]he canonical writers of the New Testament are agreed in taking Jesus' death and resurrection as the basis for their accounts of his significance. In this way, their theology is based partly on an event that took place in the full light of history, but partly on an event—or another dimension of the cross—that by definition transcends what historians can say one way or another. To be sure, the focus upon the dead and risen Lord by no means yields any single interpretation of his significance, nor does it mean that his teaching and miracles must of necessity be neglected. But it is important to understand that there is agreement in the New Testament about where to begin (158).

47. Ibid., p. 111.

48. Brevard Childs wrote, "Irenaeus did not see the rule-of-faith as the church's 'construal' of the Bible, but rather as the objective truth of the Apostolic Faith, which has been publically revealed and not concealed in a secret gnosis. There is a succession of true witnesses (IV.26.2). Its truth is unambiguous (III.2.I) and can be demonstrated in the actual history of the past (III.5.1). Yet this truth is not a static deposit from the past, but the 'living voice' (*viva vox*) of truth. Irenaeus speaks of the symphony of scripture, of its harmonious proportion (III.11.0). It provides the church with the normative criterion against which critically to measure the Gnostic distortions" (*Biblical Theology of the Old and New Testaments*, pp. 31–32).

49. A doctrine or creedal statement works "regulatively" as a rule for interpretation in second-order reflections on Scripture. It works "constitutively" when, for instance, recitation of the Apostles' Creed is employed as an element within a worship service. Sometimes, the same formal articulation can function in both fashions, as we saw in my exposition of Frei's use of the Chalcedonian pattern in chapter 5.

50. Frei, *Types*, p. 126. "[C]onceptual formulations in the form of doctrines serve as heuristic aids that serve us best when they thrust readers back to the stories themselves with new understanding," Placher clarifies the point in *Narratives of a Vulnerable God* (Louisville, KY: Westminster John Knox, 1994), p. 15. I will discuss Frei's explicit use of this threefold approach in chapter 8. See Frei, "Theology and the Interpretation of Narrative," pp. 110–14.

51. Though as we saw in chapters 5 and 6, this is a dynamic and continuous process.

52. Frei, "The 'Literal Reading,'" p. 120.

53. Ibid., pp. 144–45.

54. Ibid., p. 121.

55. Wolterstorff (*Divine Discourse*, pp. 219–20) attributes this claim to Frei and Barth.

56. Frei, "The 'Literal Reading,'" p. 143. I understand this characterization to be consistent with Frei's characterization of Barth's position, that "the possibility and even the necessity for God's assuming man unto himself by incarnating himself may be affirmed and explored *because he did so* and only for that reason" (*T&N*, p. 170). Frei endorsed this view of Barth's in his "Remarks in Connection with a Theological Proposal," *T&N*, p. 30 (cf. Hunsinger's afterword, *T&N*, p. 240).

57. Frei, "Theology and the Interpretation of Narrative," p. 108.

58. Frei, "The 'Literal Reading,'" p. 143.

59. Frei, "Response to 'Narrative Theology,'" (1985), *T&N*, pp. 208–9.

60. Frei, "Theology and the Interpretation of Narrative," pp. 113–14.

61. Frei, "Conflict in Interpretation," (1987), *T&N*, p. 163; cf. Frei, *Identity*, pp. 59–64; "The 'Literal Reading,'" pp. 140–41.

62. Greer, "A Framework for Interpreting a Christian Bible,", p. 157. Nils Dahl writes, "The basic conviction, that the death and resurrection of Jesus had happened in accordance with the Scriptures, had the double effect that the events were understood in the light of the Scriptures and the Scriptures were interpreted in the light of the

events." See Dahl, "The Crucified Messiah and the Endangered Promises," *Word and World*, 3, no. 3 (1983): 251–61 (here p. 252).

63. Perhaps we feel it to be just as natural or necessary to press Frei for the account of reference or meaning that his project must either presuppose or (by dint of logical inference) imply.

64. Brandom, "Some Pragmatist Themes in Hegel's Idealism," *Tales*, 210.

65. Ibid., p. 219.

66. Frei, "Theology and the Interpretation of Narrative," p. 110.

67. Brandom, *Articulating Reasons* (Cambridge, MA: Harvard University Press, 2000), p. 197. As the lines that follow this passage make clear, it would be incorrect to take Brandom as claiming that the normative contribution of the causal constraints exerted by the world occurs in any sense separately from, or external to, those practices through which that world is disclosed as part and parcel. Norms are creatures of practices. "The world" is part and parcel of our practices, not "outside" of them. It would be equally incorrect to ascribe to Brandom the claim that had there been no practices there would have been no world, or that had there been no fact claimers there would never have been any facts. Brandom claims just the opposite, in fact. It is a feature of our conceptual practices that we can, counterfactually, imagine what the world would be like if (and when) there were no discursive practitioners such as ourselves. But access to these states of affairs depends upon those practices. For illuminating explication of this point, see Jeffrey Stout, "Davidson, Rorty, and Brandom on Truth," in in *Radical Interpretation in Religion*, ed. Nancy Frankenberry (Cambridge: Cambridge University Press, 2002), pp. 48–49.

68. Brandom, *MIE*, p. 332.

69. *MIE*, 331. As Brandom puts it, "All our concepts are what they are in part because of their inferential links to others that have noninferential circumstances or consequences of application—*concepts*, that is, *whose proper use is not specifiable apart from consideration of the facts and objects that responsively bring about or are brought about by their application.* The normative structure of authority and responsibility exhibited by assessments and attributions of reliability in perception and action is causally conditioned" (italics added).

70. Ibid.

71. Ibid., p. 632.

72. Ibid.

73. I employ the word "text" here for the specific purpose at hand and do not mean to delimit other possible uses of the word (such as Geertz's application of it to "acted documents").

74. In Brandom's words, "the proprieties governing the application of a community's concepts are in part determined (according to the interpreter) by the actual properties of and facts concerning the things the linguistic practitioners are perceiving, acting on, and so talking about—*which are just features of their practice.*" *MIE*, p. 632 (italics added).

75. Ibid., p. 622. The operative passage reads: "Concepts conceived as inferential roles of expressions do not serve as epistemological intermediaries, standing between

us and what is conceptualized by them. This is not because there is no causal order consisting of particulars, interaction with which supplies the material for thought. It is rather because all of these elements are themselves conceived as thoroughly conceptual, not as contrasting with the conceptual. The conception of concepts as inferentially articulated permits a picture of thought and of the world that thought is about as *equally*, and in factored cases *identically*, conceptually articulated. . . . [N]oninferential dispositions (the locus of our empirical receptivity) accordingly do not constitute the interface between what is conceptually articulated and what is not but merely one of the necessary conditions for a conceptually articulated grasp of a conceptually articulated world—the world consisting of everything that is the case, all the facts, and the objects they are about."

76. Frei, "Remarks in Connection with a Theological Proposal," (1967), *T&N*, p. 32.

77. Frei, *Types*, 86–87.

78. Ibid.

79. Ibid.

80. Frei, "The 'Literal Reading' of Biblical Narrative," p. 143.

81. Frei, "Remarks in Connection with a Theological Proposal," p. 32.

82. Frei, *Types*, p. 87. Cf. *Identity*, part 4.

83. Frei, *Identity*, pp. 67, 76–77.

84. Frei, "Theology and the Interpretation of Narrative," p. 111.

85. It is an object, as Brandom puts it, that is responsively brought about by discursive practices and that responsively contributes to bringing about further such practices (*MIE*, 331).

86. Ibid., p. 332. "What determinate practices a community has depends on what the facts are and on what objects they are actually practically involved with, to begin with, through perception and action. The way the world is, constrains proprieties of inferential, doxastic, and practical commitment in a straightforward way from *within* those practices."

87. Tanner, "Theology and the Plain Sense," p. 63.

88. Ibid., pp. 68–69.

89. Stout, "Davidson, Rorty, and Brandom on Truth," pp. 40–41.

90. Brandom, *MIE*, p. 235.

91. Frei, *Eclipse*, p. 3.

CHAPTER 8

1. John Webster, "'In the Shadow of Biblical Work': Barth and Bonhoeffer on Reading the Bible," *Toronto Journal of Theology* 17, no. 1 (2001): 88. Webster expressed concerns of this sort about Frei's explication of Barth's account of the church in *Barth's Ethics of Reconciliation* (Cambridge: Cambridge University Press, 1995), pp. 217–23.

2. Frei, *Eclipse*, p. 3.

3. He signals that he is following Barth here, citing *Church Dogmatics* 1/2, pp. 722–40, 766–82 (hereafter *CD*); Cf. Frei, "Theology and the Interpretation of Narrative," *T&N*, pp. 110–14.

4. Frei, "Theology and the Interpretation of Narrative," p. 113.

5. Barth, *CD* 1/2, p. 727.

6. "Observation" is a literal translation of the term *explicatio*. David Ford, *Barth and God's Story*, pp. 24–25.

7. Frei, "Theology and the Interpretation of Narrative," p. 113.

8. Frei, *Eclipse*, p. 3; *Identity*, pp. 199–200.

9. Charles Wood, *The Formation of Christian Understanding* (Eugene, OR: Wipf and Stock, 1993), p. 75.

10. Cf. Sellars's account of 'motivating expressions' and 'ought clauses' in "Some Reflections on Language Games," *Science, Perception and Reality* (Atascadero, CA: Ridgeview Publishing, 1991), p. 350.

11. Ibid., p. 351.

12. Kelsey, "The Bible and Christian Theology," *Journal of the American Academy of Religion* 48 (September 1980): 386 (italics added).

13. Barth, *Anselm: Fides Quaerens Intellectum: Anslem's Proof of the Existence of God in the Context of his Theological Scheme* (London: SCM, [1960] 1985), pp. 24–25. See also *CD*, 4/3, p. 848, where Barth describes the gospel as "generally intelligible and explicable."

14. Auerbach, *Mimesis* (Princeton, NJ: Princeton University Press, 1953),pp. 14–23.

15. Barth, *Anselm*, p. 41.

16. Frei, "'Narrative' in Christian and Modern Reading," ed. Bruce D. Marshall (Notre Dame: Notre Dame University Press, 1990), pp. 159–60.

17. Hunsinger, *How to Read Karl Barth* (Oxford: Oxford University Press, 1991), p. 73.

18. Ibid. Hunsinger (pp. 85–86) further clarifies how this reflects the formal pattern of *Aufhebung* that structures Barth's *Church Dogmatics*: "*Aufhebung* is the Hegelian pattern of affirming, canceling, and then reconstituting something on a higher plane (a pattern whose underlying metaphor would seem to be 'incarnation, crucifixion, and resurrection')."

19. Barth, *CD* 2/1, p. 227 (Cf. "The Veracity of Man's Knowledge of God," *CD* 2/1, pp. 204–54).

20. Placher, *Unapologetic Theology* (Louisville, KY: Westminster John Knox Press, 1989), p. 134.

21. Thiemann, *Revelation and Theology: The Gospel as Narrated Promise* (Notre Dame: University of Notre Dame Press, 1985), chapter 5 (esp. pp. 107–8; here p. 105).

22. It is for this reason that an effort to account for God's "divine discourse" with the categories of J. L. Austin's speech-act philosophy risks yet another variation of what Frei called "getting the cart before the horse." On such a view, God could only be said to make a "promise" insofar as God, construed as a speaking agent, employs a proposition that takes the form of a promise. "[S]trictly and literally only persons say things, not texts. . . . Even in a metaphorical sense there is no such thing, for a text, as what it says. And so no such thing as discovering what it says," Wolterstorff writes ("Evidence, Entitled Belief, and Gospels," *Faith and Philosophy* 6 (October 1989): p. 431). Frei would be concerned that such an application of speech-act theory categories is too confining, too determinative of what can and cannot be plausibly claimed about

how the gospel accounts portray Christ, and the nature of the claims that they make on their readers. Much like the overdetermined appeal to the category of realistic narrative, Frei would likely see Wolterstorff's use of speech-act theory categories as another instance of getting the cart before the horse and then cutting the lines and claiming that the vehicle is self-propelled. So, for instance, Wolterstorff's account precludes any such thing as a "narrated promise." Theimann has demonstrated at length what it means to say that the biblical narratives make claims upon their readers (and that they narrate an act of promise, in particular). In the course of this demonstration he has shown what a sufficiently delicate use of speech-act theory looks like, that is, one in which the application of speech-act categories are oriented by his concrete engagement with Matthew's Gospel, liturgical practices, and the history of the church. This remains perhaps the most important, and yet arguably the most neglected, portion of *Revelation and Theology* (chapter 6; see also pp. 99–111). Frei alludes to the influence of James Samuel Preus's *From Shadow to Promise*, which forwards "promise" as the basis for the "normative-literal sense" in Luther's work. For a comparable account influenced by Frei, see Nils Dahl, "The Crucified Messiah and the Endangered Promises," *Word and World* 3, no. 3 (1983): 251–62. For a more trenchant analysis of Wolterstorff's use of speech-act theory, see Brevard Childs, "Speech-act Theory and Biblical Interpretation," *Scottish Journal of Theology* 58, no. 4 (2005): 375–92.

23. Thiemann, *Revelation and Theology*, p. 105.

24. Ibid.

25. Barth, *CD* 3/2, pp. 476–77.

26. Frei, "Theology and the Interpretation of Narrative," p. 112.

27. Barth to Harnack as quoted in Hans Frei, "The Doctrine of Revelation in the Thought of Karl Barth, 1909–1922: The Nature of Barth's Break with Liberalism" (PhD diss., Yale University, 1956).

28. I made the case for such an account in chapter 6.

29. Nancey Murphy cites *CD* 1/1, p. 305, as an example: "God's revelation is a ground which has no higher or deeper ground above or below it but is an absolute ground in itself, and therefore for man a court from which there can be no possible appeal to a higher court." See *Beyond Liberalism and Fundamentalism* (Harrisburg, PA: Trinity, 1996), pp. 95–98.

30. Ibid., pp. 95–100; Mark Wallace argues that there is a foundationalist dimension of Frei's project in *The Second Naiveté*,(Macon, GA: Mercer University Press, 1990), pp. 87–110.

31. Stout, *Democracy and Tradition* (Princeton: Princeton University Press, 2004), pp. 216–24.

32. Ibid., p. 216.

33. Ibid., p. 217.

34. John 20:30–31.

35. Stout, *Democracy and Tradition*, p. 217.

36. Bruce Marshall attributes this phrase to Thomas Aquinas's account of the plain sense of scripture in "Absorbing the World," Ed Bruce D. Marshall, *Theology and Dialogue* (Notre Dame: University of Notre Dame Press, 1990), pp. 69-102.

37. Frei, "Response to 'Narrative Theology,'" in *T&N*, p. 209.

38. Auerbach, *Mimesis*, p. 44. As we saw in chapter 1, Frei agrees with Auerbach that concentration upon meaning has effaced the realistic narrative, but he associated this with meaning as reference or symbolic, mythical translation. Frei differed from Auerbach in claiming that his figural reading does not expunge the realistic, literal sense, but rather extends it. On this and other important differences between Auerbach and Frei, see John David Dawson's *Christian Figural Reading and the Fashioning of Identity* (Berkeley, CA: University of California Press, 2002), chapters 7–8.

39. See Placher's introduction, *T&N*, pp. 12–13. Frei found this characteristic exemplified in *CD* 4, "The Way of the Son of God into the Far Country" and "The Royal Man," and H. Richard Niebuhr's "Toward a Definition of Christ" in *Christ and Culture*.

40. David Kelsey, *Proving Doctrine: The Uses of Scripture in Modern Theology* (Harrisburg, PA: Trinity, 1999), p. 39; Cf. Placher, *Narratives of a Vulnerable God* (Louisville, KY: Westminster John Knox Press, 1994), p. 15.

41. Barth, Ibid., pp. 722–23.

42. Frei, *Types*, 83–84.

43. Ibid.

44. Ibid., p 83.

45. Barth, "The Authority and Significance of the Bible," in *God Here and Now*, translated by Paul M. van Buren (New York: Routledge, 2004), p. 64.

46. Barth, *CD* 3/2, p. 450.

47. Ibid., pp. 442–43; Cf. *Types*, 85–91.

48. Frei, *Types*, p. 162.

49. Ibid., p. 80.

50. Cf. *CD* 4/1, pp 186–87.

51. Frei, "The 'Literal Reading' of Scripture," *T&N*, p. 122; Barth provides essential background in *CD* 3/2, p. 442. This point refers to my discussion of the emergence of the literal sense in chapter 7.

52. For a comparable statement of this claim, see K.E. Greene-McCreight, conclusion to *Ad Litteram* (esp. pp. 247–50).

53. Childs, "Speech-act Theory and Biblical Interpretation," p. 381.

54. Barth, *CD* 3/2, pp. 449, 451.

55. Barth, "The Authority and Significance of the Bible," pp. 65–66.

56. Frei, "Karl Barth," *T&N*, 170.

57. "Remarks in Connection with a Theological Proposal," *T&N*, p. 30 (cf. Hunsinger's afterword, *T&N*, pp. 240–41).

58. Frei, "The 'Literal Reading,'" p. 143.

59. Frei, "Theology and the Interpretation of Narrative," p. 108.

60. His claim at that point was that "No reference to the situation of the interpreter is necessary in understanding the text" ("Remarks in Connection with a Theological Proposal," *T&N*, 32).

61. Frei, *Types*, p. 87.

62. Frei, *Eclipse*, p. viii.

63. Frei, *Types*, p. 5; Cf. "The 'Literal Reading' of Biblical Narrative," *T&N*, pp. 144–45.

64. As we saw in the previous chapter, Frei identified two additional "informal rules" by virtue of which the literal reading exerted itself as plain throughout the Christian tradition. Second, Christian reading was to deny neither the unity of the Old and New Testaments nor the centrality of the Gospels' accounts of Jesus for organizing that unity. And third, any readings that did not contradict the first two guidelines were to be presumed permissible. Two examples of the latter that Frei pinpointed were historical-critical and literary readings. Frei found particularly useful Brevard Childs' exploration of the various ways that the *sensus literalis* had been articulated in light of these minimal parameters of agreement. See Childs, "The *Sensus Literalis* of Scripture: An Ancient and Modern Problem," in *Beitrage zur alttestamentlichen Theologie: Festschrift fur Walther Zimmerli zum 70 Geburtstag*, ed. Herbert Donner, Robert Hanhart, and Rudolph Smend (Gottingen: Vandenhoek & Ruprecht, 1977), pp. 80–95.

65. *Types*, p. 86.

66. Here Frei quotes Barth (*Types*, 86): "When the interpreter uses the scheme of thought he brings with him for the apprehension and explanation of what is said to us in Scripture, he must have a fundamental awareness of what he is doing. We must be clear that every scheme of thought which we bring with us is different from that of the scriptural word which we have to interpret, for the object of the latter is God's revelation in Jesus" (*CD* 1/2, p. 730). Barth follows this rule with four others. See 1/2, pp. 730–35.

67. Ibid., p. 734.

68. Barth, *CD* 1/2, p. 734.

69. Frei, *Types*, p. 86.

70. Barth, "The Authority and Significance of the Bible," pp. 65–66.

71. Barth, *CD* 1/2, p. 734.

72. Dawson, *Christian Figural Reading and the Fashioning of Identity*, pp. 169–70.

73. Frei, *Types*, p. 54. See Dawson (ibid.) for a superb account of the implications of this position for Frei's positioning of D. Z. Phillips in relation to Barth in *Types*.

74. Alasdair MacIntyre, *After Virtue* (Notre Dame: Notre Dame University Press, 1981), p. 207.

Index